Virginity Lost

Virginity Lost

An Intimate Portrait of
First Sexual Experiences

Laura M. Carpenter

NEW YORK UNIVERSITY PRESS
New York and London

NEW YORK UNIVERSITY PRESS
New York and London
www.nyupress.org

Library of Congress Cataloging-in-Publication Data
Carpenter, Laura M.
Virginity lost : an intimate portrait of
first sexual experiences / Laura M. Carpenter.
p. cm.
Includes bibliographical references and index.
ISBN–13: 978–0–8147–1652–6 (cloth : alk. paper)
ISBN–10: 0–8147–1652–0 (cloth : alk. paper)
ISBN–13: 978–0–8147–1653–3 (pbk. : alk. paper)
ISBN–10: 0–8147–1653–9 (pbk. : alk. paper)
1. Sex—United States.
2. Sexual behavior surveys—United States.   I. Title.
HQ18.U5C35   2005
306.7—dc22   2005011619

New York University Press books are printed on acid-free paper,
and their binding materials are chosen for strength and durability.

Manufactured in the United States of America
c 10 9 8 7 6 5 4 3 2 1
p 10 9 8 7 6 5 4 3 2 1

Contents

Acknowledgments

Like virginity loss, writing a first book is a rite of passage. I am immensely grateful to everyone whose support and guidance helped me accomplish it.

It has been my exceptional good fortune to be mentored by two outstanding and outspoken feminist sociologists. As my main adviser at the University of Pennsylvania, Robin L. Leidner taught me volumes about the science and art of sociology and showed great faith in my promise as a scholar. Constance A. Nathanson, who sponsored my Social Science Research Council–Sexuality Research Fellowship Program postdoctoral fellowship at the Johns Hopkins University Bloomberg School of Public Health, further schooled me in the sociologies of sexuality and gender and gave generously of her knowledge, advice, and time. I am honored to call these women my academic forbears—and my friends.

As a graduate student, I benefited enormously from the instruction of professors Demie Kurz, Harold J. Bershady, and Frank F. Furstenberg Jr. at the University of Pennsylvania. My colleagues and friends in the Department of Population and Family Health Sciences at Johns Hopkins also contributed to the development of this project (and of me as a scholar). More recently, I have received valuable advice and support from sociologists Sam Kaplan, Meika Loe, and Jennifer Reich and from my colleagues in the sociology department and gender studies program at Vanderbilt University. Among the latter, Jennifer C. Lena and Alison Piepmeier deserve special mention.

Among my most constructive critics and steadfast supporters have been the scholar-friends I made at the University of Pennsylvania: Gloria Y. Gadsden, Jacqueline Hart, Heidi Hiemstra, Sara B. Kinsman, Eileen Lake, Sangeetha Madhavan, Shara Neidell, Amanda Nothaft, Eva Skuratowicz, and Patricia Stern Smallacombe. Heather King Shamp and Mick Choder, friends from my undergraduate days, also helped in numerous ways.

This book would never have taken its current shape without the tough love of Ilene Kalish, my editor at New York University Press. Her critical acumen, encouragement, and considerable patience have been crucial to my ability to realize my vision for this project. Every author should be so fortunate. Salwa Jabado provided technical and emotional support. I am also grateful for the comments of anonymous reviewers at NYU and other presses.

Although my promise of confidentiality prevents me from mentioning them by name, the women and men whom I interviewed for this book deserve my deepest thanks. Many of them shared their sexual secrets with me in the hope that doing so could help make virginity loss a more positive experience for others. May their hopes in some small part be realized. I am grateful to every colleague, acquaintance, and stranger who helped me identify potential study participants; special thanks go to Carrie Jacobs and the Youth Planning Committee at The Attic.

Needless to say, I would have been lost on this journey were it not for my family and friends. Catherine Jellison and Pamela DeGeorge Hawe have seen me through more than a few rites of passage, not least the kind featured in this book. My father and stepmother, David Carpenter and Sarah Carpenter, my aunt and uncle, Barbara Carpenter Rowe and Peter Rowe, and my uncle, James Windham, have each supported me, with love, in their own indispensable ways. Peter Wittich entered my life just as this project was taking shape and has been by my side ever since. I am filled with joy and gratitude that he has chosen to accompany me across the difficult, strange, and wonderful terrain of life as a scholar and as a human being.

Finally, I want to thank my mother, Carole Windham, for shepherding me through the sometimes thorny pastures of adolescence with love. Although we've never seen eye to eye on the meaning of virginity loss, I hope that she, more than anyone, is proud of the woman I have become. I dedicate this book to her.

Introduction

The First Time

The headlines read: "A is for Abstinence" (2001), "Choosing Virginity" (2002), "Like a Virgin (Sort Of)" (2002), "More in High School Are Virgins" (2002), "1 in 5 Teenagers Has Sex Before 15" (2003), and "Young Teens and Sex" (2005). News stories about adolescent sexuality appear in the popular press like clockwork. Almost all of them focus on virginity and virginity loss, the touchstones of American conversations about young people and sex. In some stories, what is news is that teens are losing their virginity; in others, the point is precisely that they're not. More than a few accounts pause to ponder the conflicting ideas that characterize American sexual culture. As Nina Bernstein noted in a 2004 *New York Times* front-page story, today's adolescents

> cannot escape mixed messages about sex, or the complication of deciding if, when and how to sample it. They are picking from a new multiple-choice menu, where virginity and oral sex can coexist, and erotic rap makes the case for condoms.[1]

Whatever their focus, news stories about virginity loss often suggest that teens are approaching sex, especially first sexual encounters, in ways their parents can barely comprehend—in some cases, wanting to have sex at earlier ages and, in others, pledging abstinence and "saving" their virginity for marriage. Though the tone of these stories is often one of shock, or at least unease, regardless of whether teens are or are not having sex, these struggles over how, when, and under what circumstances one might "lose it" are actually nothing new.

In fact, what first got me interested in the topic was one such media story. A little over a decade ago, I was floored to see a *Newsweek* cover story proudly bearing the headline: "Virgin Cool." This pronouncement

1

knocked me for a loop. When I was a teenager growing up in suburban Maryland in the mid-1980s, the last time virginity ranked among my personal concerns, being a virgin was the antithesis of cool. Virginity, if it was spoken of, was implied by my peers to be socially backwards, prudish, undesirable—but never cool, and when Madonna's saucy song "Like a Virgin" came on the radio, friends and I winked and sang along, knowing that "like" was the operative word. I vividly remember gloating with one of my girlfriends that, should President Reagan's foreign policies trigger a nuclear war, at least we wouldn't die virgins—not like some unfortunates we knew. Virgin cool? No way.

Still, try telling that to the pair of adolescent women whose photograph appeared in my copy of *Newsweek*. Pretty and posed in body-flaunting outfits, they smiled defiantly beneath the provocative headline, as if to say, "We are too cool!" Reporter Michele Ingrassia had clearly anticipated reactions like mine. "A lot of kids are putting off sex, and not because they can't get a date," she began. "They've decided to wait, and they're proud of their chastity, not embarrassed by it. Suddenly, virgin geek is giving way to virgin chic."[2] The article went on to profile ten teenagers—eight women and two men—all heterosexual, diverse in race and religion. Some planned to remain virgins until they married, others until they were older or in love; their reasons ranged from religious beliefs to fears of unintended pregnancy and HIV. Perchance some nonvirgin readers longed to attain this novel form of chic, Ingrassia even tendered the option of "secondary" virginity, a state of renewed chastity available to "any person who . . . decid[es] to change."[3]

Had things really changed so much since I was an adolescent? That they had was, of course, the central claim of the *Newsweek* story and what qualified it as news. Many adult readers then would have assumed, as I did, that reverence for virginity was, if not quite a thing of the past, then a thing of a prim, perhaps devoutly religious, minority. As a teenager, insistent on my right to enjoy every liberty that men did, I intended to value sexual activity for its own sake, rather than for the love it might represent, as I imagined my mother's generation had done. "What if I don't want to get married?" I remember challenging my mother, then a recently divorced opponent of premarital sex. "Does that mean I should never have sex?" I could also remember reading about secondary virginity in a pamphlet from my mother's church. At the time, I couldn't fathom the possibility that anyone who'd finally gotten rid of her virginity might want to regain it. Apparently, I was wrong. All of which is to say, Americans have long viewed virginity loss through more than one lens, ever since my days as the rebellious teenager of a frustrated mother—and even before.

The uneasily coexisting stances that had my mom and me at loggerheads in the mid-1980s were the legacy of the sexual "revolution" of the late 1960s and early 1970s. A convergence of social forces at that time—the youth counterculture, women's and gay rights movements, proliferation of effective birth control methods, and climbing divorce rates, to name but a few—had helped make sex before marriage widely acceptable for men and women, albeit without wholly eradicating the erstwhile consensus that people, especially women, should remain virgins until they married.

By the mid-1980s, another series of developments had begun to work a dramatic transformation on sexual life in the United States. Starting in the mid-1970s, conservative Christians mounted a moral crusade intended to restore pre-1960s sexual norms, especially among adolescents.[4] They won a key victory with the 1981 passage of the Adolescent Family Life Act (AFLA), which mandated the inclusion of pro-abstinence instruction in federally funded sex education programs and bankrolled curriculum-development efforts. Then, in 1982, the HIV/AIDS epidemic began. Viewed at first as a disease primarily affecting gay men, by the late 1980s HIV was recognized as a threat to heterosexual adults and teens as well. Quick to capitalize on public concern about HIV, as well as their growing political clout, moral conservatives redoubled their efforts to promote abstinence-focused sex education.

Not surprisingly, entertainment and news media in the 1980s and early '90s were bursting with positive images of virgins—even as they celebrated sexual activity. Popular movies like *The Breakfast Club* (1985) and *Boyz N the Hood* (1991) prominently featured teens weighing the pros and cons of virginity loss.[5] The most famous virgin in the fictional firmament was Donna Martin (Tori Spelling) on television's teen hit *Beverly Hills 90210*, which aired from 1990 to 2000. Season after season, good-Catholic-girl Donna professed her desire to give her virginity to her husband, and various boyfriends tested her resolve, until she made love to future spouse David (Brian Austin Green) in the show's seventh year.[6] But for every Donna, there was a Brenda (Shannen Doherty) or Brandon (Jason Priestly): whatever their gender or religious convictions, none of Donna's friends remained virgins past the show's fourth season. Print media—from the *Washington Post* and *Mother Jones* to celebrity glossies like *People* and fashion magazines for women of all ages (*Seventeen, Cosmopolitan, Essence*)—likewise teemed with stories about the resurging popularity of virginity, even as they tended to depict "normal" young singles as sexually active. Young America's stance toward virginity appeared to be nothing if not ambivalent.

My interest in virginity loss as a sociological phenomenon was sparked by this rising wave of popular fascination. In 1994, when *Newsweek's* story on virginity hit the stands, I was in my second year of graduate school and eager to launch a study of my own. The mostly anecdotal appraisals of virginity loss then proliferating raised more questions for me than they resolved. Just how widespread was "virgin chic" among American youth? Did it resonate chiefly with women, as *Newsweek, Cosmo,* and *90210* seemed to suggest? Or did the smattering of virgin men now in evidence herald the imminent erosion of long-standing opposing standards for men's and women's sexual behavior? Social surveys reported that the average ages at which young Americans lost their virginity (defined by researchers as "first vaginal sex") had been steadily declining—from about 18 for men and 19 for women in the early 1970s to between 16 and 17 for both genders in 1995—while the average age at first marriage had risen, from 23 to 27 for men and 21 to 24.5 for women.[7] By these measures, at least, premarital virginity didn't seem destined to become either gender's new status quo.

But knowing the ages at which women and men began having sex couldn't tell me what virginity loss *meant* to them. Nor could such figures tell me how teens and young adults made decisions about when, where, and with whom to lose their virginity. Surely a girl who cherished her virginity might opt to lose it at age 14 if she were in love, just as a boy who felt ashamed of his virginity could reach 23 before finding a partner willing to deflower him. Furthermore, by simply equating virginity loss with first coitus, most scholars sidestepped the possibility that virginity loss could be defined in different ways. I had personally known too many people who disputed the mainstream definition of virginity loss not to see that the very definition might need to be revised. Whether giving or receiving oral sex was tantamount to virginity loss had been much debated in my high school; and the pornographic magazines my classmates and I occasionally caught glimpses of often spoke of the various "virginities" available to a single person, distinguishing, for instance, between vaginal-sex virginity and anal-sex virginity.[8] In college, hearing my lesbian friend, Nora, and her girlfriend joke about their respective sexual histories revealed a parallel lack of consensus in the lesbian and gay communities. Nora would periodically tease, "You're a virgin, you've never had sex with a man," to which Janelle would reply, "Of course I'm not, I have sex with you all the time!"

Once I began to research the topic, I found that the scholarship on early sexuality was largely silent on the meaning of virginity loss, and even more so about its definition. This silence surprised me, given how consistently American institutions — mass media, medical science, schools, religious institutions, public policy organizations, and the government—depicted virginity loss as one of, if not *the,* most meaningful events in an individual's sexual career.[9] As one advice manual for teen girls puts it, "Losing your virginity is something you'll remember your whole life."[10] In fact, of all the sexual "firsts" people can experience, only virginity loss is designated by a special term. Most of the published material I found focused fairly narrowly on the timing of first coitus or on attitudes about premarital sex, neither of which is wholly congruent with the cultural phenomenon called virginity loss.[11] Many studies, moreover, seemed uncritically to lump nonvirgin teens (so designated if they'd had vaginal sex) together with their alcohol- and drug-using peers as being "at risk" for negative outcomes from unintended pregnancy and STIs (sexually transmitted infections) to academic failure and low self-esteem.[12] Yet common sense suggested that, although sexual activity *can* pose dangers to health and happiness, many adolescents lose their virginity with few if any untoward consequences.

Ultimately, I uncovered about a dozen studies concerned with the meaning and subjective experience of virginity loss. Strikingly, none scrutinized virginity loss as a cultural phenomenon important in its own right; rather, each issued from a larger project concerning the broader contours of sexual or community life.[13] While commendable in many other respects, these studies shared two critical shortcomings. First, they dealt almost entirely with virginity loss prior to 1990, and often much earlier. Yet it stood to reason that recent changes in sexual culture—particularly HIV/AIDS, the political empowerment of moral conservatives, the rise of third-wave feminism, and the unprecedented visibility of gay and lesbian life—might have dramatically altered young people's approaches to virginity loss.

A second serious shortcoming was that the researchers typically focused on women to the exclusion of men, or targeted heterosexual people while neglecting lesbians, gays, and other sexual minorities.[14] Both patterns of omission, and the resulting narrow focus on heterosexual women, reflect enduring trends in the scientific study of sexuality and in social efforts to control it.[15] More often than not, experts, scholars, and lay observers have seen sexual activity and virginity loss among young women as problematic while considering such activity to be normal for young men. The roots of this discrepancy lie partly in women's biological capacity for pregnancy. Many have argued that if sexually active women have children outside of sanctioned relationships, a society's entire family and kinship system are threatened. It also stems from the persistent belief that women are fundamentally less sexual than men, a view that inevitably suggests that sexual women are deviant and dangerous. In practical terms, these tendencies have prompted the collection of extensive data on young women's sexuality and the development of many ways of trying to control it.

The perception that sexual prowess is fundamental to masculinity has, in contrast, deflected attention from male virginity loss. Cultural stereotypes about masculinity and femininity are reflected in the customary definition of virginity loss as occurring the first time a person has vaginal sex, an act commonly seen as something an (active) man does to a (passive) woman. This definition privileges men's experience of sexual intercourse by, in effect, requiring the presence of a penis. Some people even contend that men do not lose their virginity unless they have an orgasm; orgasms for women are seldom part of the equation.[16] Yet men themselves have clearly found some aspects of sexual activity—not least, its absence—problematic and have seen virginity loss as a significant, positive life transition. Popular tales of young men's quests to lose their virginity, preferably before it becomes an intolerable embarrassment, are legion, appearing in films from *Summer of '42* (1971) to *American Pie* (1999), novels and plays like *The Last Picture Show* (1966) and *Biloxi Blues* (1986), and "gentleman's" magazines like *Playboy* and *Penthouse Forum* (1953 to present). Periodic crusades to improve public health or morality by promoting male chastity notwithstanding, sexual activity and virginity loss have rarely been seen as carrying dire consequences for heterosexual men—at least before the HIV/AIDS epidemic began.

By a similar token, social institutions and individual observers have tended to accept as normal sexual expression between different-sex partners while marginalizing or pathologizing sex between same-sex partners. When they have not ignored gay people altogether, researchers interested in virginity loss have usually assumed that lesbigay youth define virginity loss in terms of vaginal sex.[17] Studies of early sexuality may, therefore, include gay youth who have had vaginal sex (without noting their sexual identity) while summarily categorizing those who haven't as sexually inactive. Conversely, studies that explore lesbigay sexuality in early life typically focus on initial attractions, first same- and different-sex encounters, and coming out, but rarely ask about virginity loss. Yet, recent anecdotal and popular accounts suggest that, as young gays, lesbians, and bisexuals come out at ever-earlier stages in their sexual careers, they may increasingly opt to challenge the prevailing definition of virginity loss as heterosexist.[18]

In short, despite its enduring importance on the American cultural landscape, virginity loss has largely eluded scholarly attention. A great deal remained to be discovered when I began my investigation. On the individual level, what did virginity loss mean to young Americans—and how did those meanings shape their actions and experiences? How was virginity loss related to earlier and later sexual encounters? How did men and women define it in the first place? For what reasons did people familiar with multiple ways of interpreting virginity loss prefer one over another? Were some interpretations more conducive to physical and emotional well-being?

On the societal level, I had even more questions. In what ways had the changes of the late 1980s and 1990s—the HIV/AIDS epidemic, resurgence of moral conservatism, growing lesbigay visibility, backlash against second-wave feminism and the emergence of its third wave—affected perspectives on virginity loss? What, for instance, of "virgin chic"? Had gender differences in beliefs and experiences narrowed or widened in this new social terrain—and were women or men the authors of these changes? Had an increasingly self-aware generation of lesbigay teenagers rejected virginity loss as relevant only for heterosexuals or redefined it to fit their own experiences? How did race, ethnicity, social class, and religious background enter into the mix? Studies suggested that racial/ethnic, class, and religious differences in average ages at first vaginal sex had diminished in recent decades, even as differences in subjective aspects of early sexuality persisted. Finally, what factors make virginity loss such a significant social phenomenon today, considering that many of the historical reasons for its importance have been eroded by far-reaching changes in social and sexual life?

I hope the questions I have asked, and the answers I offer here, shed some much-deserved light on the meanings of this sexual turning point and its place in the lives of diverse young men and women in the United States as a new century begins.

Asking Questions about Virginity Loss

To find out how young Americans understand and experience virginity loss, I asked a number of women and men from a variety of social backgrounds to share their personal stories with me. Over the course of 18 months in 1997 and 1998, I interviewed 61 young adults in great detail.[19] They included 33 women, of whom 22 self-identified as heterosexual, 7 as lesbians, and 4 as bisexual, and 28 men, of whom 17 described themselves as heterosexual, 9 as gay, and 2 as bisexual.[20] They ranged in age from 18 to 35 and came from diverse racial and ethnic groups, social-class backgrounds, and religious traditions.[21] All but 5 were no longer virgins when I met them. Most lived within 2 hours of Philadelphia when we met, but nearly half had grown up and begun their sexual careers elsewhere in the United States.

I deliberately chose to speak with a diverse group.[22] Interviewing roughly equal numbers of men and women, and many more lesbians, gays, and bisexuals than are representative of the U.S. population overall, permitted me to compare virginity-loss experiences across gender and sexual identities more directly than previous researchers have done. Other aspects of social identity, such as race, ethnicity, socioeconomic status, and religion, have historically also shaped individuals' approaches to sexual life. Collecting the stories of people from a wide range of backgrounds therefore allowed me to develop a more comprehensive picture of the varied meanings of virginity loss available to Americans today, and of the processes through which they come to prefer one approach over another.[23]

I also actively sought interviews with men and women who described themselves as secondary or born-again virgins (the terms are used interchangeably in popular parlance), both to broaden my vision of the meanings that could be applied to virginity and to benefit from the capacity of "exceptional" cases to illuminate deep cultural assumptions.[24] One man and three of the women I interviewed described themselves as current or former secondary virgins.

Speaking with people who came of age before the mid-1980s, as well as those who came of age afterward, enabled me to explore the impact of broad social changes on individual sexual careers and to remedy earlier studies' neglect of this younger group.[25] Just under half of the people I interviewed were born between 1962 and 1972; they were 26 or older when I interviewed them. The remaining half were born between 1973 and 1980; they were 25 or younger when I met them. Sociologists recognize that people's life stories bear the profound imprint of the context in which they grow up.[26] Everyone in the study came of age after the sexual revolution of the late 1960s to early 1970s. The "older" generation turned 13 between 1975 and 1985, the "younger" generation between 1986 and 1993. Thus, the older group learned about sex and virginity loss primarily in the era before HIV/AIDS, whereas their younger counterparts came of age during or after the transformation the epidemic wrought in American sexual life.[27] How these generational differences affect virginity-loss experiences is a theme threading throughout this book.

Another watershed moment in U.S. sexual history occurred during my study, after I had interviewed about half of my study participants. In late January 1998, allegations of a sexual relationship between President Bill Clinton and White House intern Monica Lewinsky surfaced in the news media. The ensuing controversy over whether "sex" encompassed fellatio inaugurated something of a national consciousness-raising about the definitional ambiguity of sex and, therefore, of virginity loss.[28] I suspect that this incident may change the way Americans define virginity loss, but doubt that it will alter the meanings people assign to virginity. Nor do I believe that it greatly affected people's assessments of virginity-loss experiences that had already happened.[29] However, given that the entire country seemed to be discussing the meanings and mechanics of sex, not to mention dress stains and cigars, I imagine that some of the men and women I spoke with may have been more forthcoming about the details of their sexual lives.

Because I did not identify participants using probability-based methods, my findings cannot be generalized to young Americans as a whole.[30] In particular, I cannot make claims about the *prevalence* of beliefs and behaviors in the population overall. Nor was I able to speak with enough individuals from specific racial/ethnic minority and religious groups, within broader gender and sexual identity categories (e.g., African American gay men, Jewish heterosexual women), to draw more than suggestive conclusions about the relationship of these social statuses to virginity loss. However, because my sample was quite diverse, I am confident that the range and variety of perceptions, processes, and broad patterns by gender, sexuality, and other aspects of identity that I discovered through my interviews are present among other young adults who grew up in the metropolitan United States between the mid-1970s and late 1990s.[31]

The first people I interviewed were introduced to me by colleagues, friends, and contacts at local organizations, such as a community center for gay youth. At the conclusion of these and every subsequent interview, I asked my informants if they could recommend other women and men who might be willing to share their virginity-loss stories with me.[32] This technique, known as chain referral or snowball sampling, was critical to the success of my study, for the personal introductions I received did much to help participants feel safe disclosing such intimate details to me.[33] I met with people wherever they felt most comfortable—often at their homes or workplaces, sometimes at my office. The interviews were conversational in style and lasted from one to three hours; I tape-recorded them with permission.[34] I began by asking people for basic information about their background, then invited them to tell me how they defined virginity loss and what it meant to them, now and in the past. We then discussed how, when, and from whom they learned about virginity loss and sexuality. The remainder of the interview focused on the person's own sexual history, particularly their experiences related to virginity loss. Although I sometimes had to probe for information about specific topics, such as using safer sex or birth control, most people spun richly detailed narratives with little prompting.[35]

Many diverse definitions of virginity loss were offered, as I show in chapter 2. Out of respect for this diversity, in subsequent chapters I defer to each individual's understanding of when and through what sexual acts he or she lost his or her virginity, rather than imposing the conventional definition of virginity loss on their experiences.

Understanding Virginity Loss through Metaphors

Once I began asking people about virginity loss, I heard many stories that rang familiar, but many things that surprised me as well. Having grown up in a society where the meaning and purpose of sexuality was a favorite topic of debate among everyone from my high school friends to public figures across the political spectrum, I had expected to find young women and men interpreting virginity loss in different ways. Yet I was struck by the patterns that I discovered. Although there were a few exceptions and every tale was unique in its details, all but a few of the accounts featured at least one of three metaphors, variously comparing virginity to a gift, a stigma, or a step in the process of growing up.[36] Half of the people I interviewed had, at some point in their lives, likened virginity to a gift, more than one-third had thought of it as a stigma, and just over half had ever viewed it as a step in a process. (Some study participants referred to this step as a rite of passage; I use the expressions interchangeably.) Two people described premarital virginity as an act of worship. Although other researchers have undoubtedly heard people using these metaphors to talk about virginity loss, I am the first to use them as a way of theorizing virginity loss and to recognize their importance in shaping individuals' beliefs, choices, and experiences.

Because I wanted to know how they personally made sense of and experienced virginity loss, rather than imposing my preconceived notions I used an inductive approach.[37] For example, I did not ask people whether they thought virginity resembled a gift, stigma, or process; rather, they volunteered these comparisons spontaneously as we conversed. Discovering that young Americans interpret virginity loss through these metaphors helped me to develop a more sophisticated and useful understanding of people's beliefs and behavior than has been possible through analyses linking sexual activity to broadly positive or negative attitudes toward virginity or to social characteristics (like growing up in a single-parent home). According to linguistic philosophers George Lakoff and Mark Johnson, people routinely use metaphors to make sense of everyday life; they expect the phenomena juxtaposed in a metaphor to resemble one another in meaningful ways.[38] In my study, I found that people who invoked the same metaphor took strikingly similar approaches to virginity loss, sharing distinctive sets of expectations, preferences, and practices—which, in turn, reflected social conventions for gifts, stigma, and rites of passage more generically. (I use the terms metaphor, understanding, interpretation, approach, script, and frame as synonymous.)[39]

Interpretations of virginity loss are also affected by gender and other aspects of one's social identity. As sociologist Judith Lorber has noted, however, when researchers expect to find differences by gender, they can often (if inadvertently) overstate those differences while neglecting to explore important similarities across gender.[40] I have therefore tried to identify general patterns of beliefs and behavior before examining the effects of social identity in order to illuminate the complex relationship among gender, sexuality, and virginity loss. Although participants' interpretive preferences differed by gender and sexual identity, "atypical" interpretations were more common than previous studies have suggested.[41] What is more, people who favored the same metaphor understood and experienced virginity loss in very similar ways, regardless of their social identities. Yet, gender, sexuality, and other aspects of identity did lend distinctive nuances to virginity-loss stories within interpretive groups, in some cases affecting individuals' feelings of control over their experiences.

The young men and women I interviewed were, as a rule, familiar with different interpretations of virginity loss. Yet most of them favored a single metaphor for virginity rather than blending interpretations or switching frequently between them. This is not to say that their approaches were static or wholly bounded, however. About one-third reported adopting a new interpretation of virginity at some point in time, typically in response to new life events. Moreover, in practice, the boundaries between the metaphors and the experiences of the women and men who invoked them were fluid, even indistinct. My descriptions of these interpretive stances should, therefore, be understood as ideal types.[42]

Of course, these metaphors are a part of our culture.[43] More broadly, it's important to note that as men and women move through the world, they draw on their culture to help make sense of their experiences; to guide them as they confront various problems; to learn how to become particular kinds of people; and to differentiate themselves from others.[44] In a heterogeneous culture such as that in the contemporary United States, a single phenomenon can often be understood in multiple ways; such is the case with virginity loss.[45] Gender, sexuality, race/ethnicity, social class, and religion shape individuals' understandings of virginity, both because people learn about the world from others who share their social identities and because cultures deem particular understandings appropriate for particular kinds of people.[46] People possess many social identities simultaneously—one can be female, Jewish, working class, and the daughter of divorced parents as well as a popular high school cheerleader with a committed boyfriend—and, in that sense, must negotiate among conflicting sets of beliefs and expectations. Individuals may, of course, resist or reject what is expected of people "like them"; but they typically face sanctions for doing so. For instance, girls can be labeled "sluts" if they have sex without love and boys can be labeled "wimps" or even gay should they not have sex early in their adolescence. How ideas about gender, sexuality, and other identities influence one's understanding of virginity loss is a central theme of this book.

Over the course of the twentieth century, extensive social and cultural changes "eroded and destabilized long-standing relationships to create a more fragmented and individualized society."[47] Formerly, life trajectories were largely dictated by social statuses like gender; today, Americans enjoy considerably more latitude. Just two generations ago, for instance, many middle-class White women felt constrained to choose between marriage, children, and homemaking and practicing a "feminine" profession while remaining a chaste spinster; today, they may embrace those traditional versions of feminine identity or adopt "progressive" forms of femininity by delaying or forgoing marriage, becoming single mothers or remaining "child free," and pursuing hitherto masculine careers. In this way, to the extent that metaphors for virginity are associated with particular versions of gender, sexuality, and other identities, the experience of virginity loss becomes a vehicle through which people can cultivate preferred versions of social identities.[48] Therefore, in addition to examining how social identities shape interpretive choices around virginity, this book also explores how people actively choose and use metaphors for virginity to construct and enact social identities.

Which metaphor for virginity loss a person favors matters for other reasons as well. My research shows that different understandings of virginity loss promote certain sexual beliefs and behaviors which, in turn, can have different effects on one's physical health and emotional well-being. Importantly, some metaphors for virginity are more conducive to emotional and physical well-being—before, during, and after virginity loss—than others.

I will also consider how my research can inform the ongoing debate about sex education in U.S. public schools. Since the mid-1980s, two major models of sex education have been vying for dominance: those that emphasize sexual abstinence and those that present a more comprehensive array of information. In addition to providing different types and quantities of information about pregnancy and STI (sexually transmitted infection) prevention, the two approaches tend to promote specific interpretations of virginity. Abstinence-focused curricula typically depict virginity as a gift to be given in marriage and frame the stigma metaphor as an unacceptable alternative, while comprehensive sex education curricula often present virginity loss as a step in a process. My comparative analysis of the differential effects of the gift, stigma, passage/process, and act-of-worship metaphors—among people who, like the vast majority of young Americans, have not remained abstinent until marriage—speaks to this debate.

Many of the factors that historically made virginity loss significant have lost much of their salience and force, due to extensive changes in social and sexual life, the secularization of American society, feminism, and development of highly effective contraceptive methods, to name but three. Yet, everyone I interviewed believed that most Americans see virginity loss as a momentous life event and almost all of them had personally seen their own experiences as very meaningful. I contend that Americans currently accord tremendous significance to virginity loss because of the role it plays in the construction of identity and in the establishment of adulthood.[49] My interviews suggest that there are costs as well as benefits to investing virginity loss with such importance, however. By considering the reasons for virginity loss's significance today, this book helps reveal how broad social changes and individual biographies intersect, especially in light of evolving understandings and experiences of gender, sexual identity, and adulthood itself.

Plan of the Book

Before we can discuss how virginity loss is understood and experienced in America today, it's important to examine how it has been interpreted, defined, and experienced in the past. Virginity is an ancient concept, and over the centuries Western peoples' understandings of virginity loss have evolved to fit their ever-changing societies. The same social forces have also helped to transform people's conduct—including when, where, and with what types of partner they lose their virginity. I chart these changing interpretations and experiences in chapter 1. Understanding how young women and men define virginity loss is fundamental to understanding how they experience it. Chapter 2, therefore, focuses on the diverse definitions used by the people who took part in my study. As I will show, generation, sexual identity, and gender shaped their definitions in important ways.

With this foundation in place, I turn to the beliefs and experiences of young Americans today. In chapters 3, 4, and 5, I tell the stories of young women and men who interpreted virginity as a gift, a stigma, or a process/passage. For convenience, I will refer to them, respectively, as "gifters," the "stigmatized," and "processers." Almost everyone I spoke with approached virginity loss through one (or more) of these three metaphors. However, my interviews and reading of popular culture also revealed the emergence of a distinctive fourth metaphor, one that frames premarital virginity as an act of worship. This metaphor, and the increasing prominence of abstinence-only sex-education programs, are the subjects of chapter 6.

I conclude the book by returning to the questions raised in this introduction, showing how my research has helped to answer them. At the heart of chapter 7 is a comparative analysis of the effects the gift, stigma, process/passage, and act-of-worship metaphors have on young people's physical health and emotional well-being. Through this analysis and an examination of the relationship between these metaphors and the major approaches to sex education, I connect my scholarship to the ongoing debate about sex education in America. I close with a discussion of the enduring social significance of virginity loss, and its implications for individuals and society overall.

It's now been over a decade since that 1994 "Virgin Cool" headline made me do a double take. Thinking, reading, and writing as well as talking to so many people about their own experiences with virginity loss has been an incredibly fascinating and, at times, deeply moving experience. I have heard stories about sexual experiences that virtually no other scholar has ever recorded and I have been repeatedly surprised by my own assumptions and challenged to see virginity loss in a different light. Writing this book has been an absorbing, instructive, and revealing experience for me. My hope is that reading this book will prove to be the same.

1

A Brief History of Virginity Loss

In the summer of 1999, not long after I'd conducted the last interview for this book, Universal Pictures released a movie about four high school boys determined to lose their virginity by the night of their senior prom. *American Pie* took box offices by storm, launching the careers of half a dozen young actors, and ultimately spawning two commercially success-ful (if increasingly vapid) sequels.[1] If anyone had doubted that young Americans saw virginity loss as a significant experience, here was confir-mation that they did.

On the surface, *American Pie* resembles countless other teen sex come-dies. Its plot centers on a group of male friends who feel stigmatized by their virginity and long to eradicate it with maximum haste and minimum embarrassment. Jim (Jason Biggs) scarcely seems to care whether he loses his virginity with a sexy exchange student, geeky marching-band flutist, or homemade apple pie.[2] Likewise mortified, Paul Finch (Eddie Kaye Thomas) tries to disguise his virginity through a series of elaborate sub-terfuges before finally being initiated by his classmate Stifler's stunning mother (Jennifer Coolidge), in an apparent homage to *The Graduate*. The young women in the movie, by contrast, hope to bestow their virginity on loving partners, in romantic surroundings. Vicky (Tara Reid) refuses to have sex with longtime boyfriend Kevin (Thomas Ian Nicholas) until he can say that he loves her; and Heather (Mena Suvari) repeatedly rebuffs the attentions of star athlete Oz (Chris Klein) until he proves that he's in-terested in her as a person.

Yet, the movie also features characters who defy gender norms. Jessica (Natasha Lyonne) respects her friend Vicky's desire for a "special" vir-ginity-loss encounter but makes a point of warning her that vaginal sex is seldom perfect the first time, effectively presenting virginity loss as a step in a learning process. In a truly revolutionary move for a teen comedy,

Jessica also suggests that Vicky might be more inclined to have sex if she were having orgasms during foreplay, thereby arguing that women should make virginity loss contingent on sexual pleasure. Michelle (Alyson Hannigan) likewise flouts traditional feminine ideals. Having announced that she agreed to be Jim's prom date because he was a "sure thing," she brusquely deflowers him, then disappears.[3] Nor do the film's young men fully conform to traditional ideas about masculinity. Oz decides it is worth remaining a virgin if he can keep Heather's trust and affection; and mutual virginity loss appears to enhance Kevin's love for Vicky.[4] Sherman (Chris Owen) frames virginity loss as a rite of passage; having spent the night with a girl, apparently having sex, he declares, "Say good-bye to Chuck Sherman the boy. I am now a man."

The teenagers in *American Pie* take diverse approaches to virginity loss, even though they are all White, middle-class, and heterosexual. When I first saw the movie, having just interviewed 61 young Americans about virginity loss, I was struck by how much it reflected the patterns I saw in my research. The fictional youth interpreted virginity through the same metaphorical lenses as the women and men I interviewed, comparing virginity to a gift, a stigma, and a step in the process of growing up; and they exhibited a similar combination of conformity and resistance to traditional gender ideals. In depicting virginity loss as a site of competing and even contradictory beliefs, *American Pie* epitomized a phenomenon that captivated many lay and academic observers at the time. As sociologist Steven Seidman and others have noted, in the last decades of the twentieth century American sexual culture entered a period of unprecedented diversity.[5]

Yet, many of the meanings currently assigned to virginity have been in circulation in Western cultures for centuries.[6] Indeed, as I researched the history of virginity loss, I saw how previous generations of Americans had also invoked the gift, stigma, and process/passage metaphors. In this chapter, I chart evolving understandings, definitions, and experiences of virginity loss from the time British colonists arrived in the "new world" until the present.[7] Understanding the processes through which different approaches to virginity loss have emerged, come to prominence, and fallen out of favor will provide a useful backdrop against which we can unravel contemporary patterns and begin to consider what might transpire in the future. My account relies chiefly on secondary sources, although I also incorporate selected primary materials and draw representative illustrations from popular culture.

Before proceeding, some words of clarification are in order. The scientific study of sexuality is a relatively young discipline, launched in the 1880s by medical scholars and psychologists such as Richard von Krafft-Ebing and Havelock Ellis.[8] Although the first surveys of sexual beliefs and practices in the United States were fielded in the 1890s, sex research remained relatively moribund until the 1920s and 1930s; even then, scholars seldom collected data from unmarried men and women. Research focusing on sexual life before marriage grew exponentially in the 1960s and 1970s, motivated initially by a narrow concern with the psychological adjustment of (mostly White) college students and, starting in the early 1970s, by mounting social anxiety about adolescent pregnancy and, from the mid-1980s, HIV/AIDS. Marriage, birth, and other legal records can provide some "hard" data on sexual attitudes and conduct before the scientific era; however, for the most part, what we know about bygone periods comes from prescriptive literature (sermons and advice manuals), idealized texts (novels and songs), and personal documents (diaries and letters). These sources offer considerable insight into the sexual ideals of the past but only indirect evidence about actual human behavior. Contemporary studies indicate that most people's sexual behavior conforms broadly to their beliefs—for example, teenagers who disapprove of premarital sex are less likely to engage in it—yet discrepancies are not uncommon.[9] It is also important to note that the sexual patterns that prevail among marginalized social groups—racial/ethnic minorities, people who desire same-sex partners, the economically disadvantaged—often differ from patterns among dominant groups and are frequently absent from, or misrepresented in, the historical record and even scientific scholarship.[10]

The Roots of Colonial American Beliefs

In the United States, ideas about virginity loss are firmly rooted in the Christian tradition of venerating premarital virginity, which White colonists brought with them from Europe.[11] This tradition evolved from ancient Jewish, Greek, and Roman beliefs and customs. While by no means uniform, these cultures all valued virginity in unmarried women and believed virgins of both genders to possess special powers, such as invulnerability to injury or death.[12] The English words *virgin* and *virginity* derive from the Latin "virago," meaning "maiden," and entered the English language in the 1200s, followed by the expressions *to keep* and *to*

lose "virginity" around 1390. The oldest uses of the term *virginity* referred to "abstinence from or avoidance of all sexual relations" and
"bodily chastity . . . esp[ecially] as adopted from religious motives."[13]

Most early Christian theologians claimed that Adam and Eve were
born virgins and that their first sexual encounter helped unleash sin into
the world.[14] Believers who wished to live a sinless life were accordingly
encouraged to embrace virginity, preferably as a permanent state. For
those souls who could "not control themselves," Paul of Tarsus, perhaps
the best-known proponent of lifelong virginity, advocated sexual activity
within marriage over failed celibacy outside it in the famous phrase, "It
is better to marry than to be consumed with passion."[15]

All early Christians were encouraged to embrace sexual abstinence.
Both genders were thought to experience sexual desire, but abstinence
was understood in gender-specific ways. The term "virgin" customarily
referred to women, whereas "chastity" was the favored expression for
men, implying that sexual purity and abstinence were innate in women,
but had to be cultivated by men.[16] From about the twelfth century on,
women's physiology was believed to allow for a more complete virginity
than men's, insofar as "the female body [was] hollow and therefore capable both of containing the divine and being sealed to exclude all other
influences."[17] More practically, since virginity precluded marriage, it ap-
pealed to women seeking independence from men and freedom from the
dangers of childbirth. The popular thirteenth-century poem, "Hali Mei-
denhad," describes virginity as "the one gift granted you from heaven;
give it once away and you will never recover another in any way like it"
and counsels women to reciprocate God's largesse by "giv[ing] yourself
to Him"—or, failing that, to a husband.[18] In contrast, medical scholars
warned men that, Christian teachings notwithstanding, sexual continence
was injurious to their health.[19] Ambivalence about men's virginity—typ-
ified by Saint Augustine's prayer, "Give me chastity and continence, but
not just now"—has characterized Western thinking ever since.[20]

When early Christians deigned to define virginity loss, they emphasized spiritual rather than physiological criteria. The spiritual state of
chastity was typically held to be superior to, and more fragile than, the
physical state of virginity.[21] Ideally, chastity and virginity overlapped; but
more than a few writers differentiated between people who remained
spiritual virgins despite compromises to their physical integrity (e.g.,
through rape) and those who preserved their physical virginity but had
been unchaste in thought or deed (e.g., through lustful fantasy or mas-

turbation).[22] That said, for most of European and U.S. history, rape was believed to result in virginity loss.[23] On the rare occasions medieval Europeans delineated physical criteria for virginity loss, they tended to argue that penile penetration would result in virginity loss whereas foreplay and masturbation would merely be "corrupting."[24] Sexual acts between same-sex partners were viewed as sinful and unchaste but probably not as compromising virginity.[25]

Virginity's prestige suffered severely with the Protestant Reformation and rise of scientific secularism in the sixteenth and seventeenth centuries.[26] English Protestants tended to disdain religiously motivated celibacy as "reeking of Popish superstition" and to view sexual expression as normal and desirable for both genders, so long as it was intended for reproductive purposes within marriage.[27] Public concern with men's virginity diminished further in this period, while the association between masculinity and sexual activity was reinvigorated. Authors such as William Shakespeare and Ben Johnson encouraged young women not to protect their virginity unduly (even as they applauded the virginity of their queen, Elizabeth).[28] In the first scene of *All's Well That Ends Well*, for instance, the rakish Parolles scoffs at Helen's lament that, prevented from marrying her true love, "I will die a virgin," and boldly denounces virginity as

> against the rule of nature. To speak on the part of virginity is to accuse your mothers, which is a most infallible disobedience. . . . Virginity breeds mites, much like a cheese . . . is peevish, proud, idle, made of self-love, which is the most inhibited sin in the canon.[29]

By the eighteenth century, a subculture that not only accepted but actively celebrated sexual immoderation in men had developed among some secular elites.[30] The most (in)famous of these libertines, Casanova, recommended "humoring" women who refused to lose their virginity by engaging in mutual masturbation or fondling without penetration.[31]

Nonelite men apparently took the virginity of future wives fairly seriously, however, not least because they could ill afford to reject social conventions.[32] Young women, too, continued to value and guard their virginity—until marriage, but not as an alternative to it. According to medievalist Kathleen Coyne Kelly, "[A]fter the English Reformation, virginity was generally viewed as a temporary stage through which a young girl passed on the way to chaste marriage. Virginity was a valuable commodity, but it had a very limited shelf-life."[33] In short, the Enlightenment did not revolutionize beliefs about virginity, but rather brought secular reasons for valuing it to the forefront.

As the spiritual connotations of virginity diminished, unmarried men and women gained greater license to engage in noncoital intimacies. Demographic and literary evidence, such as the memoirs of farm laborer John Cannon, indicates that, by the late 1600s, an Englishman who limited his (heterosexual) love affairs to kissing, fondling, and mutual masturbation could congratulate himself on "studious avoidance of the sins of fornication and adultery" and rest assured that his women partners would be "considered a virgin on marriage."[34]

The Colonial Period to the Early Republic

The men and women who settled British America were mostly Protestants and, as such, valued virginity chiefly in its premarital guise.[35] In the early colonies, social norms forbade sexual activity before and outside of marriage for both genders, as well as nonreproductive practices like masturbation, oral-genital sex, and contact between same-sex partners. Yet church and court records suggest that prohibitions on premarital sex were weakly enforced among betrothed couples and that premarital pregnancies, theoretically anathema, were almost always resolved through marriage, usually with the support of social, legal, and religious authorities.[36] Courting couples had opportunities to experience physical intimacy through the custom of bundling, in which a marriage-bound couple would spend the night together in bed fully clothed, and through moments of privacy stolen in fields and barns.[37]

White colonists typically defined their sexual morality in opposition to that of Native Americans and people of African descent, both enslaved and free, whom they routinely derided as sexually promiscuous, amoral, and animalistic.[38] Many indigenous American and African cultures did, in fact, hold less restrictive views on nudity and premarital sex than the Christian colonists. But rather than accepting different norms and practices as alternative moral systems, White rulers used them to justify racial oppression. As slavery became entrenched in the late 1600s, most colonies passed laws forbidding interracial sex and marriage.

In the mid- to late 1700s, the growing popularity of Enlightenment philosophy, which promoted an ethos of individual responsibility, began to erode church and state authority over sexuality, an erosion hastened in turn by the social disruptions of the French-American and Revolutionary Wars.[39] With fewer formal controls, young people enjoyed greater opportunities for sexual exploration before marriage. A dramatic increase in premarital pregnancy in the late 1700s—from about one in five first births from 1701 to 1760 to about one in three between 1761 and 1800 —indicates that this exploration not infrequently included vaginal sex.[40]

These developments carried different implications for women and men. The abdication of legal, social, and religious authorities not only permitted the sexual freedom that resulted in more premarital pregnancies, but also made it increasingly possible for men to abandon single women whose children they had fathered. Demographic and socioeconomic trends exacerbated women's plight. By the late 1700s, men in America no longer outnumbered women, as they had in the early colonial period, making it increasingly difficult for women to marry. Women remained economically dependent on men and marriage, however, and illegitimate births lost none of their stigma. Women who lost their virginity prior to marriage in the late eighteenth century therefore risked far more than men did, and were far more vulnerable than their sisters had been just decades before. This increasing vulnerability, along with other broad social changes, helped bring about the Victorian era in sexual culture.

Passionless Women and Mixed-up Men, 1830–1890

Reflecting social concerns of the day, the early nineteenth century saw a proliferation of cautionary books, stories, and ballads about young White women "seduced and ruined" by lustful men.[41] Among the most popular of these was Susanna Rowson's novel, *Charlotte Temple*. The plot is simple and tragic. Fifteen-year-old Charlotte Temple, a schoolgirl in Chichester, England, is "pure and innocent by nature" until handsome Lieutenant Montraville sets about seducing her.[42] Although Charlotte knows that "religion [and] duty, forbid [me]," when Montraville promises (deceitfully) to marry her, she agrees to follow him to his new post in America.[43] Charlotte soon becomes pregnant; but Montraville grows bored with "the woman whom he had . . . robbed of innocence" and abandons her to marry a rich man's daughter.[44] With no means of support and rejected by every soul she petitions, Charlotte winds up destitute, ill, and immensely repentant for the irrevocable loss of her virginity/honor, "the only gem that could render me respectable in the eye of the world."[45] When her father arrives to bring Charlotte home, it is too late; he forgives his daughter as she dies in his arms, scant days after giving birth to a healthy child. A remorseful Montraville surfaces in time to apologize to Mr. Temple, then suffers "fits of melancholy" until his death.[46]

Lest readers fail to appreciate the moral of her tale, Rowson provided explicit instructions: "[L]isten not to the voice of love, unless sanctioned by paternal approbation: . . . then kneel down each morning, and request kind heaven to keep you free from temptation."[47] These directives encapsulate nineteenth-century Americans' stance toward young White women's sexuality. As rates of illegitimacy and abandonment climbed due to weakened social prohibitions and socioeconomic changes, community leaders and laypeople began to view sexual passion in women with suspicion. Many concluded, like Rowson, that women could be best protected not by merely restraining their sexual passions but by actually lacking them altogether. By the 1830s, the belief that women were essentially passionless, even within marriage, would become a defining feature of mainstream American sexual culture.[48]

Although proponents of female passionlessness spoke in universal terms, in practice the ideology applied chiefly to White women and did little to disrupt prevailing perceptions of Black and Native American women as inherently lascivious. Middle-class reformers also thought poor and working-class White girls particularly prone to compromising their virtue, and took pains to warn them accordingly. *Charlotte Temple,* for example, was printed in "numerous editions . . . specifically targeted for working-class readers" throughout the 1800s.[49] Yet, biases in the historical record make it difficult to determine whether the sexual beliefs and practices of less-privileged groups actually differed from those of the White middle class.

Suspicion of women's sexuality was not the only social support for the ideology of female passionlessness. Protestant revivalists in the "Great Awakening" actively encouraged women to advance the greater social good by harnessing their inborn asexual spirituality to control men's innate carnal desires.[50] The doctrine of separate spheres that developed as industrialization removed paid labor from the home, granting men responsibility for the public sphere of work and politics and relegating women to the private sphere of home and family, also bolstered the view of women as passionless by widening the gulf between women's and men's experiences and opportunities, sexual and otherwise, especially in those families with the financial means to enact it. Still more support came from health reformers such as Sylvester Graham. Believing that men who succumbed to lust risked depleting their limited reserves of bodily energy, resulting in ill health, impotence, and the decline of civilized society, Graham and his disciples admonished women to apply their chaste natures toward curbing men's sexual impulses, before and during marriage.[51]

The same social forces helped foster new ideals for men's sexuality. Religious prescriptions for male premarital virginity, as espoused by revivalists, were nothing new; but Graham's model of health suggested that men could also reap economic benefits from pre- and postmarital continence. Self-restraint in all walks of life appeared key to men's success in the burgeoning industrial economy.[52] Many American Victorians came to see sexual continence as a sign of strength and masculinity, the ideal man as "an athlete of continence, not coitus, continuously testing his manliness in the fire of self-denial."[53] Yet, old notions of male "sexual necessity" persisted. Well into the 1890s, many middle-class Whites believed that adult men could maintain neither their health nor their masculinity without discharging sexual energy, and even some physicians recommended "fornication as a cure for masturbation and other ills."[54] Red-light districts flourished in American towns and cities throughout the 1800s, despite organized opposition.[55] Some fathers "proudly sent their sons off to bawdy houses to establish their masculinity"; and early sex surveys found that a sizable minority of men in the late 1800s had paid to lose their virginity before marriage, though moral decency required that they did so discreetly.[56]

In short, despite the close fit between the ideals of feminine passionlessness and masculine continence, a sexual double standard ruled the day. Victorians defined virginity primarily in terms of moral, rather than physical, criteria during this period, and those criteria grew more conservative over time. By the late 1800s, popular stories frequently featured heroines who lost their virtue seemingly without engaging in a genital sexual act. Some middle-class moralists even declared kissing and hand-holding to be unacceptably intimate prior to betrothal.[57] Virginity/virtue was fragile, and the line between pure and fallen women was absolute.[58] Blame for premarital sex invariably fell on the woman: either she failed to deploy her virginal innocence in a sufficiently deterrent manner, or she hadn't been innocent in the first place. Youths' behavior, especially women's, appears to have conformed broadly to ideals, with rates of pre-marital pregnancy among White women declining dramatically between 1830 and 1850.[59]

Even as Victorian beliefs about gender and sexuality distanced women from men, they helped foster intimate relationships between people of the same sex.[60] This was especially true for middle- and upper-class Whites, who had the means to segregate the genders, and for women in particular, given their socialization to value the affective dimensions of life. Same-sex friendships in the Victorian era could be quite romantic and frequently included physical demonstrations of affection, some of which may have been erotic in nature. Lovers had a strong incentive to keep sexual aspects of their relationships secret, however, for even though engaging in same-sex activities wouldn't be interpreted as a form of pathology until late in the century, it *was* viewed as perverse and sinful. The widespread assumption that same-sex friendships were asexual, especially among naturally passionless women, probably made it easier to conceal erotic expression when it did occur.

Middle-class Whites tended to believe that they alone could achieve sexual morality, although the historical record provides evidence to the contrary. Most Whites denigrated Africans and their descendants as sexually depraved.[61] Yet, the life histories of former slaves suggests that enslaved Blacks' own standards for sexual conduct before marriage, which evolved out of African traditions and adopted Christianity, were far from licentious.[62] Black parents rarely permitted youth to court until late adolescence and they strongly favored long-term monogamous unions over casual sexual liaisons. Nonmarital births among African Americans were neither uncommon nor cause for shame, however, due to a combination of enduring African values, the absence of an incentive to ensure legitimacy for inheritance purposes, and, most important, slaves' lack of practical control over their own sexuality. Owners interfered with courting and could prohibit or force marriages, often with the goal of augmenting their human property.[63] When enslaved women were raped by White men, they had no redress. Under these circumstances, it was impossible for Blacks to valorize virginity in the same terms as Whites did. After Emancipation, African Americans gained greater control over their own sexual lives, albeit within a context in which White authorities tacitly condoned the rape of Black women and lynching of Black men on suspicion of sexual desire.[64] Many slave marriages were formalized and the majority of southern Blacks continued to discourage promiscuity while forgiving premarital virginity loss.[65] African Americans who aspired to middle-class status, however, increasingly adopted the more restrictive sexual standards favored by middle-class Whites as one means of defusing racist stereotypes and gaining social mobility.[66]

White reactions to the sexual cultures of Mexican Americans in the U.S. Southwest and East Asian immigrants in the West, from about 1850, resembled their reactions to Black and working-class White sexuality. Heavily influenced by Roman Catholicism, Hispanic sexual culture placed great value on unmarried daughters' virginity. However, Mexican American youth commonly courted and danced in public, activities that White Victorians interpreted as licentious and immoral.[67] Chinese, Japanese, and other Asians who immigrated to the U.S. West as laborers were not permitted to bring their families, so Asian American communities were overwhelmingly male, save for a small number of female sex workers.[68] Although most East Asian cultures traditionally value virginity, White Americans interpreted the sexual regime that resulted from their immigration policies as evidence of Asian women's promiscuity and Asian men's asexuality or, alternately, depravity.[69]

The Development of Dating, 1865–1900

The Victorian approach to virginity loss was disrupted by the rapid social changes that took place at the end of the nineteenth century, although divisions by gender, race, and social class remained. Theodore Dreiser captured the spirit of the era in his 1900 novel, *Sister Carrie*. The story begins in 1889, a time when rapid industrialization was drawing thousands of young men and women from rural America to the nation's cities, where they hoped to achieve financial and social independence. Yet, as the 18-year-old heroine, Carrie Meeber, discovers soon upon arriving in Chicago, turn-of-the-century America offered few gainful *and* honorable employment options for women who lacked or refused economic support from fathers or husbands. When illness forces Carrie from a hard-won factory job, she defies her sister's command to return to the family home in small-town Wisconsin and agrees to set up housekeeping with her new friend, dapper salesman Charles Drouet, who promises to marry her once his finances improve. Their disparate reactions to the new arrangement, including Carrie's loss of virginity, speak volumes about the gendered sexual mores of the time:

"Oh," thought Drouet, "how delicious is my conquest."

"Ah," thought Carrie, with mournful misgivings, "what is it I have lost?"[70]

Her moral frailty exposed, Carrie is subsequently seduced and nearly ruined by a married friend of Drouet. By the end of the novel, she has rejected this shiftless man and achieved fame and fortune as a stage actress, albeit apparently at the expense of love and contact with her family.

Although Dreiser's book shares *Charlotte Temple*'s status as a cautionary tale for virgin women and an indictment of sexually predatory men, the fact that Carrie ultimately prospers in spite of her sexual transgressions indicates how much American sexual culture was transformed in the space of a century.[71] Industrialization and urbanization were the chief engines of change. Starting at the end of the Civil War and accelerating after 1880, tens of thousands of young White working-class men and women, most of them single, migrated to cities eager for work in the burgeoning industrial economy. A parallel, albeit smaller, migration occurred among young working-class African Americans in the South.[72] Young urbanites enjoyed relative anonymity and freedom from the watchful eyes of kin and close-knit communities. Opportunities for young women and men to socialize unsupervised expanded tremendously, especially as growing numbers of single women began to work for pay.[73]

Urbanization and industrialization fostered a consumption-oriented economy in which virtually all aspects of life, including sexuality, could be turned into commodities. Risqué novels and picture magazines proliferated, as did commercial pastimes like dance halls, amusement parks, and nickel cinemas. Such amusements helped give rise to an urban working-class youth leisure culture, first among Whites and a few decades later among Blacks, which in turn profoundly changed the nature of working-class courtship.[74] In the late 1800s, upper- and middle-class youth pursued heterosexual romance through a system of social calling, whereby marriageable daughters invited eligible men to visit in the security of their parents' homes. Unable to access the material requisites of social calling —parlors, pianos, and privacy—working-class youth devised the "date."[75] Instead of being received in would-be Juliets' homes, working-class Romeos invited young women out to theaters, dances, and other public venues. Dating introduced an explicit monetary component to courtship and, since men, as "hosts" and higher-wage earners, customarily paid, tipped the balance of power in men's favor.

The advent of dating did not appreciably alter prevailing beliefs about premarital virginity, but it did affect sexual behavior. Previous generations of youth had indulged in some amount of sexual contact before marriage, typically kissing and perhaps necking. But the privacy of dates and anonymity of urban settings made more intimate sexual activity increasingly possible and, by all evidence, more common. Kissing and necking became increasingly acceptable for White couples of all classes; however, petting remained not quite respectable and was probably largely confined to betrothed pairs.[76] Although most unwed White couples apparently stopped short of intercourse, climbing rates of premarital pregnancy indicate that an increasing number of young women were losing their virginity before marriage.[77] Class differences in courtship customs suggest that this increase in premarital sex was concentrated among working-class youth, who had more opportunities to indulge and fewer disincentives not to.

Worried that dating and the permissive sexual practices of working-class youth and new immigrants would contaminate their own offspring, White and African American community leaders launched a series of crusades to shore up the sexual standards they held dear.[78] White activists' various efforts—to establish homes for "wayward" girls, raise the age of sexual consent, and curtail the circulation of "obscene" literature—coalesced into a national, broad-based social-purity movement, with mostly female leaders and a critique of men's sexual privilege at its core.[79] Suffragists and organizations like the Women's Christian Temperance Union roundly criticized men's social and economic power over women, dismissed the popular view of men as innately lustful, and demanded adherence to a single sexual standard reflecting contemporary expectations for women. Yet, their pet strategy for enhancing women's sexual autonomy backfired. The campaign for "voluntary motherhood"—the right of married women to refuse sex in order to avoid pregnancy—ultimately encouraged ordinary men and women to think of sex as separate from reproduction and to accept artificial birth control, two preconditions for women to lose their virginity before marriage with impunity.[80] Black leaders likewise struggled to curb sexual "immorality" and to promote a single, conservative sexual standard, but their critique centered more on Whites' power over Blacks than men's power over women, with the aim of achieving "racial uplift," counteracting racist stereotypes, and stemming racist violence.[81]

Public support for a single sexual standard did in fact increase among the White and Black middle classes in the 1890s; but, in practice, the double standard reigned as before. Women were still expected to marry as sexually inexperienced virgins, while young men enjoyed considerably more latitude.[82] In fact, as the consumer-oriented economy and rise of bureaucratic corporations made self-control less crucial for men's professional success, sexual prowess—demonstrable through virginity loss—began to replace sexual continence as "essential to the worth" of White middle-class men.[83] Black middle-class men, by contrast, were still expected to exercise sexual restraint; but they were probably also more likely to have sex before marriage than Black middle-class women.[84]

Same-sex relationships were also affected by shifting social circumstances. As small numbers of middle-class White women began to gain economic independence through higher education, some of them rejected marriage to men in favor of committed live-in relationships with other women. At least some of these "Boston marriages" were explicitly erotic.[85] Urbanization facilitated the development of close, potentially erotic relationships among men, who could and did live together in city boarding houses, away from community scrutiny.[86]

Extending the "New" Sexual Culture, 1900–1945

In the popular imagination, 1920s America is inhabited by the sexy flappers and reluctant-to-settle-down new men immortalized in the fiction of F. Scott Fitzgerald and by the proudly sexual women and unorthodox men described by Black blues singers like Bessie Smith.[87]

Although less celebrated than Fitzgerald, Percy Marks created an exceptionally detailed account of the changing sexual customs of White college youth in his 1924 novel, *The Plastic Age*. When the book's protagonist, Hugh Carver, arrives at Sanford College, he gains immediate favor "for his shy, friendly smile, his natural modesty, and his boyish enthusiasm."[88] But when it comes to sex, small-town Hugh is "pathetically ignorant . . . consumed with curiosity." Though attractive to women, he had kissed his hometown sweetheart, Helen, only once, "a silly peck on the check."[89] His roommate, Carl Peters, is a charming reprobate by contrast. A "good-looking, sophisticated lad" from a nouveau-riche family,

Carl bedecks his side of their room with "photographs of the 'harem'" and freely admits, "I drink and gamble and pet."[90] When Carl implies "by sly innuendos that there wasn't anything that he hadn't done," Hugh feels "a slight disapproval—and considerable envy."[91] Yet, he is relieved to find out that Carl, too, is a virgin.

But it isn't long before Carl loses his virginity, one drunken night on summer vacation. Hugh finds him "neither better nor worse for his experience," and thus increasingly questions his own "very strict" sexual standards.[92] But he's not sure what path to follow. Some of his classmates applaud men like Carl and "hate to admit they're pure," while others speak ill of "dirty" fellows who "chase around with rats" (cheap women) or even disapprove of petting altogether.[93] Hugh wavers, neither wanting to be a virgin when he marries nor wishing to have sex without love. Over time, he learns to flirt and pet with sophisticated girls and falls in love with Cynthia Day, blithely ignoring warnings that "Cynthia runs with a fast crowd."[94] After a heady evening of dancing and drink at the Sanford junior prom, Cynthia asks Hugh to "take me somewhere."[95] They are interrupted before they can have sex, and Cynthia subsequently ends the relationship, fearing that they are motivated by "sex attraction" rather than love. A year later, despite the possibility that Cynthia has lost her virginity with another man, still-virgin Hugh considers her worthy of a marriage proposal (which she declines).

Mainstream American beliefs about virginity loss had clearly changed since the days of *Sister Carrie*. By the mid-1920s, Victorian standards no longer governed the sexual lives of White middle-class youth, although the precise details of the new sexual regime remained open to debate. Middle-class youth were embracing the hitherto working-class practices of dating, extensive sexual intimacy before marriage, and a weakened double standard.[96] Conventional morality still favored premarital virginity, especially for women. But nonvirgin women like Cynthia Day were no longer automatically labeled immoral or unmarriageable; and the growing equation of masculinity with sexual prowess prompted more than a few middle-class men to follow their working-class brothers in rejecting premarital virginity as a personal ideal and using "boastful talk of sex conquests" to "confirm their masculinity among other men."[97] The moral definitions of virginity loss that prevailed during the Victorian era had fallen by the wayside, in favor of primarily physiological definitions equating virginity loss with first vaginal sex.[98]

Underlying these new approaches to virginity loss were the growing consensus that marital love ought to be erotic and that women were sexual by nature. The socioeconomic changes of the late 1800s had, along with the suffragist and social-purity movements, greatly expanded education opportunities for women of all social classes and brought White middle-class women into the paid labor force in record numbers. At the same time (and not unrelated), fertility among native-born Whites plummeted, aided by the popularization of birth control.[99] Perceiving the White American family to be in crisis, many turn-of-the-century social critics recommended a new type of marriage, emphasizing personal fulfillment over family formation and perpetuated by bonds of companionship and erotic affection.[100] Positing "a satisfying sex life" as "essential for" rather than antithetical to "a satisfying marital union" would not, in turn, have been possible if middle-class Americans had not begun to embrace the new theories of sexuality, advanced by the likes of Sigmund Freud and Havelock Ellis, which proposed that all humans were inherently sexual and that sexual repression of either gender caused more harm than good.[101]

In this context of growing gender equality and recognition of women's sexuality, many young White middle-class women saw cultivating sexy, feminine personas as a means of demonstrating their independence and modernity (a practice encouraged by the burgeoning mass media and advertising industries).[102] The dawn of "sex appeal" did not, however, disrupt the prevailing belief that women's virginity represented a gift ideally given at marriage. The "typical" White college woman interviewed by journalists Dorothy Bromley and Florence Britten "did not intend to go the limit with any boy because she believed in 'giving her whole self when she married'"; and advice manuals noted regretfully that some girls, "when in love," believed that virginity "is the only thing they have to give."[103]

However, some young women (primarily the highly educated) were beginning to interpret virginity loss as a *rite of passage*, or step in the process of growing up, a potentially egalitarian view popularized in the late 1920s by Margaret Mead and other anthropologists.[104] In Bromley and Britten's estimation, such women were "in almost as great a hurry to cast aside their virginity as their grandmothers were to let down their skirts and put up their hair."[105] A few young women even seemed to feel stigmatized by their virginity, like the Midwestern girl who said of her own first lover, "I felt apologetic about being a virgin, and thought that the man was doing me a favor."[106]

For their part, many men clearly still wished to be their wife's first and only sexual partner. "I realize how selfish it is on my part," wrote one of Bromley and Britten's respondents, "but I feel that 90 per cent of men will demand the same."[107] However, many also expressed willingness "to forgo virginity in a wife who has been sincere in her past love."[108] The increasing acceptability of nonvirginity in women derived in large part from cultural ideals linking love, marriage, and sexuality; for if sexual intercourse was to be seen as an appropriate expression of committed love, then premarital virginity loss could be forgiven when inspired by an "all-consuming love" (especially if a couple were engaged).[109] Still, a woman's social class and race often determined whether she received the benefit of the doubt. Expert and popular literature of the 1920s and 1930s perpetuated the image of working-class women and women of color as uniquely prone to using their sexuality for material gain and losing their virginity "without reflection and without motive, in an almost animalistic manner."[110]

For White middle-class men, the chief effect of the new theories of sexuality was that injunctions to repress their sexuality were replaced by warnings that, in the words of Freud, "complete abstinence in youth is often not the best preparation for marriage. . . . Women sense this, and prefer among their suitors those who have already proved their masculinity with other women."[111] Although outright rejection of the Christian ideal of male premarital chastity placed a man "just beyond the bound of respectability," Bromley and Britten reported that many a man who remained a virgin in college felt "inclined to think I am something of a sissy."[112] "Decent" young men, epitomized by Hugh Carver, were expected to prefer sex with love over sex for its own sake. By the mid-1930s, many young women claimed to prefer sexually experienced husbands. The majority of the women in Bromley and Britten's survey

discounted their future husband's virginity. Those who intended to wait for marriage argued that they would want to be initiated into the great and rather terrifying adventure by a man who had got beyond the fumbling stage. They would prefer that he had not been initiated by a prostitute, but they would draw the line only at a man who was diseased.[113]

Alongside these prevailing perspectives, the belief that virginity loss represented a rite of passage gained currency even faster among young men than among their female counterparts.[114] Many held that, in the words of sexologist Albert Ellis, a man who does not "seek out sex satisfactions prior to marriage . . . is not smart . . . not really a man."[115] The net result of these developments was the narrowing, but by no means the disappearance, of the sexual double standard.

These "modern" understandings of virginity emerged in concert with the development of a middle-class youth culture in which dating played a prominent role.[116] The expansion of secondary education after about 1900 and the contemporaneous recognition of adolescence as a distinct and precarious life stage effectively isolated youth from adult society and encouraged them to defer adult responsibilities like marriage.[117] In addition to its inherent pleasures, dating represented a welcome emblem of generational difference; and the postponement of adulthood allowed young people to emphasize sociability over spouse-seeking. Dating was further popularized through the increasingly national mass media and facilitated by new technologies like the telephone and automobile.[118]

African Americans experienced the social trends that changed understandings of virginity among Whites in a context of persistent racism and restricted economic prospects. In the early 1900s, serial monogamy and semipermanent cohabitation were the norm among urban working-class and poor Blacks, largely because they were unable to achieve the economic stability that facilitated marriage.[119] Under such circumstances, extolling premarital virginity made little sense. Between 1916 and 1930, over 500,000 African Americans migrated from the rural South to the industrial cities of the Northeast and Midwest, greatly expanding the Black working class and fostering a vibrant urban entertainment culture.[120] Working-class youth took advantage of the resultant opportunities to date, pet, and lose their virginity before marriage (granted, premarital virginity had not previously been stressed among working-class Blacks, especially men), while leaders of the middle-class "Talented Tenth" renewed their calls for premarital sexual propriety and enjoined their daughters *and sons* to think of their virginity as a gift.[121] Young middle-class Black men, for their part, appear to have voiced strong support for the conservative standards with which they were raised, even as they had sex before marriage at higher rates than any group of their peers.[122] Yet, it was not long before dating became the norm among middle-class urban African American youth.[123] (In the rural South, where Jim Crow laws, poverty, and geographic isolation denied Black youth access to the venues of formal dating, they continued to court at picnics, church, and work.)

As middle-class youth adopted dating, their relationships grew more intimate sexually. They had been raised to view love as erotic and women as sexual; and the private nature of dates allowed for greater sexual freedom than had calling. Hand-holding and kissing, which had become conventional parts of White middle-class courtship by the First World War, were joined by the mid-1920s by necking and petting.[124] Even in small cities like Muncie, Indiana, half of high school boys and one third of girls had participated in "petting parties," according to wife-and-husband researchers Helen and Robert Lynd.[125] Intimate sexual activity began to occur at earlier stages of courtship among middle-class African Americans as well. Comparing youth of late 1800s to their 1930s counterparts, one former slave said, "They courted then just like they do now. Only they wasn't fast like they are now."[126]

Many unmarried youth felt that they could pet to a point just short of vaginal sex (but often to orgasm) without compromising their virginity. Indeed, doing so became so common in the 1920s that it garnered its own appellation: *technical virginity.*[127] For example, Ben Hecht's 1921 novel, *Erik Dorn,* describes pretty flapper Mary James as "technically a virgin. . . . She guarded [her chastity] with a precocious skill, parading it through conversation, hinting slyly of it. . . . She had learned the trick of exciting men with her virginity."[128]

The same factors that made petting more prevalent, along with minor challenges to the ideal of premarital virginity, led to a dramatic increase in the number of young Americans losing their virginity before marriage. Although premarital virginity loss had not been uncommon among any group of men since the late 1800s, it now became more the rule than the exception.[129] Rates of sex before marriage remained lower among women, but climbed steeply—from about 14 percent of White women born before 1900 to about 40 percent of those born later.[130] (Changes among Black middle-class women were probably less pronounced, given continuing pressure to uphold the code of "chastity and model womanhood.")[131] Most women who lost their virginity before marriage did so discreetly, with the men they intended to marry. Their "conservatism" was no doubt fueled by the higher social value placed on women's virginity, as well as by laws and customs impeding unmarried women's access to contraception.[132] Even so, the changes in women's behavior were so substantial that many middle-class men who came of age after the 1910s began their sexual careers with "respectable" women, whereas young men of previous generations had by and large limited their conquests to prostitutes or women of lower status than their own.[133]

The increasingly erotic nature of love and the growing tendency to define individuals in terms of their sexuality helped give rise to the understanding of homosexuality as referring to a type of person, "encompassing emotions, dress, mannerisms, [and] behavior"—albeit a psychologically troubled person—rather than "a discrete, punishable offense."[134] Labeling and repression of homosexual men and women increased in the short run—many states criminalized consensual sodomy, for instance—but also fostered the group consciousness that ultimately inspired the gay rights movement.[135] The blossoming of homosexual subcultures in urban centers in the 1920s and the increasing appearance of homosexual themes in popular culture—plays like *The Captive* (1926), novels like *Well of Loneliness* (1928), and Harlem songs like "Bull Dagger Woman"— helped more young gays and lesbians to recognize their desires and realize that they were not alone.[136] At the time, it was believed that having only same-sex affairs would guarantee virginity at marriage.[137] But the gradual increase in the visibility and acceptability of homosexuality that began in this era was crucial to the emergence of present-day ideas about same-sex virginity loss.

Toward the Brink of Sexual Revolution, 1945–1965

American sexual culture took a conservative turn in the late 1940s and 1950s, thanks to a prosperous economy and widespread longing for security after the deprivation and uncertainty of the Great Depression and Second World War. In the 1930s, many young Americans had seen marriage as a somewhat distant goal, not least because they could ill afford to assume responsibility for families of their own. The rapid expansion of white- and blue-collar employment opportunities after the Allied victory greatly reduced economic disincentives to marriage. Between 1939 and 1951, the average age at first marriage fell from 23 to 20 for women and from 27 to 23 for men. By 1959, 47 percent of U.S. women were marrying before their nineteenth birthday.[138] Changes in the timing of marriage affected the timing and nature of dating. In the 1920s and 1930s, young people didn't begin dating until late adolescence and most dated as widely as possible, reserving exclusive relationships until they were seriously contemplating engagement.[139] But as ages at marriage crept downward, many youth felt compelled to start searching for Mr. or Miss Right at age 12 or 13. "Going steady" with a single partner replaced sociability as dating's chief aim.

Postwar parents worried, not without reason, that going steady would lead to sex before marriage. Steady couples paired up for months or years and typically saw themselves as more committed than those who were merely dating, often adopting many of the trappings of betrothal—monogamy, endless hours together, and exchanging visible tokens such as rings—even though the arrangement was understood to be temporary.[140] Steadies therefore enjoyed ample incentives and opportunities to engage in escalating sexual intimacies. Secluded "Inspiration Points"—sites where couples could "make out" (the new term for petting) in parked cars—sprang up across the nation.[141] "Good girls" were expected to restrict petting to committed love relationships and to preserve their virginity until marriage. As one young woman told a Gallup pollster, "Virginity is one of the greatest things a woman can give to her husband."[142] Young men, in contrast, were tacitly encouraged to "sow their wild oats."[143] Adult authorities sought to curb teens' sexual activities by tightening curfews and rules, especially on women—measures that tended to enhance the appeal of early marriage, given the sexual liberty it allowed.[144] Many experts argued that couples who felt "ready for sexual intercourse . . . *should* marry" and even berated reluctant-to-marry couples for "moral cowardice."[145]

The 1953 motion picture, *The Moon Is Blue,* perfectly captures the prevailing beliefs about virginity in this era.[146] When the film's wholesome heroine, 22-year-old Patty O'Neil (Maggie McNamara), accepts a dinner invitation from handsome stranger Don Gresham (William Holden), she agrees to have a predinner drink at his apartment on the condition that he not try to seduce her. In her estimation, "girls" who visit bachelors' homes must either be "willing to lose their virtue" (i.e., virginity) or "to fight for it"—and she declares herself a steadfast member of the latter camp. Despite his playboy persona, 30-year-old Don also draws a sharp line between good women and bad. Only the night before meeting Patty, he broke his engagement to cool and elegant Cynthia Slater (Dana Addams) because she tried to seduce him. Patty's professed virginity does little to deter Don from his attempts at seduction—at first. But in the ensuing comedy of mistaken intentions, Don is won over by Patty's innocence and quirky charm, not to mention her nurturing personality and considerable domestic skills. The movie concludes with Patty accepting his proposal of marriage (and planning to give up her acting career).

Many young Americans shared Patty and Don's beliefs about virginity and marriage and strove to emulate them in their own lives. However, as in the 1920s and 1930s, cultural ideals linking love and sexual expression had the unintended effect of encouraging committed couples to have sex before marriage. Nearly four-fifths of the men and half of the women who came of age in the 1940s and 1950s lost their virginity before they wed.[147] Middle-class men and women were less likely than their working-class counterparts to lose their virginity before marriage, probably because they had more to lose—college, career, and a "good" marriage—through unintended pregnancies.[148] Within social classes, Black men were more likely than White men to have sex before marriage, but Black and White women behaved in very similar ways.[149]

The tension between ideals and conduct around virginity was one of several postwar sexual paradoxes that set the stage for the sexual "revolution" of the late 1960s.[150] This tension had existed in the 1920s and 1930s, of course; but the American public had largely been able to ignore it until the publication of Alfred Kinsey and colleagues' *Sexual Behavior in the Human Male* in 1948 and *Sexual Behavior in the Human Female* in 1953. Collectively known as the Kinsey Reports, these hefty compendiums of sexual habits became surprise best-sellers.[151] Many readers were shocked to learn, from an ostensibly scientific authority, that over half of the women interviewed for the study—and many more of the men —had lost their virginity before they married.[152] The Kinsey studies also shook the widespread assumption that homosexual desire and activity were rare, with the claim that as many as one in three men and one in ten women had experienced an orgasm with a same-sex partner.[153] These revelations helped facilitate the evolution of urban gay communities, which had already received a boost from the sex-segregated employment and relative freedom of the war years.[154] Still, virginity loss remained equated with vaginal sex and "homosexually inclined" youth often felt isolated and found their desires difficult to name. It is likely that most gay and lesbian adults who came of age in the 1950s and 1960s began their sexual careers with other-sex partners.[155]

The commercial success of the Kinsey Reports points to another postwar paradox: the growing sexualization of commodities and commodification of sexuality during an era of sexual conservatism.[156] *The Moon Is Blue* is a case in point. Although the film seems remarkably traditional from today's perspective, depicting virginity as women's ticket to wedded bliss, in 1953, Hollywood Production Code officials refused to certify it on the grounds of its "unacceptably light attitude toward seduction, illicit sex, chastity, and virginity."[157] When director Otto Preminger decided to release *Moon* without official approval, it became one of the year's top-grossing films. As with the best-selling Kinsey books, the public's favorable response to *Moon* hints at a permissive undercurrent running just beneath the era's conservatism. Not coincidentally, 1953 also marked the premiere of the remarkably successful, sexually explicit men's magazine, *Playboy,* which from its inception unequivocally celebrated bachelors' sexual escapades and tended to portray male virgins as effeminate losers.[158]

Thanks to corporations' realization that sex sells, plus the first stirrings of second-wave feminism (Betty Friedan's *Feminine Mystique* was published in 1963), it wasn't long before women could purchase their own fantasy of a sexy singles lifestyle. The indisputable queen of this new regime was Helen Gurley Brown, whose irreverent 1962 advice guide, *Sex and the Single Girl,* and revamped version of *Cosmopolitan* magazine (from 1965) explicitly refuted the prevailing view that sex outside of marriage brought women nothing but despair. Brown didn't seek to devalue women's virginity per se, but she denounced the good girl/bad girl dichotomy, asserting that it was perfectly acceptable for an unmarried "girl" to say "yes" "when a man 'insists.'"[159] She also expressed profound distress at the effects of traditional sexual socialization on American women: "One fine day—maybe on her wedding night but probably before—she will want to unlock her chastity belt and she won't be able to find the key."[160]

The Revolution Begins, 1965 and Onward

The permissive undercurrents reflected in the sexual paradoxes of the Cold War years, along with major demographic changes, ultimately helped produce the sexual revolution of the late 1960s and early 1970s. The baby boomers—the immense cohort of children born between 1946 and 1964—were the chief architects of this transformation.[161] Having grown up in a time of material abundance, members of this generation rarely had to abandon school for work during adolescence (with the exception of the truly poor), and they enjoyed unprecedented leisure time and disposable income. Advertisers and consumer-goods manufacturers were quick to capitalize on this fact: the youth market, touting products that emphasized teens' difference from adults, quickly came into its own.

By the mid-1960s, U.S. college campuses swelled with record numbers of students. Able to postpone adult responsibilities, influenced by the Beat and Hippie subcultures, and appalled by American involvement in Vietnam, many White college-age boomers lashed out against what they saw as the complacent conservatism of older generations. Rejecting their parents' cherished sexual norms formed a key strand in their rebellion. Black students likewise took up arms, though their rebellion focused more on the failure of the civil rights movement to deliver racial equality than on parental values per se.[162] Different motivations notwithstanding, White and African American youths' sexual beliefs and behaviors changed largely in concert.

Where their parents had drawn a veil of silence around premarital virginity loss, making it seem less common than it was, American youth in the late 1960s advertised their nonvirginity and openly rejected premarital chastity as an ideal. They were also willing to lose their virginity with partners they didn't expect to marry—to engage in what sociologists John Gagnon and William Simon memorably described as *pre*-premarital sex —and at earlier ages on average.[163] Other scholars reflected that, although approaches to virginity loss had changed, it continued to mark a key social transition, one that had, along with driving and drinking, largely taken the place of such traditional, but increasingly delayed, markers of adulthood as marriage and entry into the paid labor force.[164]

Changes around virginity loss were especially dramatic among young women, in part because standards for men were less conservative to begin with, in part because of the development of the Pill and IUD (intra-uterine device), and in part because the feminist movement's demand for complete equality enhanced women's ability and desire to breach traditional sexual standards.[165] Young men, for their part, felt the effects of a new model of masculinity, brought about by the weakening of adult authority and rigid gender norms, which favored a more egalitarian ethos in professional and personal life.[166]

Yet, the sexual double standard did not fade away. In fact, a new version rapidly crystallized, whereby casual sex was deemed acceptable for men but women were expected to make sex—thus virginity loss—contingent on love or at least strong affection, and preferably the title of girlfriend.[167] Many young women complained of being treated as "out of it" for delaying virginity loss, but those who wished to maintain "good" reputations still found it necessary to proceed with caution.[168] Still, from the late 1970s on, scholars observed a small but growing cadre of teenage girls actively resisting the new double standard, eagerly forsaking virginity loss with a beloved partner for "getting it over with," as did so many men.[169] Young men found that the freer climate simply made losing virginity more imperative, at earlier ages, than before.

Racial/ethnic differences in attitudes about virginity and ages at first vaginal sex began a steady diminution in the late 1960s, apparently due to growing racial equality and integration.[170] Social-class differences likewise narrowed, as middle-class Americans embraced increasingly liberal attitudes about sexuality and gender, and working-class and poor youth gained material incentives to postpone sex (or otherwise avoid pregnancy) during the 1960s expansion of higher education.[171] Yet, some differences persist into the present day. On average, African American adolescents become sexually active at earlier ages than Whites, who become sexually active before Latino/as, who in turn become sexually active before Asian Americans.[172] Overall approaches to sexuality also appear to differ by race and ethnicity, with Black men tending to favor a recreational stance, Black women and Latinas thinking of sex in more traditional/relational terms, and Latinos and Whites favoring a relational approach.[173] However, recent studies suggest that socioeconomic status affects adolescents' sexual conduct more profoundly than racial/ethnic background, with working-class and poor teens initiating sex earlier than their middle-class counterparts and, once sexually active, using birth control less often.[174]

An ironic effect of the late-1960s shift toward more permissive standards for virginity loss was an apparent increase in the number of youth, primarily women, who regretted losing their virginity so much that they decided to postpone further sexual encounters until some point in the future. Scholars in the 1970s called this pattern "regretful non-virginity" or "secondary virginity"; neither term caught on among lay people until the mid-1980s, when conservative Christian groups began to promote secondary virginity and coined the synonym "born-again virginity."[175]

The sexual revolution also inspired new approaches to petting. In the mid-century, heterosexual couples rarely engaged in fellatio and cunnilingus before marriage, and then only after they had engaged in vaginal sex.[176] But as public discussions of sexuality became increasingly explicit and varied in content, more and more heterosexual Americans became aware of oral sex—popular media from Dr. Alex Comfort's best-selling manual, *The Joy of Sex* (1972), to the pornographic crossover hit, *Deep Throat* (1972), positively celebrated it—and began incorporating oral sex into their own sexual repertoires. By the mid-1980s, many adolescent peer groups saw oral sex as an activity compatible with retaining (technical) virginity.[177]

Yet another sexual sea-change that began in the late 1960s involved Americans' understandings of homosexuality. Catalyzed by the riot that ensued when the New York police raided the gay bar, Stonewall Inn, in the summer of 1969, gay men and lesbians began to organize and vocally demand an end to their social and legal oppression. Key early victories included the American Psychiatric Association's 1974 decision to drop homosexuality from its list of mental disorders and the abolition of many state antisodomy laws.

Like the generation before them, many gays and lesbians who came of age in the 1970s and 1980s began their sexual careers with different-sex partners and appeared to share the mainstream culture's belief that virginity loss was irrelevant to same-sex encounters. This belief is exemplified in nationally syndicated advice columnist Abigail (Dear Abby) Van Buren's pronouncement, in 1983, to a young woman who'd "had a few affairs with females": "Technically you are a virgin. . . . (A few lesbian experiences during one's adolescence does not necessarily a lesbian make.)"[178] But the post-Stonewall generation developed its own standards and rituals, including coming out: the public proclamation of one's homosexual or bisexual identity that has since become an almost obligatory rite of passage for lesbigay women and men.[179] As the visibility of—and tolerance for—lesbigay sexuality increased, the average age at coming out declined significantly, from about 22 for gay men and 25 for lesbians in the early 1970s to about 17 and 20 (or even younger), respectively, in the mid-1990s. Equipped earlier to identify their own desires as well as potential same-sex partners, more and more lesbigay youth would begin their sexual careers with same-sex partners, and at earlier ages on average.

Virginity Loss after HIV/AIDS

The "liberated" sexual culture of the late 1960s and 1970s had barely taken root when it met with a series of critical challenges. As early as the mid-1970s, moral conservatives, led by the Christian right, mounted a series of crusades intended to reverse the gains of second-wave feminist and gay-rights activism and the increasingly permissive tone of sexual culture overall.[180] Focusing on what was widely perceived as an epidemic of adolescent pregnancy, moral conservatives helped secure the 1981 passage of the Adolescent Family Life Act (AFLA), which required that federally funded sex education programs present maintaining virginity until marriage as a contraceptive option. When, in the late 1980s, HIV/AIDS was recognized as posing a threat to heterosexual adults and teens, social conservatives redoubled their efforts to implement abstinence-focused sex education in public schools and launched a public service campaign extending the popular antidrug slogan, "Just say no," to premarital sex.

Calls for more restrictive sexual standards in the 1980s also came from a very different quarter: radical feminists, such as Andrea Dworkin and Catharine MacKinnon, who sought to combat sexual violence against women by such means as prohibiting pornography and sex work.[181] Opposing their efforts were feminists like Ellen Willis and Carole Vance, who stressed the need to expand women's sexual liberties, even if that meant accepting their right to engage in potentially harmful practices.[182] In the divisive debate that ensued, many feminists felt compelled to choose between being either "for sexual pleasure" or "against sexual danger." Such a context encourages women to frame virginity loss as purely liberating or entirely perilous. The tension between these positions rekindled in the 1990s, when young feminists fighting acquaintance rape were denounced by social critics like Katie Roiphe for embracing victimhood and by observers like Wendy Shalit for inviting assault by abandoning "feminine" modesty.[183] By the end of the decade, self-described "third wave" feminists were advocating an intermediate position, decrying inequality in heterosexual relationships while insisting that heterosexual sex offered opportunities for pleasure and exploration.[184] Such a position implies a more complicated vision of women's virginity loss.

The same period saw similar tensions around same-sex sexuality. The 1990s and early 2000s were marked by unprecedented lesbigay visibility and political gains for lesbian, gay, and queer activists. Popular media featured a growing number of gay and lesbian characters and themes, from kisses between women on L.A. Law (1991) and Roseanne (1994) to the Emmy-winning sitcom Will and Grace (1998 to present); Olympic diver Greg Louganis and New York Giants linebacker Roy Simmons publicly revealed themselves as gay in 1994 and 1992, respectively; and unprecedented numbers of openly gay people ran for U.S. Congress in 1998. Yet, moral conservatives continued to vilify same-sex sexuality. Anti-gay legislation proliferated at state and federal levels, Congress passed the Defense of Marriage Act in 1996, and House conservatives proposed the Federal Marriage Amendment to the U.S. Constitution in 2002 and 2004.[185] Nor did hate crimes against gays abate; the 1998 murder of University of Wyoming student Matthew Shepard was merely the most prominent. Expanded visibility and ongoing opposition together transformed the experiences of lesbigay teens of the post-HIV generation. In contrast with their older counterparts, they have come out at younger ages, increasingly identified as gay or bisexual before becoming sexually active, and embraced participation in public protests and Gay Pride marches as rites of passage.[186] These trends appear to harbor potential for changing the ways young people, both lesbigay and straight, conceptualize and approach virginity loss, as we will soon see.

Overall, permissive and restrictive stances toward virginity coexisted uneasily in the 1990s and early 2000s. Moral conservative efforts curbed, but by and large did not reverse, the liberalizing tendencies of the late 1960s and 1970s. Although a majority of American teens continued to approve of sex before marriage and to engage in vaginal intercourse during high school, the average age at first sex leveled off around 1990 and rose slightly toward the end of the decade, especially among men.[187] Yet even as men's and women's ages at virginity loss have converged, studies of the subjective aspects of early sexuality suggest several enduring differences. Most notably, young heterosexual women are more often disappointed by and/or feel a lack of control at virginity loss than young men; but some recent studies suggest that disappointment and "feminine" interpretations of virginity may be increasing among adolescent men.[188]

It is in this context of sexual diversity and tension that I set out to examine in depth how young Americans define, interpret, and experience virginity loss at the turn of the twenty-first century.

2

Defining Virginity Loss Today

When I asked people how they would define virginity loss to someone who had never heard of it—"Say, to a visitor from another planet"—the vast majority of the heterosexual women and men I interviewed gave replies like Lavinia Thompson's.[1] A 30-year-old African American paralegal, Lavinia answered simply, "[Virginity loss is] the first time having sex." It became clear from her responses to subsequent questions that when Lavinia said "sex," she meant vaginal intercourse. A few heterosexual people I spoke with remarked that beliefs about oral and anal sex vis-à-vis virginity were somewhat ambiguous; fewer still raised the possibility of virginity loss with same-sex partners.[2] Heterosexuals who spontaneously mentioned same-sex virginity loss typically had lesbigay friends who had brought the issue to their attention or had undergone professional training emphasizing sensitivity to lesbigay concerns (e.g., as a psychotherapist).[3] Charlotte Brandt, a 28-year-old White fund-raiser, described the evolution of her definition of virginity loss:

> My first immediate reaction is, between heterosexual people. And it would be penetration, vaginal penetration, with a penis. . . . And I think that that was my definition of it . . . probably until I was in my early to mid-twenties. When, not only did I start having gay friends, but then I actually thought about them having sex. And so, you know, a female friend of mine who's a lesbian, who's never had sex with a man, is she a virgin? No, she's not a virgin.

The fact that most heterosexual men and women assumed that virginity loss constituted vaginal intercourse highlights the degree to which heterosexuality is taken for granted in American society. This tendency serves to perpetuate the pattern poet/scholar Adrienne Rich calls "compulsory heterosexuality," whereby sex between women and men is assumed to be the norm and anything else is discouraged, disparaged, and rendered virtually invisible (or worse).[4]

In contrast, although many of the lesbigay people in my study also began by glossing virginity loss as the first time a person had sex, they invariably proceeded to question the very definition of "sex." Twenty-one of the 22 gay and bisexual men and women I interviewed claimed that a person could lose her or his virginity through oral and/or anal sex as well as through vaginal intercourse. The single exception was Miranda Rivera, a 29-year-old Puerto Rican lesbian teacher. Miranda saw virginity as irrelevant to sex between women and felt that women who have never had sex with men can take pride in having retained their virginity. She explained, "A woman loses nothing when she goes to bed with another woman. . . . But somehow there's something lost, in terms of men, you know, like her honor." [5]

Some lesbigay people saw oral and anal sex as resulting in virginity loss only between same-sex partners, but the majority favored applying the same standards to every possible pairing. As Seth Silber, a 19-year-old gay White college student, explained:

> See, I define sex as, you know, not . . . just genital contact. But also not necessarily, you know, strict penis-vagina penetration. Um, I think of oral sex as sex, and I think of anal sex as sex, and I think of vaginal sex as sex. Those are kind of, like, the three things that I think of as sex.

Seth said he'd lost his virginity when he first exchanged oral sex with a girlfriend, at age 15, about a year before he came out (though he didn't think of himself as losing his virginity at the time). Notably, the generations differed, with lesbigay participants born between 1962 and 1972 being more likely to distinguish between acts with same- and other-sex partners than were their younger counterparts.

Whether or not they differentiated between the acts involved in same- and other-sex virginity loss, gay and bisexual men and women who offered same-sex inclusive definitions were effectively arguing that same-sex practices should be not just accepted, but accepted on the same terms as heterosexual practices. These sentiments contrast with those of previous generations of lesbigay people, who by and large accepted the conventional equation of virginity loss with first vaginal sex and therefore either assessed their own status in terms of coitus or deemed virginity irrelevant to their experiences (as did two of the oldest gay men I interviewed).[6] Choosing to expand the definition of virginity loss to encompass same-sex activities appears to be a recent development, resulting from gay rights activists' success in enhancing the visibility and acceptability of lesbigay sexuality.

Activists' successes have also been instrumental in enabling the current generation of lesbigay youth to recognize and express their sexual identity at earlier ages, often without experimenting with heterosexual sex. Several of the youngest gay men in my study proudly spoke of challenging traditional definitions of sex in public school health classes. Ettrick Anderson, a 19-year-old gay African American student, recalled that, in the Philadelphia-area middle school he attended:

> My health teacher [and] I once had this huge argument during class because she defined intercourse as "Male inserts A into female's B," and that was it. And I disagreed with that. And I asked her, "Well, you're forgetting a bunch of people." And she said, "No." And she almost kicked me out of class.

Increasing awareness of and tolerance for lesbigay sexuality have also affected heterosexuals' definitions of virginity loss. Although few straight men and women voluntarily mentioned same-sex virginity loss, when I asked for their opinions, three-fourths said they believed that both women and men could lose their virginity with same-sex partners.[7] People born between 1973 and 1980 were much more likely than those born between 1962 and 1972 to favor lesbigay-inclusive definitions of virginity loss. Yet, in contrast to their lesbigay counterparts, the majority of heterosexuals posited different standards for virginity loss with same- and other-sex partners. A typical response came from Meghan O'Brien, a 22-year-old White college senior:

> I guess virginity has to be defined within each type of relationship, like woman-woman, man-man, heterosexual. I don't know . . . I never really thought about it. Because it's not as clear-cut and defined, I don't. People haven't really ever set terms on that type of thing. I guess I would say . . . if that is their form of sex, if that's . . . their way of making love . . . I think probably no, they wouldn't be a virgin.

That opinions on this point should differ by sexual identity is not surprising, given that heterosexual men and women typically lack the personal incentive for and intense commitment to promoting equality across sexual identity that characterizes so many lesbigay lives.

Defining Other Kinds of Genital Sex

Everyone I interviewed agreed that a woman or man would lose their virginity the first time they engaged in vaginal sex, provided that they had not previously engaged in another type of genital sex. They also agreed that virginity loss had to involve at least some sort of genital contact between two people. However, manual genital stimulation alone was not sufficient to constitute virginity loss in the eyes of even my most inclusive informants. Deborah Sherman, a 29-year-old White lesbian, explained that, although she would categorize intimate nongenital touching as "sex," she favored less expansive criteria for virginity loss:

> I want to be more open than that. I want to say, "Oh, you can hold hands," or, "You can, you know, touch each other for a while and there goes virginity." But I think, I think I'm going to go for the genital option there [laughs].

Nor did I speak with anyone who believed that a woman whose hymen had been broken without sexual contact would have lost her virginity.[8] In defining virginity loss primarily in terms of physical acts rather than moral propriety, the men and women in my study were following a pattern that has prevailed since the early 1900s.

Opinions differed as to whether oral and anal intercourse could result in virginity loss, depending especially on the sexual identity (and sexes) of the virgin and partner and of the person offering the definition. Several of the gay men I spoke with mentioned a lack of consensus in the gay community as to whether oral sex between men "counts" as sex or as virginity loss. According to Ettrick Anderson:

> A lot of people break it down by like, the acts that correspond to your sexual orientation. . . . So if you're a gay male, you're supposed to have anal sex because that's what gay men do. And if you're a gay woman, then you're supposed to have oral sex, because that's what gay women do. And so those become, like, markers for when virginity is lost. So . . . I could probably go out and find like, twenty queer boys in this building

who would say that, if someone's never had anal sex, then they're still a virgin, if they're a gay male.

Yet, 6 of the 9 gay men (including Ettrick) and both of the bisexual men in my study argued that a virgin man would lose his virginity by engaging in fellatio with another man. Opinions varied according to men's personal preferences. The 3 gay men who insisted that gay virginity loss entailed anal intercourse all enjoyed the practice, or expected to. Fernando Garcia, a 21-year-old gay Cuban American performing-arts student and self-described virgin, said:

> Personally, I don't look at oral sex as, like, capping virginity. . . . If that were the case, then I wouldn't be a virgin. I think, oral sex for me doesn't pass that line of, like, losing virginity. It's like still sexual behavior, but it's not like, going all the way.

The remaining men saw anal sex as considerably less appealing. As Seth Silber explained:

> Well, I haven't, um, had anal sex. I've tried, it just seemed too painful. . . . And since I haven't had, like, vaginal sex, I've just had a fair bit of oral sex [laughs]. Like, I know that in people's eyes, I'm a virgin, but . . . I think of myself as sexual, I think of the things I've done as sex. I don't, like, see the word virgin as applying to me.

To men like Seth, it made no sense to call themselves or other sexually active people virgins. All of the bisexual women and lesbians I interviewed (except for Miranda) believed that a virgin woman could lose her virginity by engaging in cunnilingus with another woman (as opposed to, say, requiring digital penetration).

In contrast to lesbigay men and women, most of whom claimed that oral and anal sex would result in virginity loss for any combination of partners, the majority of heterosexuals I spoke with placed oral sex between men and women squarely in the category of foreplay—"That's . . . fooling around, in my terminology," said Marty Baker, a 26-year-old White retail manager—or argued that while oral sex might be sex, it wouldn't amount to virginity loss. More than half of heterosexual women and men argued that female-male anal intercourse would not result in virginity loss. As Karen Lareau, a 21-year-old White student, explained, "I guess [hetero anal sex] would go along the same lines as oral sex. . . . Sex has always been defined to me as the vaginal way. . . . As far as virginity goes." A few individuals excluded male-female anal sex from their definitions of virginity loss because they saw it as perverse or demeaning. Wendy Hargrave, an 18-year-old White student, declared, "Yes, it's sex, but I personally think that anal sex is, like, degrading. So if that's happening, it's not really . . . giving anybody else that little piece of you." The practice of classifying anal and oral intercourse as (heterosexual) foreplay dates to the late 1600s, with explicit "rules" appearing around the turn of the twentieth century, as in marriage manuals defining petting as "literally every caress known to married couples but does not include complete sexual intercourse."[9] It seems, then, that former President Bill Clinton is far from alone in distinguishing fellatio from "real" sex.

Yet, for the heterosexual people who claimed that anal intercourse *would* result in virginity loss between a man and woman, the key issue was the physiological or emotional *resemblance* between anal and vaginal sex. As Kate O'Connor, a 24-year-old White radio producer, put it, "What [anal sex] involves is so close to vaginal intercourse that you might as well just be doing that. . . . I've always heard of kids who do that, so that they won't, quote, lose their virginity, and it's kind of like, well, isn't that just a minor technicality?"

Straight men and women who had not engaged in fellatio or cunnilingus before their first vaginal sexual experience were considerably more likely than those who had done so to perceive oral sex as potentially resulting in female-male virginity loss.[10] Paul Duval, a 25-year-old Haitian American bookstore clerk who'd had vaginal sex before any other kind of genital sex, said, "Personally I don't consider someone who's done basically just everything except vaginal-penile intercourse [should] try to pass themselves off as a virgin." Paul and Kate were two of only a handful of heterosexuals who pointedly disparaged the behavior often called "technical virginity." More than half had, in fact, acted in ways consistent with maintaining technical virginity—that is, they had repeatedly had manual, oral, or anal sex with partners before the partners with whom they lost their virginity.[11] Gay and bisexual women and men almost necessarily saw technical virginity in a different light, insofar as they typically viewed oral and/or anal sex as resulting in virginity loss (especially between same-sex partners).

As I noted in the Introduction, I had interviewed only 36 people when allegations of a sexual relationship between President Bill Clinton and

White House intern Monica Lewinsky came to light. At the time, I wondered whether the ensuing national dialogue on the definitional ambiguity of sex would affect the way people defined virginity loss, thereby biasing my later interviews. Fortunately, this did not seem to be the case. Of the 25 people I interviewed after January 1998, only 5 spontaneously mentioned the Clinton-Lewinsky controversy, suggesting that it was not particularly salient to their understandings of virginity loss. More important, only 6 of the 25 self-identified as heterosexual. My "pre-Monica" interviews had indicated that most if not all lesbigay women and men had questioned the prevailing equation of "sex" with vaginal-penile intercourse while they were coming out, typically long before we met. In effect, then, only heterosexual people were "at risk" for redefining virginity loss as a result of the scandal; and I could discern no differences between the definitions I heard before and after January 1998. In the long run, however, the Clinton-Lewinsky controversy may alter popular definitions of virginity loss. For example, media accounts suggest that, after the impeachment proceedings, adults increasingly worried that teenagers saw engaging in oral sex as consistent with retaining their virginity.[12]

Pinpointing Personal Virginity Loss

Not surprisingly, the kinds of sexual activities people identified as resulting in their own loss of virginity also differed by sexual identity. Fifty-six of the 61 people I spoke with described themselves as non-virgins. All 37 of the nonvirgin heterosexual women and men said that they had lost their virginity by engaging in vaginal sex, as did 4 of the 5 nonvirgin bisexual women and men. In contrast, only one of 8 nonvirgin gay men and 4 of 6 nonvirgin lesbians lost their virginity through vaginal sex.[13] Two lesbians reported losing their virginity the first time they exchanged cunnilingus with a woman. Five gay men and one bisexual man lost their virginity through oral sex with other men; one gay man (Seth) lost his virginity when he exchanged oral sex with a woman; and two gay men lost their virginity through anal sex with men. Few of the people who lost their virginity with same-sex partners had ever engaged in vaginal sex, and those who had understood these encounters as distinct from virginity loss, popular definitions notwithstanding. Abby Rosen, a 33-year-old White lesbian science librarian, emphatically declared that the first and only time she had vaginal sex with a man, after several sexual relation-ships with women, "I didn't consider myself then losing my virginity."

Women and men who had lost their virginity with a different-sex part-ner did so on average between the ages of 16 and 17, in all but one case through vaginal sex. The women were just slightly older than the men when they lost their virginity—16.8 compared with 16.5—which is con-sistent with recent survey estimates.[14] Boys who lost their virginity with other boys (through oral or anal sex) were somewhat younger on aver-age, between 13 and 14, while girls who lost their virginity with other girls (through oral sex) were slightly older, about age 19. These figures are consistent with recent research finding that gay and bisexual boys' first erotic encounters with same-sex partners (including kissing) occur earlier than do lesbian and bisexual girls' (at about age 13 and 15, respectively, on average).[15] (Reliable estimates of the ages at which self-identified les-bigay youth first have genital sex with same-sex partners do not exist, to my knowledge.)

Exceptions: Nonconsensual Sex and Secondary Virginity

In categorizing certain sexual acts as resulting or not resulting in virgin-ity loss, the women and men I spoke with were following the century-old practice of defining virginity loss in primarily physiological terms. But when it came to two specific scenarios—nonconsensual first sexual en-counters and secondary virginity—many of them preferred to assess in-dividuals' virginity status based on social and psychological criteria.

Just under half of the people I interviewed believed that a virgin who was forced to have sex would no longer be a virgin, an assertion they based on physiological grounds. According to Danice Marshall, a 28-year-old heterosexual African American nurse practitioner:

> To say someone is a virgin or not does not have to do with whether or not they had an intimate relationship with the perpetrator or the partner. If you're no longer a virgin, it's just because of the fact that a penis en-tered a vagina.

Discontent with this aspect of the definition of virginity loss was com-mon, however. Said Karen Lareau, "It's not the way that I would . . . de-fine losing your virginity . . . in a romantic kind of world. [But] it would definitely be intercourse, so I wouldn't consider them a virgin. Unfortunately."

The remaining half claimed, in contrast, that nonconsensual sex could not result in virginity loss, or could do so only in a technical sense. Some said that this was because rape was not "really" sex. Matt Bergquist, a 24-year-old White heterosexual engineer, explained:

> For some reason I don't think of rape and molestation . . . as sex in the same way. I guess losing your virginity is at least partially defined by the experience you gained about sex and relationships. And I think that there's so much that's strange about [coerced] encounters that they may not really fall into that category.

Others suggested that virginity loss depended on volition. In the opinion of Carrie Matthews, a 20-year-old White heterosexual nursing student:

> I see virginity as definitely something that you can choose into, and people . . . don't get to choose into rape. . . . If their only sexual experience has been something like a rape, I would call them a virgin even though technically something did happen.

Both arguments give social and psychological changes equal weight as physiological experiences in determining whether a person has "truly" lost her or his virginity.

The women I spoke with were considerably more likely than the men to exclude nonconsensual sex from their definitions of virginity loss. Nearly two-thirds of the women said that rape could never or could only technically constitute virginity loss, compared with only half of the men. This stands to reason, given women's greater susceptibility to rape and the fact that a larger proportion of women in the study had personally been the victims of sexual assault—8 of 33 women, compared with one of 28 men. Every one of the nine former victims maintained that virginity could not be lost through coerced sex.[16] Gender differences in beliefs about nonconsensual sex and virginity loss probably also stem from women's greater familiarity with the feminist argument that rape is an act of violence rather than a sexual act. First voiced in the 1970s, this claim has spread through magazine articles, support groups, and events such as Take Back the Night marches.[17] In fact, I found a generational difference, with only one-third of women and men born between 1973 and 1980 believing that coerced sex could result in virginity loss, compared with over half of those born between 1962 and 1972. This pattern suggests that this feminist understanding of rape is gradually being incorporated into mainstream understandings of sexuality and virginity loss.

For many of the people I interviewed, social and psychological criteria also overshadowed physiological ones when it came to the possibility of regaining virginity. Half believed that under no circumstances could a person become a virgin, or lose their virginity, more than once. Although some made this argument on physiological grounds, others pointed to experiential factors. As Tony Halloran, a 21-year-old White heterosexual busboy, saw it:

> I've seen commercials about [born-again virginity], but I don't see how they do it. Like, they can't forget that experience. . . . They'll always have that memory of when they lost their virginity, for the first time. So I don't see how they can become a virgin again.

Experiential factors also figured prominently in the reasoning of the other half of participants, who believed it *was* possible to be a virgin more than once. Most of these men and women saw renewing virginity as an emotional, psychological, or spiritual matter. As Terence Deluca, a 27-year-old White heterosexual heating and air conditioning mechanic, put it:

> There is a different feeling when you love somebody and when you just care about somebody. So I would have to say if you feel that way then I guess you could be a virgin again. Christians get born all the time again, so . . . when there's true love involved, yes, I believe that.

Women were twice as likely as men to contend that a person could potentially resume her or his virginity. This is not surprising, for, as we will see, women are more apt than men to sympathize with (or to have personally felt) the desire for a second chance at virginity loss—in part because women typically place greater value on having "special" virginity-loss experiences and in part because women are more often disappointed with virginity loss.[18] Women born after 1972 were substantially more likely than those born between 1962 and 1972 to argue that a person could be a virgin again, suggesting that the conservative Christian notion of secondary (or born-again) virginity has infiltrated mainstream U.S. culture through abstinence-focused sex education curricula, mass media campaigns, and growing membership in conservative denominations. Men's opinions did not differ by age.

A handful of people I spoke with mentioned a third domain in which nonphysiological criteria for assessing virginity status may be gaining importance: the spiritual. Some conservative Protestants claim that almost every non-genital sexual activity, including kissing and perhaps even looking at sexually explicit magazines or movies, is tantamount to virginity loss. This argument essentially represents a resurrection of Victorian thought. Dana Hagy, a 30-year-old White heterosexual homemaker and born-again Christian, explained: "Some people even say if you've looked at—obviously these people, I think, are radical—if you've looked at a pornographic magazine, well now you're not a virgin anymore, in some sense, in innocence." Dana was one of four conservative Protestants who told me that this perspective was circulating in their religious communities; all four quickly declared that they personally rejected it.

On Second Thought . . .

Definitions of virginity loss do not change only at the broad societal level; people can also revise their perspectives over time. Almost two-fifths of the women and men I interviewed informed me that they had, at some point, rethought the way they defined virginity loss. The majority of them were self-identified lesbigay men or women who had begun to include same-sex encounters in their definitions of virginity loss when they began questioning and rejecting heterosexual norms during the process of coming out. Several heterosexual people also told me that they had added same-sex virginity loss to their definitions after they'd discussed sex with lesbigay friends or undergone career training that sensitized them to GLBT concerns. Gaining more firsthand sexual experience inspired a few other heterosexuals to redefine sex *and* virginity loss. Heather Folger, a 28-year-old White office worker, told me that, although as a teenager, "I probably would've said, 'Yeah, [having only oral sex] would still make you a virgin.' . . . Not ever having done it, you know, not knowing what it really entails," when she started having oral sex, some years after losing her virginity, she decided that fellatio and cunnilingus were just as much sex as vaginal intercourse. A similar pattern was observed by psychologists Stephanie Sanders and June Reinisch; they found that young adults who had engaged in coitus were more likely to include oral- and anal-genital contact in their definitions of "sex."[19]

More Than One Virginity Loss

Given the myriad changes in understandings of sex and sexuality in recent history, one might expect that American youth would be on the verge of abandoning the concept of virginity loss as outdated or irrelevant. My research suggests that, on the contrary, young people are in the process of redefining virginity loss. Although vaginal sex still epitomizes virginity loss to most Americans, the definition is expanding and becoming more flexible, inclusive, and individualized overall. I observed a clear generational difference among the men and women I interviewed, with those born between 1973 and 1980 being more likely to allow for the possibility of virginity loss between same-sex partners, to exclude nonconsensual sex from their definitions, and to accept the possibility of resuming virginity than were people born between 1962 and 1972.

The increasing visibility of lesbigay people and new patterns of coming out brought about by gay rights activism and the HIV/AIDS epidemic have also contributed to new definitions encompassing virginity loss between same-sex partners. Feminist theories of rape have paved the way for definitions that exclude nonconsensual sex, while the resurgence of conservative Christianity has helped to popularize the idea that virginity can be regained and lost anew. Although today's young Americans follow their post-Victorian forbears in defining virginity loss primarily in terms of specific bodily acts, social and psychological criteria are enjoying a renaissance with respect to nonconsensual sex and secondary virginity. Criteria emphasizing spiritual and moral contamination may be making a comeback among a minority of very conservative Christians.

In addition to redefining virginity loss in response to a changing social landscape, young Americans are also in the process of interpreting virginity loss in more individualized ways. The women and men I spoke with made sense of virginity loss through four primary metaphorical frames, comparing virginity to a gift, a stigma, a process/rite of passage, or an act of worship. Although these metaphors have historically been associated with particular genders, religious beliefs, and other aspects of social identity, my research suggests that these links are weakening and growing more flexible over time. In the next few chapters, I will explore in depth the most common ways that virginity loss is understood today. Each chapter examines the distinctive constellations of beliefs and behaviors associated with a metaphor, showing how they produce characteristic trajectories—some positive, some negative—before, during, and after virginity loss.

3

A Gift of One's Own

Was Britney Spears really a virgin until the age of 21? From 1992 to 1994, preteen Britney epitomized wholesome American girlhood as a Mouseke-teer on Disney TV's revival of *The Mickey Mouse Club*. The young girls who admired Spears then helped propel her to superstardom a few years later, buying her first album and mimicking her wardrobe and dance moves by the millions. When Spears's debut single reached No. 8 on *Bill-board*'s pop charts at the end of 1998, she was not yet 17.[1] By 2000, the 18-year-old Spears boasted a decidedly sexy public persona, strutting the stage in skin-tight leather while crooning lyrics like "I'm not that inno-cent" and "I'm a slave for you."

In the first flush of success, Britney embraced the job of teen role model, explaining to a reporter from *Rolling Stone,* "You want to be a good example for kids out there and not do something stupid."[2] Among her exemplary attributes were regular church attendance and disapproval of smoking, drinking, and premarital sex. A fawning 1999 biography told of the 17-year-old innocently flirting with members of the popular boy band 'N Sync while on tour as their opening act, and "blushing" to admit that she'd kissed "[f]ive or six" boys in her lifetime.[3] Most famously, Brit-ney openly shared her desire to remain a virgin until she married. "I'll try not to have sex before marriage," she told one interviewer. "My girl-friends always say once you do that, there are so many other emotions in-volved, and I can't deal with that right now."[4] Britney's purported home-town sweetheart, Reg Jones, confirmed her claims in a British tabloid, saying, "She treasures her virginity above fame and fortune."[5] In short, whether as a result of her small-town, Southern Baptist upbringing or as a move calculated to reassure her young fans' parents and her own cor-porate sponsors, Spears described her virginity as something she trea-sured, or as a gift.

Some male fans took Spears's avowed chastity as a challenge. In 2000, when the singer was just 18, a wealthy American businessman reportedly offered to give her over $7 million if she would lose her virginity with him. Britney was outraged, telling journalists, "It's a disgusting offer. He should go and have a cold shower and leave me alone. . . . I want to wait until I get married before I sleep with anyone."[6] Her reaction, perfectly understandable for any young woman not keen on a career in prostitution, took on an additional resonance given her understanding of her virginity as a gift. The women and men that I spoke with who drew on this metaphor invariably appraised virginity as a very valuable gift, based on its uniqueness, nonrenewability, symbolic import, and status as an extension of the giver's self.[7] Typically, people see the value of a gift as reflecting the worth of its recipient and, accordingly, bestow the choicest gifts on the special individuals in their lives. Recipients conversely tend to interpret gifts as tokens of their own value in the eyes of the giver. When a virgin who views virginity as a gift decides to give her virginity to a specific partner, she is effectively declaring that he (or she), and their relationship, are valuable and unique. From the perspective of the gift metaphor, virginity is far too special to be purchased by a stranger; it is literally priceless.

Spears was lauded from many quarters for publicly taking such a traditionally feminine stance on virginity. A typical magazine columnist commended her for being "very sexy" but still having "strong principles and religious views."[8] Even officials from the Church of England praised Britney as "a great ambassador for virginity," in the wake of her confessed crush on her royal contemporary, Prince William.[9] Those who lauded Spears seemed to suggest that if all young women similarly valued their virginity, teen pregnancy, AIDS, and even welfare-dependency would become problems of the past. In a decade that had seen a proliferation of virginity-cherishing young women in American mass media—Donna Martin on TV's *Beverly Hills 90210* being the best known—Britney was the reigning queen of Virgin Cool.

But it wasn't long before the pop star's increasingly sexy image—with ever-skimpier stage outfits, more suggestive dance routines, and steamier song lyrics—and her advancing age raised doubts about her virginity status. By 2001, Spears was 19 years old, 2 years past the age at which half of American women of her generation have had vaginal intercourse.[10] But the chief challenge to Britney's assertions came when she and her boyfriend of one year, singer Justin Timberlake, bought a $3 million Hollywood mansion together. Spears told *US Weekly* that, although she was "very in love" with Timberlake, "I want to wait to have sex until I'm married. . . . But it's hard."[11] In light of the couple's cohabitation, her claims to virginity seemed implausible at best.

Speculation about Spears's virginity reignited when she and Timberlake broke up in early 2002. Within months, Justin had publicly refuted Britney's avowals of virginity and—not surprisingly, given the stigma often associated with virginity in men—done what he could to dispel perceptions that he might be a virgin, for instance, appearing in the company of sexy, presumably nonvirgin, women such as pop icon Janet Jackson.[12] Spears, for her part, couldn't seem to decide what image to project. As 2002 progressed, she was observed smoking cigarettes, giving the finger to paparazzi, and remarking on the similarity between her life and the sex-soaked TV series *Sex in the City*.[13] In September, *People* magazine quoted an increasingly defiant Britney as saying, "Who really cares if I've had sex? . . . It's nobody's business. . . . If I mess up, I'm human . . . I'm no different than anyone else my age."[14] Finally, in a tell-all interview for *W* magazine in August 2003, Spears confessed:

> I've only slept with one person my whole life. . . . It was two years into my relationship with Justin, and I thought he was the one. . . . But I was wrong! I didn't think he was gonna go on Barbara Walters and sell me out.[15]

Most difficult was forsaking the permanent bonds that giving her virginity had seemed to promise:

> We were together so long and I had this vision. You think you're going to spend the rest of your life together. Where I come from, the woman is the homemaker, and that's how I was brought up.

Spears's tale indicates some of the risks inherent to gift giving. Scholars have discerned three intertwined obligations: to give, to receive, and to reciprocate.[16] To label gift giving as an obligation may seem peculiar, since common sense dictates that gifts are by definition voluntary. Indeed, they are. Yet, gifts are also, paradoxically, virtually mandatory in certain social circumstances—such as between family members on birthdays, Christmas, or Hanukkah. Accepting a gift is likewise nearly compulsory, not least because refusing a gift entails symbolically refusing the giver.

The most potent obligation is reciprocity, that is, if someone gives you a gift, you are expected to give that person a gift in return, usually one of roughly equal value.[17] That gift will, in due course, inspire another gift from the original giver, which must in turn be reciprocated, and so on into the foreseeable future.

Gift giving fosters social solidarity in two ways. Slight variations in the type or value of gifts ensure a continuing balance of debt between partners, which in turn promotes an ongoing relationship.[18] By exchanging presents on a continuing basis, two people tend to strengthen the bond between them. Solidarity is also fostered by the emotional and symbolic value that gifts carry in addition to their material worth. As French sociologist/anthropologist Marcel Mauss noted, gifts are "often personified," imbued with the spirit of the giver. Insofar as this essence is transferred along with the gift, it helps forge a "sort of spiritual bond" between the giver and recipient.[19] Givers today can seldom force unwilling recipients to return their gifts and therefore are always somewhat beholden to recipients.[20] This uncertainty encourages would-be givers to assess the worthiness of potential recipients with great care.

As just one of the latest, and most famous, episodes in the social construction of virginity as a treasured possession, Britney Spears's story is emblematic of the experiences of many of those with whom I spoke. Her views on virginity seemed to be most influenced by her gender and religious background, her parents' and peers' beliefs, and her commitment to her first serious relationship. As I will show throughout this chapter, for people who conceive of virginity as a gift—or "gifters," as I will call them —each of these factors plays an important role in the decisions that culminate in virginity loss and in retrospective evaluations of virginity-loss experiences.

Of these factors, gender is perhaps the most important. Whether they celebrated Britney's virginity or scoffed at her claims, the public's fascination with her sexual status underlines the enduring salience of women's virginity in American culture. Similar speculation has dogged other attractive young female celebrities, notably Brooke Shields some twenty years earlier.[21] Such running commentary about virginity status does not seem to attach itself to comparably young and attractive male celebrities, however, and if it did, it would likely involve speculation as to their heterosexuality. The belief that women's virginity is a gift, which informs the classic double standard for sexuality, can probably be traced back to women's historic status as property transferred from fathers to husbands at marriage.[22] The young bride was expected to be a virgin on her wedding night, though her groom was not.

Although women are no longer literally "given away" by their fathers, ideas about "saving yourself" and "waiting for the right one" still figure prominently in many women's approach to virginity loss.[23] The women I interviewed were considerably more likely than the men to have compared their virginity to a gift at the time they lost it (or ever).[24] However, more than a few of the men, especially the youngest ones, also described their virginity as a gift. This chapter explores how women and men used the metaphor of gift giving to guide their early sexual careers and to construct their gender and other identities.

"Whenever You Find the Right Person"

Kelly Lewis describes losing her virginity as one of the most romantic episodes in her life. A 24-year-old office assistant by day, Kelly spends her evenings studying to become a certified physical therapist. Her peaches-and-cream complexion, dark shoulder-length hair, and bright smile give her the look of the pretty girl-next-door. She grew up in a small city about 2 hours' drive from Philadelphia, where she now lives with her boyfriend. When I asked Kelly what virginity meant to her, she replied:

> [Virginity is] supposed to be something special and cherished and wonderful and something to keep and you give to someone who is . . . I don't know if lose is the right word. . . . I'll say you give to someone, whenever you find the right person.

While she describes virginity as a valuable gift, she is quick to point out that she and her high school friends hadn't seen virginity as intrinsically precious, but as special because of what happened when you gave it to someone.[25] "We valued it . . . not that you should keep it forever," she said. "Like, we saw value in sharing it, having sex with someone."

Kelly believed that being in love was an essential precondition for virginity loss, but that being married was not. "Love—I guess that's the reason why you're supposed to keep your virginity," she said. "Until you find someone that you love. You know, the specialness of it." This stance was typical of gifters. Although every one of them emphasized the importance of love, barely a handful thought it would be ideal to remain a virgin until

marriage.[26] By contrast, relatively few of the women and men who preferred the process and stigma metaphors declared that virginity loss
should be reserved for love, and only one advocated virginity at marriage.[27]

Envisioning virginity as a gift to be bestowed on a special love, rather
than on a husband, helped Kelly reconcile her parents' different beliefs
about the meaning of sex. Kelly's mother was the more traditional of her
parents by far. A homemaker who remarried within a year of divorcing
Kelly's father (when she was 8), Kelly's mother encouraged her daughter
to think of sex as something special meant to be shared by married couples only. In fact, one of the few personal sexual details Kelly could recall
her "very quiet, close-lipped" mother disclosing was the fact that she'd
had sex with, "only your father," and her second husband.[28] In contrast,
Kelly's father, an attorney, to whom she'd always felt closer, "Never really had any ideas, like 'Oh, don't do it, it's wrong.' I mean, when you've
been divorced three times, what can you tell somebody?" In his apartment, "there were images of sexuality all over the place, or of women. . . .
He was into . . . *Playboy,*" and he was "very open to talk." He spoke of
sex primarily in terms of physical pleasure—the stereotypical masculine
stance—leading Kelly to expect that sex would "feel good." Faced with
these contrasting perspectives, Kelly decided that she wanted sex to be
about more than just physical sensation, but that she would never be as
prudish as her mother seemed to be.

Kelly and her friends believed that giving your virginity to a special
boyfriend would bring you closer and create a more intimate and lasting
relationship. One reason this would happen, Kelly suggested, was that
virginity loss involved sharing a unique and valuable part of yourself.
"You're giving it to someone, but it's yours," she explained. "You're not
really losing . . . possession of part of yourself, because it's still a big part
of yourself." Two-thirds of gifters made similar claims; hardly anyone
who saw it as a stigma or process concurred.[29] Indeed, scholars have observed that, when people see a gift as comprising part of the self—as
many see virginity—they often perceive it as part of an "extended self"
which, when shared between giver and receiver, helps bind them together.[30]

Not surprisingly, Kelly felt it was crucial to be choosy and to save her
virginity for someone special. Remarks about waiting for the "right" or
"perfect" partner, based on such criteria as love, commitment, and "spe-

cialness," peppered gifters' stories—but were virtually absent among people who viewed virginity as a process or a stigma. Many gifters also believed that it would be ideal for a couple to lose their virginity together. To their way of thinking, exchanging this most-precious gift would not only forge an especially strong bond between partners, but would also ensure mutual reciprocation.

On the surface, reciprocating a partner's gift of virginity with one's own appears to violate social norms discouraging the giving of identical gifts. For example, if you give someone a ring for her birthday and then she gives you the same ring for yours, she has effectively canceled your obligation to reciprocate, along with the opportunity to continually strengthen the ties between you.[31] Yet the high regard my interviewees had for mutual virginity loss suggests that virginities are not perceived as of exactly equal value, suggesting that virginity is seen as part of a person's unique self.

But for gifters, the giving of one's virginity in exchange for another's is not enough. According to the men and women I spoke with, a deeper emotional commitment to the erstwhile virgin should also be given. Danice Marshall, a 28-year-old heterosexual African American nurse practitioner (and evangelical Christian), drove this point home. In discussing her decision not to give her virginity to Roger, a "very handsome" boy she dated when she was 15, she said:

> I knew I didn't want to become one of his statistics. . . . I would ask him to give me a reason why I should have sex with you. . . . And, he could not give me a valuable, you know, like [he said], "It would feel good." And [I said], "But you can't guarantee me, give me something concrete." . . . And so I knew that I didn't want to have my first experience with a guy that would view me [as] a notch on the bedpost. That . . . gave me another thing to look at when I decided who I was going to . . . choose to lose my virginity with.

Such vigilance was crucial in sparing Danice and like-minded virgins from echoing Britney Spears's lament, "I didn't think he was gonna . . . sell me out."[32]

Kelly went on casual dates with a few boys her freshman year in high school, kissing all of them and letting one touch her breasts, "He unhooked my bra and that was a big deal!" In her sophomore year, she started dating Dave, and they fell in love. At 16, Dave was 2 years older than Kelly, but not much more sexually experienced. Kelly recalled their first, fumbling forays into heavy petting:

> He took off my underwear. . . . He touched me and . . . [trails off]. But, I mean, I didn't even know what he was going to be looking for. I had no clue. I mean, I had never used a tampon, I had no idea. And I don't think he had any idea either!

Engaging in increasingly intimate sexual acts with at least one boy- or girlfriend was universal among people who interpreted virginity as a gift. In effect, these women and men treated each successive stage of sexual intimacy as an increasingly valuable gift in an ongoing exchange, with virginity loss representing the most precious gift of all. Taking a gradual or incremental approach to sexual activity allows virgins to assess their partner's ability and willingness to reciprocate. Someone who responds to less-valuable gifts—such as kisses and petting—with deepened affection and commitment can be better trusted to reciprocate more valuable ones, including virginity. Gradually escalating sexual activity therefore helps virgins to minimize, though not to eliminate, the risk of having the gift of their virginity go unreciprocated.

Kelly had been dating Dave for almost six months when, after careful soul searching and consultations with her friends, she decided she wanted to give him her virginity. Choosy as she was, everything about him seemed "right." They were in love and, over their months together, Dave had proven his ability to give of himself emotionally to her. Not surprisingly, since one of the few gifts deemed commensurate to virginity was a partner's deepened love and commitment, almost everyone who saw virginity as a gift opted to lose her or his virginity with a beloved, long-term boy- or girlfriend.[33] They also tended to date their partners considerably longer before virginity loss than did people in the stigma and process groups—about 6 months on average, compared with one and 4 months, respectively.

As it turned out, Dave would also be able to reciprocate Kelly's gift of virginity with his own. He shyly revealed this detail, much to Kelly's delight, when she disclosed her own virginity. Like every gifter, Kelly was very open with her friends and with the boys she dated about her virginity and the importance she placed on it.[34] Between romantic partners, such revelations served as reminders of virginity's value and of the necessity of reciprocity. In contrast, those who preferred the passage metaphor rarely expressed pride about their virginity, while many who saw virginity as a stigma worked hard to conceal their status.

Dave and Kelly first tried to have vaginal sex during a party at a friend's house, sneaking off into the nearby woods while the other guests remained indoors. But, she recalled:

> It just wasn't working. We had no idea what we were doing, it was dark . . . there was no foreplay, no nothing, it was just like, "This is what we're supposed to do, let's just do it." And, I think it was a combination of one, it hurt, two, I got scared. And so we stopped. And he was okay with that. And I was certainly okay with that. And so that was it. And we kind of like, laughed, you know, "Oh well."

They tossed the condom they'd been using into the underbrush and went back to the party. One reason the encounter failed may have been its motivation, for, as Kelly explained, she and Dave longed for the closeness they thought virginity loss would bring them far more than they felt inspired by physical desire. Giving emotional considerations precedence over physical ones was typical of people who interpreted virginity as a gift. The desire for physical pleasure figured much more prominently in the decision making of people in the stigma and process groups.

Although Dave's penis had been partway inside her vagina, Kelly didn't want to consider that night as the time she lost her virginity. She remembered thinking, "'This hurts, it's horrible, this is not what it's supposed to be.' And so I don't consider that being, like, the first time I had sex." Close calls of this nature were quite common among—indeed, *unique to*—women and men who interpreted virginity as a gift.[35] They serve as evidence of these individuals' intense desire to lose their virginity not only with the "right" or perfect partner, but also under perfect circumstances—that is, in relatively romantic surroundings and free from fumbling or worse. Whereas someone eager to lose her virginity (someone who saw it as a stigma, for instance) might have interpreted partial vaginal penetration as virginity loss, Kelly emphatically did not. This wasn't because she hoped to lose her virginity with a different boy—she intended to give her virginity to Dave all along—but because she didn't want the special experience she expected to remember forever to be flawed. The intense desire of people in this group for "perfect" virginity-loss encounters was, I imagine, exacerbated by the cultural tendency to treat virginity loss as a uniquely important, irreproducible event. Or, as Danice Marshall put it, "[T]his is something you can't take back."

After their attempt at sex, Kelly and Dave resumed their routine of going to movies and parties and petting on the way home. They were still in love and being together mattered far more to them than sex. Every month or two, they would fight and break up, then get back together after a few days had passed. But on one occasion, almost a year after their close call, instead of reuniting with Kelly, Dave started dating someone else. Devastated, Kelly tried to rekindle their relationship; but Dave proved immune to her pleas. After 2 months, convinced that Dave had given his virginity to his new girlfriend, Kelly, now 15, resolved to get him back however she could. She felt certain that having sex would inoculate their relationship against interlopers, so one afternoon she cornered Dave and declared, "I want to get back together so we can have sex." Though flustered by Kelly's bluntness, Dave also wanted to give their relationship another chance. They went on a few dates and at last had sex.

When she shared this experience with me, Kelly could recall every detail, right down to the turquoise panties she wore. "The things you remember!" she laughed. In her eyes the encounter had been nearly perfect, despite ending abruptly and falling short of the physical marvels she'd expected. "It didn't hurt," she said, "but it wasn't like everything that, you know, everybody told me it was going to be." Emotionally, however, giving her virginity to Dave surpassed Kelly's dearest dreams. Having sex felt loving and very intimate, and it even seemed to add some much-needed glue to their relationship—their periodic breakups came to an end. Ten years later, Dave confessed to Kelly that her suspicions had been misplaced, he hadn't given his virginity to his temporary girlfriend. Kelly was still thrilled to know that Dave had reciprocated her gift of virginity not only emotionally, but also with his own. In fact, gifters were more likely to lose their virginity with fellow virgins than members of any other interpretive group—hardly surprising, given how many held mutual virginity loss as an ideal.[36]

Kelly and Dave used condoms when they tried to lose their virginity, when they actually did, and whenever they had sex thereafter. For the most part, Kelly told me, they had been concerned with preventing pregnancy, rather than HIV, which they hadn't then seen as a threat to heterosexuals like themselves. Gifters were more likely to practice some form of birth control or safer sex at virginity loss than any other group in my study—four-fifths of them did. Largely this seemed to be a by-product of the intimacy enjoyed by people in committed romantic relationships, which helps them discuss and prepare preventive measures in advance. Such comfort may be particularly crucial for young women. According to scholars, many young women fail to use contraception or practice safer sex out of fear that preparing for sex will mark them as promiscuous or easy.[37] Young women in committed love relationships may, by contrast, feel "permitted" to acknowledge the possibility that they might have sex, which in turn is a prerequisite for preparing for safer sex.

Kelly and Dave had a sexual relationship for nearly two more years. Such enduring relationships were especially common among gifters. Those who remained with their partners did so, on average, for 2 years after virginity loss, compared with 6 and 8 months for their counterparts in the stigma and process groups, respectively.[38] Throughout those 2 years, Kelly relished playing expert adviser to her girlfriends who were still virgins—a role enjoyed by many women who felt they'd lost their virginity in ways befitting their vision of virginity as a gift. Gradually, Kelly began to get more physical pleasure from vaginal sex; but the emotional rewards remained more important to her. As a case in point, she recounted a conversation with her father when she was 16 or 17:

> He asked me . . . you know, "Are you having sex." "Yes." And he asked me, "Why are you having sex?" And I think, you know, I gave an answer like, "It feels good." It did feel good, but . . . I think that was what I thought I was supposed to say.

Breaking up with Dave did not diminish Kelly's conviction that sex was meant to be shared with a special person. When she decided to have sex with her next serious boyfriend, a romance that began in college, she found she had to relinquish "the idea of being with only one person" that had been so important to her. She explained:

> When I had another partner, it was something like I, I actually said good-bye. . . . I guess I thought of the first person that I was with as being pure and whole and good and wonderful. Maybe a lot of what people think about being a virgin. And then when I . . . was with another person, I gave that part of it up.

Her first time with her second lover was, Kelly said, one of the three most significant sexual experiences of her life, along with losing her virginity, at 15, and her first orgasm, at 23.

Kelly's ideals and experiences were undoubtedly shaped by her gender and sexual identity, albeit in ways that might easily remain invisible, since her approach is widely perceived as natural for heterosexual women (especially if they are White). The overwhelming majority of people who viewed virginity as a gift self-identified as heterosexual, like Kelly, or as bisexual.[39] Lesbians and gay men, by contrast, rarely compared virginity to a gift. I believe this may be because a model of virginity loss that revolves around traditional understandings of femininity and masculinity has relatively little appeal for people who desire same-sex partners.[40]

"[A] Mutual Amount of Giving, on Both Behalves"

Some young men did interpret virginity as a gift. What first struck me about Bryan Meyers was his self-deprecating boyish charm. An 18-year-old White college freshman, Bryan had clean-cut good looks, with short sandy hair and bright blue eyes. He approached our conversation with an earnest politeness, but it was easy to imagine him playing the class clown. When I thanked him for agreeing to be interviewed, he laughed and said, "What college guy doesn't want to talk about sex?" Lest I get the wrong impression about what kind of sex he meant, he described himself as "totally hetero." He was born and raised in upstate New York, where his mother and father both worked as public-school teachers.

Given the masculine bravado lurking just below Bryan's good-kid surface, I was somewhat surprised to hear him describe virginity loss in terms almost identical to those used by Kelly—terms overwhelmingly associated with femininity in American culture. When I asked how he would define virginity loss to someone who'd never heard of it before, he replied that, after "describ[ing] it clinically, you know . . . whether penetration has taken place,"[41] he would explain that virginity is

> something that you have for yourself, you know, it's like, "This is yours," . . . and you finally decide who you're going to give this to. And that's, you know, you hope that that person really appreciates it. . . . [W]ith all the diseases and whatever going around there's such a heightened awareness these days of . . . just saving yourself. . . . It's even funny

that they use those terms. I mean it's like, saving yourself as if, as if you're giving you. And I guess that's kind of true. So . . . I think that people consider it giving of themselves to do this, and I think that that's definitely important to them.

Although he believed that a person should be in love with his or her virginity-loss partner, Bryan saw no point in waiting until marriage. People who do are "making a mistake if they think that they're ready for somebody, and just because they said they're not going to do it 'til they get married, and then they wait."

Bryan is a classic gifter. In fact, his feelings about reciprocity were more emphatic and considered than those of most people in this group. As he put it:

> I think that [there] definitely has to be just trust and, most importantly, reciprocity. I think that there has to be . . . [a] mutual amount of giving, on both behalves, because then, for something special like that to happen and . . . you feel that you are not . . . loved as much as . . . you love this other person, and you actually decide to have sex with this person, I think you kind of feel slighted.

Bryan suspected that his approach set him apart from many young men. "I'm different from a lot of my guy friends," he said, ". . . they still don't have a clue." Bryan's story can help us see how men who defied gender conventions by likening virginity to a gift both resemble and diverge from women who share their beliefs and from men who do not.

One way Bryan differed from Kelly was the means through which he arrived at his position. He didn't think that popular media had influenced his opinions, nor that his religious background had had much of an impact. Raised as a Methodist by parents who rarely went to church, religion has never played an important role in his life. Yet, like Kelly, he felt that his parents and peers had profoundly influenced his beliefs. His mother and father had always encouraged him to think of sexual expression as an aspect of love, but said little about virginity per se until he was in high school. When he was a freshman or sophomore, his mother advised him to "wait until you're ready" and really in love (she didn't mention marriage). From her perspective, Bryan said, that advice "backfired" —for by the time she gave it, Bryan felt ready for sex and chose to interpret her words as a stamp of approval.

Bryan's high school peers expressed a range of beliefs about virginity, with different cliques disposed toward different stances.[42] Whereas his own friends, the academic-track kids, were usually supportive of peers who remained virgins, the "dickheads"—that is, the rougher crowd—tended to disparage virginity and virgins, especially if they were boys. In that heterogeneous context, having an accepting peer group was probably critical to Bryan's ability to interpret virginity as a gift at an age when many boys begin to see it as a stigma. Bryan's high school circle was probably more supportive of the gift metaphor than most, for he belonged to a student group that sought to promote AIDS awareness through programs that often included pro-chastity rhetoric.

> [W]e did some skits and things like that, you know. We were proponents of virginity and, you know, staying, keeping, you know, "The best thing is abstinence," and that catch-line. And so I think that's when . . . we started talked about [sex and virginity loss] seriously, was once it actually started happening.

Although Bryan couldn't recall whether the group had supplemented their own skits and posters with a ready-made curriculum, his description of their positions and certain phrases he used—like "staying pure"—suggest the influence of abstinence-focused sex education programs like Sex Respect, which celebrate chastity and tend to frame virginity as a gift.

Ironically, Bryan's involvement in the AIDS-awareness group did more than sustain his beliefs—it introduced him to his first girlfriend and eventual virginity-loss partner. An 18-year-old senior, Heather shared 16-year-old sophomore Bryan's zest for balancing studiousness and fun. He was thrilled when she agreed to date him exclusively: "[F]or some reason . . . I had always wanted a girlfriend. . . . I'd rather be loved and have that little cuddly-ness with just one person than go on lots of dates and stuff."

Before dating Heather, the sum total of Bryan's sexual experience amounted to "kissing and a few, like, up-the-shirt fooling around." He and Heather kissed on their early dates, then, "Four or five weeks into it, we started having a little bit of fun"—that is, touching one another's bodies beneath their clothing. By the time they had been dating 4 months, "That's when things started getting really hot and heavy," they were very much in love. "And it was the good kind, too," Bryan explained. "There's just something about high school love that you just can't find anywhere else." The physical side of their relationship proceeded in increments, just like Kelly and Dave's. Bryan summarized: "We went through the whole mutual masturbation thing, and then oral sex . . . and a week later, we had sex." He was perfectly content to take things slowly, not least because virginity was unique and its loss so consequential. "Considered that it's a one-time thing, and bang, once you do it, it's like, never again . . . you want to make sure it's something done right. Something special," he said.

Heather was also a virgin, and it delighted Bryan to think that they could lose their virginity together. "I thought it was great," he said. "There was no other way I would have wanted to do it, honestly." The pair assessed one another's feelings about having sex through humorous yet pointed banter:

[T]he first month or two months, we kind of made the obligatory, like, "Oh, well, we don't have to have sex," statements. . . . And I think that most people say that just to reassure the person, so that they don't think that they're going to be forced to do anything against their will. But eventually [laughs], we tossed those statements out the window.

Some of the humor stemmed from the fact that Heather was 2 years older, and thus had waited longer to have sex. Said Bryan:

When we would talk about it, I was like, "I really need it [sex]." And she's like, "Well think of that with two more years added to it." And I'd be like, "Oh, man, I couldn't handle that." And, you know, jokingly, but still there's a little bit of truth to the jest.

As it turned out, Bryan was, at age 16, the first of his close male friends to lose his virginity.

Despite anticipating that they'd probably have sex before long, Heather and Bryan resisted planning a specific encounter. "I didn't want anything to seem contrived," Bryan explained. "I just didn't want to . . . book an hourly rate hotel with mirrors on the ceiling or . . . drive off to [a] public road . . . and do it in the back of the car." Even so, he reflected, "We had to have maybe said a little bit, because we had condoms." Their care in preparing for safer sex, facilitated by their close relationship, was further fostered by their coming of age during a period of heightened awareness about HIV/AIDS, and, more specifically, by their mutual involvement in AIDS education. Even so, like many people I spoke with,

Bryan had worried about STIs "initially, but once we trusted that we both were virgins, then that really became no concern." Eventually, Heather began using the birth control pill.

An opportunity to have sex spontaneously arrived when a friend threw a party while his parents were out of town. "A little bit of alcohol was flowing, and we all stayed over . . . that's when it happened," Bryan recalled. The experience unleashed a tumult of emotions:

> When I was doing it, I didn't know what the heck was going on. . . . It was just so unbelievable that this, like, this *thing* you talk about your whole life is actually happening. And honestly, I think that . . . it's not as, like, as mind-blowing as you expect it to be. Because it's just like, "This is it? I'm actually doing this, I'm actually, losing my virginity? . . . It's as easy as this?" You know, it's just so weird. . . . Afterward it actually was better, felt better than while it was taking place. Just because, you know, wow, we had just shared this thing, and isn't that nice. So . . . directly afterwards, it was very, very cool.

Bryan was, in fact, surprised to find virginity loss so positive and satisfying. For, despite hoping for a romantic and special encounter, Bryan harbored unusually low expectations for a gifter. He'd found it hard to imagine that the intimacy he would gain could outweigh his feelings of irrevocable loss.

> I didn't expect anything good, honestly. Because you kind of think, "Wow . . . there it is, I just did it. Never do that again anymore." So it's not a very nice feeling to think about that. But then when you start thinking about, you know, with whom you did this, then you're just like, "Well, I'm glad . . . that, for me, it was a nice experience." Because I've heard so many horror stories that, you know, I'm glad that I did it right.[43]

Heather and Bryan continued to have sex after that first night, but "not very often. . . . [I] probably could count the number of times on all the digits I have on my body." One reason they had sex so seldom was that the possibility of an unintended pregnancy loomed in the back of Bryan's mind. "I would've shot myself," he said. "It's just terrible to even think about it." It was also difficult to find suitable places for sex, since they both lived with their parents.

Bryan and Heather dated for 2 years altogether. "Some of the best times of my life were with her," he said. In his senior year of high school, he decided to end the relationship in order to date someone else, "but . . . after I had spent a little bit of time with that person, I was like, 'This sucks, I want to go back.'" Heather demurred, however, and Bryan eventually "found somebody else." When I met him, he'd been dating his new girlfriend for 5 months and knew he was in love. Like Kelly, Bryan saw sex with a second partner as a significant event, meriting the same careful approach as virginity loss:

> I think that every time you get into a new relationship . . . you start at zero. . . . You're with somebody and it's, sex is something that you do between two people, so it's like . . . the turning point happens in the relationship, not—rather than in the individual.

The similarities between Bryan's and Kelly's stories underline how much men and women who shared an understanding of virginity as a gift had in common. Yet, the gift metaphor has not shed its associations with femininity; it takes on different nuances when invoked by women and men. When young men choose to approach virginity as a gift, they are, in effect, rejecting a traditional version of masculinity for a more relational, sensitive stance. Insofar as this "new" masculinity seems feminine by comparison, it may connote homosexuality. I imagine that awareness of this connotation was one factor prompting Bryan's emphatic assertions of heterosexuality at several points in our interview. However, only two of the gay men and one of the bisexual men I interviewed had ever interpreted their virginity as a gift. This pattern challenges the popular assumption that gay relationships must mimic heterosexual ones, a stereotype scholars and gay activists have long derided as a myth.[44]

Bryan's tale also reveals how profoundly people's sexual careers are influenced by the historical context in which they come of age. Only 18 when I interviewed him, Bryan belongs to the same generation as Britney Spears and other paragons of Virgin Chic. The "younger" men and women with whom I spoke, just children when the HIV/AIDS crisis began, learned about sexuality and virginity entirely in the era of safer sex and "just say no." They were, moreover, born after second-wave feminism had profoundly altered mainstream American ideas about gender and sexuality.[45] Men born between 1973 and 1980 were nearly as likely as similarly aged women to have ever been gifters (about half had), whereas only one of the men born 1962 and 1972 had ever favored the gift metaphor (compared with two-thirds of the "older" women). The "new" style of masculinity that evolved in response to the feminist and youth counterculture movements has, I believe, enabled young men to interpret virginity as a gift without sacrificing their masculine identities.[46] Furthermore, group and individual efforts to prevent the spread of HIV/AIDS, including the infusion of conservative Christian sexual ideology into popular culture and sex education curricula, have prompted young men to approach sexual activity with greater caution than in the past—for instance, by increasingly eschewing casual sex.[47]

The upbeat narratives of people like Bryan and Kelly do not hold true for all gifters. The following profiles explore the experiences of virgins whose paths diverged from their hopes and expectations.

"It Was Weird to Feel Like This Is Something That Might Be Bad, You Know?"

Although Karen Lareau shared Kelly and Bryan's understanding of virginity, she differed from them in one critical respect: she consciously chose to give her virginity to a man with whom she was not in love. A tall, White 21-year-old, Karen was the proud captain of her university's varsity volleyball team. When I spoke with her, she was just months away from receiving her bachelor's degree in geography, an interest she attributed to moving a lot while growing up.

Ever since she was a girl, Karen told me, she had thought of virginity as being "kind of like this special gift that you have to give to someone. And . . . besides the physical act . . . a lot of emotional things that go along with it." Her beliefs about virginity had, she supposed, been shaped by the "family values and religious values" espoused by her parents. Devout Episcopalians, they took a traditional approach to family life—Dad did the breadwinning as an environmental engineer, while Mom took care of the home—and were not only young when they married, but also virgins. Mrs. Lareau in particular encouraged Karen and her sister to emulate her example; virginity was, along with romance, a frequent topic of their mother-daughter heart-to-hearts. Karen, who remained active in church during college, was not alone in tracing her views on virginity to her religious identity. Among the people I interviewed, devout members of mainstream Protestant denominations and practicing evangelical and fundamentalist Christians were disproportionately likely to interpret virginity as a gift. Indeed, other researchers have found that devout and/or conservative Christian youth are more apt to disapprove of premarital sex, and to lose their virginity at later ages, than their less-religious peers.[48]

Despite agreeing with her mother that a woman should give her virginity to a man she truly loved, Karen wasn't so sure that there'd be only one true love in her life. She also doubted whether it would be realistic to wait until she was married, given how much the world had changed since her mother was 21. Then, she pointed out, people "look[ed] down on you if you [weren't] a virgin," whereas now

> it's almost kind of the opposite. Like, people look down on you if you *are*. Not really look down on you, but ask you, "Well, why?" you know. "Why are you?" And just, it's not a common thing anymore to be a virgin when you're married.

Karen decided that virginity loss should happen in "a relationship where you can say that you actually love the other person. . . . Someone you've been with for a while and know that you're hopefully going to be with in the future . . . even if you do sleep with one or two people before you find, like, the one that you're going to be with." Her friends in middle and high school—in North Carolina and Texas, respectively—had agreed. In Texas in particular, Karen said, virginity was prized and romantic relationships were slow-paced and serious:

> You date, you see each other, things move slowly, and people are going more towards marriage. A lot of my friends down there are, like, seriously, seriously involved with someone. A couple of them are even married.

Karen's high school had been small and so close-knit that everyone knew which of their peers were virgins—the vast majority—and which were not. Although she and her friends never lacked for dates, Karen was the only one who'd had a serious boyfriend, though not until twelfth grade. "I guess I would consider myself kind of late for starting a lot of this stuff," she said, "because until my senior year . . . I'd only just kissed a guy." Her "first experience with, like, fingering and stuff like that" was with her high school boyfriend, Jim. Looking back, she wondered if maybe she should have given him her virginity, too. "It was a great relationship that we had. . . . We were physically definitely very ready!" But, for a variety of reasons, Karen and Jim didn't have sex.

> I really thought about it with him. And we were right there a couple of times. But he didn't press me on it and I just didn't do it. It definitely wasn't that I didn't want to. I think it was just because he never really just said, "Do you want to have sex?" Because if he had said that, I probably would have said yes [laughs]. . . . And I think it was kind of like, I was kind of naive about a lot of those things, too. Like he was, like I say, my first time for a lot of that sort of stuff, so I wasn't really . . . sure about a lot of things and, you know, never even had oral sex with him. . . . And there weren't, you know, my peers around me weren't really having sex. And we were like the one really serious couple, so it wasn't like I was comparing myself to anyone else.

When she left Texas to attend college in New Jersey, Karen found herself surrounded by peers whose ideas about virginity differed sharply from her own. "Here," she said, "things just go so quickly . . . guys move really fast and—really different from Texas." Although her college friends *said* they saw virginity as precious, Karen thought their behavior —especially their frequent casual sexual liaisons—suggested otherwise. Gradually, she began to question her own beliefs. She explained:

> It was weird to feel like [being a virgin] is something that might be bad, you know, 'cause it's always something that I thought would be really good. . . . And none of my friends are like, "Oh, that's bad that you're not having sex." They're like, "That's great that you're still a virgin." But you'd hear them talking about all their experiences and you're like, "Wow, I'm missing out" [laughs].

Karen used several strategies to manage her conflicting emotions. Although she shared her feelings with close women friends who were sexually active, she particularly sought the support and advice of fellow virgins. Her college roommate, also a virgin, was a key source of reassurance. "[E]very once in a while," Karen said, they would remind one another, "'Well, virginity is still around,' you know, 'It's okay,' you know?" With people she didn't know well, or didn't expect to become close to, Karen took advantage of the relative anonymity afforded by a large university and the widespread assumption that college-age virgins are few and far between; most of her peers assumed she was sexually active. It wasn't that she'd stopped taking pride in her virginity, she insisted, she just wanted to avoid being teased by people who saw virgins as socially backwards or boring. Intentionally concealing virginity was very unusual among people who saw virginity as a gift and unique to Karen among the women in this group.

Karen also practiced what many call "technical virginity." While still a virgin, she said,

> I'd done everything—well, not anal sex, but like—besides actually having vaginal intercourse. I'd had oral sex before [with four men] and a lot of just, like, heavy petting and, you know, stuff like that. . . . I've hooked up with quite a few people since I've been [at college], and they've all been on various levels of intimacy, depending on how long I've been . . . with them.

In short, she felt comfortable engaging in sexual activities she defined as foreplay with men she deemed unworthy of her virginity, so long as she always stopped short of vaginal intercourse. (Karen was one of six gifters who did "everything but" have sex while purposely remaining virgins.)

Like everyone who interpreted virginity as a gift, Karen felt she'd been choosy about her sexual partners. She carefully considered whether boys she dated might eventually merit the gift of her virginity. Physical and emotional "readiness" both figured in her equation as necessary, but not sufficient, conditions. On the one hand, Karen said, "There's . . . sexual attraction. You know, that's very important. . . . Otherwise, I wouldn't even consider it." On the other hand, she acknowledged, "A lot of people . . . I've wanted to have sex with [physically] but . . . it wouldn't have been appropriate to have sex with them because it wasn't a relationship or anything like that, it was just a hook-up." She elaborated:

> It's like everything has to come together. If you just do one thing, like, emotionally you're ready, but you're not sexually attracted to them, then there's no point in doing it. And, like, you're usually sexually attracted to them but emotionally you know that it would be a stupid thing to do. You end up hurting yourself otherwise.

Karen was unusually cognizant of her sexual desires for someone who interpreted virginity as a gift. Remaining a virgin for several years longer than most gifters may have given her more time to develop a thorough sense of her sexual needs. Indeed, scholars have found that young women (and men) who first have vaginal sex at relatively older ages report enjoying it more than their younger counterparts.[49]

Karen's coping strategies notwithstanding, after almost 3 years at a university where casual sex was the norm, hardly any of her friends remained virgins and she began to feel increasingly "weird," almost stigmatized. Her story echoes research suggesting that virgins' behavior is influenced more strongly by friends' actual sexual conduct than by their opinions.[50] To alleviate feeling odd, Karen decided, at age 20, that she ought to lose her virginity, even if she couldn't do so in a way befitting her lifelong ideals. At the time, she had been sexually involved with a close friend, Chip, for about 6 months. Over that period, their sexual encounters had grown progressively more intimate, eventually including cunnilingus and fellatio. Karen liked Chip, but didn't love him, nor did she consider him her boyfriend. Yet, she stressed, "It wasn't like I felt like it was a one-night stand or anything." She reasoned:

> From the very beginning, he was always like, "I want to make love to you, I want to have sex with you." And I think that I finally was just like, well . . . I was curious, I really wanted to have sex, I was very attracted to him. I knew that emotionally we weren't in the type of relationship that was really going to pay out . . . but I guess I just put that aside for a while.

Despite her decision to settle for a less-than-ideal partner, in choosing someone she cared about and whom she trusted to remain her friend after sex, Karen was more selective than many who interpreted virginity loss as a stigma or a rite of passage. Chip, at 21, wasn't a virgin; but Karen made sure that he knew she was. Beyond sensitizing him to the magnitude of her decision, she believed her truthfulness had encouraged him to be more attentive to her needs. "He was really cool about it and helped me along and stuff like that," she said with a grin.

Like Bryan, Karen resisted planning her first time in advance, even though she'd determined that it would happen with Chip. One evening, after attending a basketball game, she and Chip started "fooling around" and he asked her if she wanted to try vaginal sex. "Okay," she replied, "but you have to use a condom." Unlike many of her friends, for whom vaginal sex had been painful at first, Karen found it pleasurable:

For me it was a great experience. . . . I guess that's because I probably, you know, fooled around with enough guys and . . . had other things done, that I wasn't going to be sore from it. . . . I guess I was . . . hoping that it would be a good time [laughs]. But didn't know.

Karen's experience confirms researcher Sharon Thompson's claim that young women who recognize their sexual desires and make sexual activity contingent on them are more likely to find pleasure in virginity loss than are women who deny or disregard their desires.[51]

Although Karen felt some remorse at missing the special experience she'd once dreamed of, she didn't regret her decision—at least not at first. She'd even felt a bit relieved not to be a virgin anymore. When she told her closest friends what had happened, they were supportive and understanding.[52]

Karen continued to spend time with Chip, and to have sex with him now and then, for several months. In her mind, he was never more than a friend; but, she said, "I think *he* actually did think that we were in a relationship for a while." She explained:

He's like, "Well, you know, if I could be with someone right now, it would be [you], but . . . I have to sort things out first before I can think about being with someone." So . . . he wasn't giving me emotionally what I needed, I mean . . . 'cause emotionally he wasn't stable himself.

Karen wasn't disappointed that Chip couldn't reciprocate her gift by "being with" her, because she had never expected him to be more than her friend. As time passed, however, she began to feel troubled about other aspects of her experience. In particular, she said:

[J]ust knowing that . . . it wasn't really a real relationship—it was a good friendship, I guess you would say. . . . And then some of the other, the reasons why. . . . The [nonvirgin] girls in my house, and wanting not to be a virgin anymore. And I kind of felt bad about losing that desire, actually to be a virgin. And I thought that maybe that was kind of a wrong reason to lose my virginity. Just wanting not to be one.

By the time of our interview, Karen felt she had come to terms with these discomfiting feelings. She was also happy that, in her current relationship, she had made choices about sex that were more consistent with her beliefs. She'd begun dating Dean a few months after her affair with Chip faded, and this time, Karen said, it was "for real." Dean was different from the other men at her school, she explained, and they shared similar beliefs about sex as well as similar sexual histories:

> [H]e's only been with one other person, too. So it's really, really cool. Like, I was really excited when I found that out. . . . [We're] on the same level. And he's had, you know, his first was in a really serious relationship, so. He's kind of the serious relationship type [laughs]. Which is nice. Like, I'm ready for that now.

Karen and Dean waited to have vaginal sex until they had been dating, and in love, for nearly a year. Although she forswore any desire to go back and do things differently, Karen admitted: "If I had been a virgin, going into this relationship . . . I wouldn't have thought twice about it. Because it's just something, like, that happened really naturally and was great." In fact, she confided, she hoped that she and Dean would be engaged by the time they graduated. Karen was unusual among gifters in linking marriage and sex so closely, probably as a result of her religious faith and the conservative sexual culture of her Texas upbringing. Surveys show that sexual attitudes are markedly more traditional in the South than in the Northeast and Mid-Atlantic, in part because many more southerners are conservative Christians.[53] Public-school systems in the South are also more likely to teach abstinence-focused sex education curricula.[54]

Karen's story highlights the importance of social context in shaping young Americans' sexual careers. When she was surrounded by friends and peers who shared her view of virginity as a gift, Karen found it easy to behave as she believed. But in an atmosphere where few people felt as she did, she began questioning her convictions and, eventually, set them aside long enough to have sex with Chip. In some ways, Karen rued her decision—for instance, she knew she'd lost the opportunity to strengthen her relationship with Dean by giving him her virginity—but for the most part, she expressed satisfaction with the choices she'd made. That she *herself* decided to diverge from the ideal "script" for giving the gift of virginity is crucial to understanding her relative satisfaction—as will be made apparent by comparing Karen's experience to that of a young woman whose *partner* refused to reciprocate her gift.

"*I Think I Thought It Would Make Me Maybe Feel Love for Him That I Knew I Didn't Have*"

Like everyone in this group, Julie Pavlicko had longed to bestow her virginity on a loving partner who would cherish her all the more for her gift. She had trusted that, by being prudent and picky, she could guarantee that her virginity would go to a special and appreciative recipient. But Julie's carefully selected boyfriend decided not to acknowledge, much less return, her gift. For Julie, virginity loss was nothing short of devastating.

With long, elaborately styled blond hair and heavily made-up green eyes, Julie looked younger than her 25 years. We met at her apartment in suburban Philadelphia, near the retirement home where she'd worked as a counselor for almost 3 years. Julie had grown up in a semirural area about an hour away. Her father and mother had worked on the assembly lines of several small manufacturing plants until their recent retirement. She was single—"but looking!"—and had no children.

For as long as she could remember, Julie had believed that losing her virginity with someone would be a way of saying, "I really love this person, I want to give this part of myself to him." She had often heard that women felt a special connection to the man who "took" their virginity and that a husband or boyfriend who received a woman's virginity would love her, and she would love him, even more than before. In Julie's eyes, virginity loss was much more than a physical act. "When you are giving to someone like that, it's not just your body, it's, you know, your mind, your heart," she said.

Julie's family had attended twice-weekly services at an independent fundamentalist church when she was growing up, and she and her sister had gone to church schools until ninth grade. Although she still believed in God and many teachings from her parents' church, by the time I spoke with her Julie no longer belonged to that or any other congregation. She had no doubt that her religious upbringing "really shaped the way that I thought about sex." Church lessons about sex tended toward the implicit, she said:

> I can't remember, specifically, anybody ever sitting down and saying, "Okay, you can't have sex because God says it's wrong." . . . Nobody ever came out and specifically said that, but they kind of danced around the subject. "You shouldn't date guys," you know. "Every date is a potential mate" [laughs]. . . . You weren't allowed, you weren't supposed

to be holding hands, you weren't supposed to go over to [each other's] house.

These messages, typical of conservative Protestant guidance on sexuality in the 1990s, made a deep impression on Julie, as they did on many of the conservative Christians I interviewed. In fact, of the ten I spoke with, six interpreted virginity as a gift—although many of them, like Julie, rejected the strictest elements of church teachings on sexuality.[55]

Julie's parents conveyed their beliefs about sexuality in even less explicit ways. Julie explained:

> I knew . . . they wanted me to be a virgin until I got married. You know . . . it just wasn't accepted in our culture, in our church, whatever. And I'm sure they thought, you know, "She's our little girl." . . . They never talked about [sex] to me, and I think a lot of it was because they didn't want me to know anything about it. Like if some, like, steamy scene came on TV, "Oh, gotta change that," you know [laughs]. It was really, like, kind of looked down upon.

As a teenager, Julie felt able to talk about sex more openly with her friends, though they all kept personal details to a minimum. Her church friends harbored more conservative opinions about virginity than her friends from public high school, but both groups of young women talked about "when you should lose your virginity, who you should lose it to, why you should do it." Television, movies, and magazines offered another source of information about sex, one which tended to depict women and men's virginity in starkly different lights. Julie said:

> There's a couple of movies that I can recall for, you know, hormonal little 16-year-old boys. . . . And most of those were, like, comedies. It was looked upon like, "Oh, it's really funny," and, you know, "He's just out of control!" But when they have the shows with the women [such as *Beverly Hills 90210*], it's very serious. You know, it's not like, "Oh, this is really funny, that she's losing her virginity."

Such gendered standards had hardly seemed unique to media images; in fact, they'd been taken for granted by everyone Julie knew. "I think people, I think society puts a much higher value on a woman's virginity," she said. "And for a guy it's just, you know, something to get over. Have a real good time and keep going on down that road." It was also taken for granted (never questioned, in fact) that virginity loss could only take place between a man and a woman.

By the time they were 14 or 15, Julie and many of her friends had decided that it would be okay to give your virginity to someone you loved but probably wouldn't marry. As Julie put it:

> If you get to be 25, 26 years old and you meet this man that you really love and you're still a virgin, and you want him to be the one, I think that's great. . . . If you can wait that long and eventually get married and, you know, on the wedding night, that's incredible! But if you're like, 15, 16 years old, and you're with this guy, and you think that you . . . really love him, and then you go ahead and sleep with him, I think that can be good, too.

Julie and her friends' willingness to bend the ideal of virgin marriage with which they'd grown up, despite their conservative religious beliefs, suggests how thoroughly the sexual liberalization of the 1970s and 1980s permeated American society.

Julie started dating when she entered high school. She did little more than kiss her first boyfriend, partly because she was young, nervous, and inexperienced, and partly because she wasn't in love with him. She recalled their encounters as involving

> mostly just kissing, petting . . . not anything below the waist. He was a lot older than I was, he was [17] and I was, like, 14. . . . And I was really nervous about it because . . . he was really, other than . . . the little guy that I held hands with in kindergarten, you know, it was really the first guy that I really had any kind of, like, romantic type feelings for.

Julie met her second boyfriend, Scott, when they were both 15. The captain of his high school's junior varsity basketball team, Scott was handsome and popular, if also self-centered and "very, very conceited." At the time, Julie thought she "really loved him," but "also knew that it wasn't going to last forever."

Scott wanted to have sex shortly after they started dating, but Julie told him she was a virgin and not ready to go all the way. He claimed that he'd had sex with previous girlfriends, but Julie later discovered that that was a lie. "He had told me that he had been with one person before that," she said, shaking her head. "But I later found out that he hadn't been, and he was just telling me that so that he would look . . . more like a boy, I guess." Julie was, along with Kelly Lewis, one of three women in this group who eventually found out that their boyfriends had pretended to be nonvirgins before they had sex, suggesting that the boyfriends saw virginity as a stigma (concealing virginity from sexual partners is characteristic of men in the stigma group). Approaching virginity loss from apparently different perspectives had few, if any, repercussions for Kelly and Dave; but it mattered a great deal for Julie and Scott.

Despite Julie's initial refusal, Scott continued to pressure her for sex. She vividly remembered his entreaties, and the subtext underneath them:

> He was like, "Oh, Jule, you know you really should because." Uh, what was the reason? Something about . . . the end result of it was, "If you don't, then I'm going to leave you." . . . I mean, I think that had a lot to do with it. But I think it was more phrased like, "Then you'll show me that you really care about me." You know? I think that was more of what the phrasing was. But it was that underlying, you know, "If you do love me then you will, if you don't then you won't." It was that kind of thing.

In their first 5 months together, Julie and Scott became increasingly sexually intimate, until genital petting was a part of almost every date. This routine, and what Julie saw as its inevitable conclusion, was one of the reasons she decided to give Scott her virginity. She explained:

> I remember we talked about it a lot. . . . And I remember, we'd go to the movies and, you know, we'd be kissing and whatever. And it just seemed like, you know, we had gone so far, and there was like, nothing else to do. We obviously could not get married at that point in time [laughs].

The fact that Scott's affection for her seemed to intensify with every sexual encounter further convinced Julie that he would be the right boy to receive her virginity. Sexual desire played little part in her decision; in fact, it was virtually absent from her recollections.

What happened when Julie acquiesced to Scott's request left her stunned and upset. Physically, she found vaginal sex neither pleasurable nor painful; and she didn't worry about pregnancy because they used a condom. Nor did having sex alter Julie's state of mind. She said:

I thought it was going to feel a lot different, and I thought it was going to be more painful. I thought that . . . like, the floods were going to open and blood was going to, you know. I thought it would make me feel different.

What really surprised her was Scott's reaction. Rather than being grateful, he questioned her truthfulness!

After it happened, he was like, "Are you bleeding?" You know, it was like, "Is it happening? Do you feel different?" And I was like, "No, not really" [laughs]. . . . And he was really upset about that. Because he thought for sure that I lied to him. And that he hadn't been my first. And I remember thinking back on that and saying like, "You dick," you know? 'Cause, I mean, it, at the time it meant a lot to me. That I was . . . doing this with him. But then again, it was like, "You know what? You think I lied to you." So. You know, "Why, obviously it didn't mean that much to you, 'cause you don't trust me enough to believe me."

Scott's behavior, if less than admirable, nonetheless makes sense in light of social expectations for gifts. As Julie's boyfriend, Scott may have felt that he deserved the gift of her virginity, and thus that she cheated him out of it.[56] Or he may have disagreed with her as to which of them gave the first truly significant gift—was it the affection and commitment Scott bestowed as Julie's boyfriend, or the virginity she presented out of her feelings for him?—and therefore about who owed what to whom.[57] What ensued between them suggests that, when exchange partners disagree about the sequence or value of gifts, the interpretation of the more powerful party—in this case, the older, more popular, male Scott—will prevail.

Furthermore, because givers typically proffer gifts that reflect the recipient's value to them, Scott may have taken Julie's ostensible failure to give her virginity as a sign that he wasn't worth very much to her. Because receiving a valuable gift enhances a person's social status, some men and women may even seek to increase their own worth by "taking" someone's virginity. Tony Halloran, a 21-year-old busboy from an Italian-Irish family, told me about just such a scenario. Despite personally seeing his virginity as a stigma, Tony was still a virgin at age 20. When the older sister of one of his friends discovered his status, she asked Tony to give his virginity to her. He said:

The way she phrased the question was, "Can I be the first one? Can I take your virginity?" And I was like, "Yeah." And she . . . felt special, I guess. And even afterwards, I remember her saying that I would always remember her. Because she was my first.

Several gifters suggested a less mercenary reason for seeking to be a recipient: having enjoyed their own virginity-loss encounters, they wanted to give someone else a similarly positive experience.[58]

Julie was deeply hurt that Scott believed she had deceived him. She was also devastated to find that, contrary to her expectations, her gift neither enhanced their love nor strengthened the bonds between them.

> I thought it would make me feel differently about him. I thought it would make him feel differently about me. I thought it would make *me* feel differently about me. But it didn't really. . . . Because he assumed that I lied to him. It certainly didn't change our relationship. It didn't make it better, it didn't make it worse.

When I asked how she had expected their relationship to change, she said she thought

> that it would be different, there would be a lot more caring. . . . I think I thought it would make me maybe feel love for him that I knew I didn't have. Maybe it would, like, give us a fresh connection that we didn't have. Whether it be physical or mental or. . . . You know, there was, there was nothing added to the relationship. No more caring, no more nurturing, no more nothing!

Nothing Julie could say or do seemed to change Scott's mind. Yet he made it clear that he wanted to keep dating (and having sex). Julie struggled to cast aside her feelings of distress and impotence; she even had sex with Scott a few more times. Though he had behaved reprehensibly, she reasoned, the fact that she'd shared a special part of herself with him made it worth trying to stay together. Efforts at maintaining unsatisfactory relationships are, in fact, one of the less savory consequences of perceiving virginity as part of the self—especially for people who feel, like Julie, that transferring that part entails an irrevocable loss.[59] When, for example, Danielle Rice, a 27-year-old White heterosexual telecommunications technician, told me that she spent 6 years with the "very abusive" boyfriend to whom she gave her virginity, I couldn't help but wonder whether she had, on some level, been reluctant to leave him because he possessed what she described as "something of mine . . . that I can only give up once," a part of herself she would be forced to abandon along with him.

When Julie's anger with and distrust of Scott hadn't subsided after a month, she decided to end their relationship. Ashamed of her poor judgment in choosing him, and sure that it would reflect badly on her, Julie kept her virginity loss secret from everyone but her two closest girlfriends, to whom she turned for sympathy and advice. Her reaction mirrored that of every woman whose partner failed to reciprocate her gift.

A few months later, Julie started dating a new boy at high school. Though less popular than Scott, Dan was far more considerate and respectful. He and Julie made sure they were really in love before they even contemplated having sex, and they dated for more than 2 years in all. Yet this positive experience did not dispel Julie's sense that the way she lost her virginity had fundamentally changed who she was as a sexual being. Scott's failure to recognize or return her gift showed Julie just how little control she'd had over their sexual liaisons, and she carried that sense of disenfranchisement into later relationships. Having given away her virginity to someone who clearly didn't appreciate it, Julie felt diminished in value, so much so that she believed she was no longer special enough to refuse sex with less than special men. After Dan, Julie went through what she described as a "pretty promiscuous" phase. In college, she recalled, "I had a roommate that, she was a virgin, and she'd [be], 'Jule, how can you sleep with that guy? . . . You just met him!' But I'd do it, you know. It didn't really matter much to me." Such feelings of lost self-worth are a major hazard of perceiving virginity as part of the self.

By the time I met her, Julie was trying to take what she hoped was a healthier approach to sexual relationships. She explained:

I have accepted myself and I'm happy with myself. And I think I know at this point that I don't need somebody else to make my life, you know, complete. . . . [Now] I don't want to be involved with anybody until I find someone that I'm really happy with. You know, somebody that I want to have sex with mentally and physically. . . . It's not just going to be like, wham, bam, see you later.

In ultimately deciding to postpone having sex until she met someone really special, Julie resembles those who describe themselves as secondary virgins—but she declined to apply that label to herself.

Although she declared herself glad to have learned a lot from the way she lost her virginity, Julie's regret and disillusionment were palpable 10 years later. In a plaintive voice, she said, "You know, you had asked about, was there anything I would change. Well, I wish I could have felt more . . . I wish it would have been, like, this so special moment in my life."

Julie's story underscores the tremendous importance of reciprocity for gifters and demonstrates the degree to which a virgin's sense of having controlled her own destiny could color her subsequent sexual career. In a society in which many people do not view virginity as a gift and where informal social control is relatively weak, recipients enjoy power over givers, specifically the power not to reciprocate. Virgins who favor the gift metaphor therefore run the risk that their *partners* will determine what happens when they lose their virginity. I found that people whose partners reciprocated their gifts, like Kelly, and those who personally chose to forgo reciprocation, like Karen, were generally satisfied with their virginity-loss experiences and went on to approach later relationships much as they had their first—for instance, by continuing to predicate sex on love and commitment. In contrast, virgins who felt taken advantage of by nonreciprocating partners described themselves as Julie did, not only as emotionally upset by their experiences, but also—and more disturbingly—as unable to assert themselves in subsequent relationships as well.

Julie was one of four women who told me that they felt disempowered sexually after their "special" boyfriends refused to reciprocate their gifts of virginity—gifts the boyfriends had coerced or tricked them into giving. It appears that these young men more or less consciously used the dual nature of gifts, as voluntary yet obligatory, to their own strategic advantage.[60] When Scott pressured Julie to give him her virginity, he stressed romantic partners' obligation to give one another gifts while ignoring the definition of gifts as voluntary. Julie was effectively trapped between two conventions of gift giving; and the understanding that prevailed was, significantly, the one promoted by Scott, the more powerful partner by virtue of his gender. In this way, the gift metaphor tends to reproduce current patterns of gender inequality.[61]

A man's greater power prevented a fifth woman from controlling her virginity-loss experience in a different way. Miranda Rivera, a 29-year-old Puerto Rican lesbian who works as a teacher, lost her virginity at age 21 when she was raped by an acquaintance. She had already come out as a lesbian to herself, but not to all of her friends. Miranda was angry and bitter that she hadn't been allowed to determine when—much less whether—she gave her virginity to a man. (She was the only lesbigay person I interviewed who believed that a woman could only lose her virginity with a man.) She said:

> It was like a double kind of a transgression, you know? Because I hadn't had any sexual experience before, with a man or a woman, and there was the physical thing of it, [the] invasion and, the virginity thing. . . . This guy took the choice away from me.

Because Miranda lost her virginity through rape it would have been impossible for her to have had a positive experience; yet her belief that virginity is a gift appeared to magnify her dissatisfaction.

Unlike Julie, Miranda did not feel sexually disenfranchised *following* virginity loss. In fact, the experience strengthened her resolve to have sex only on her terms. Several years after being raped, and after two serious sexual relationships with women, Miranda decided to intentionally give what had been taken from her. "Virginity then became a matter of, like, going to sleep with someone willingly," she explained. "So . . . I did have a sexual encounter with a guy for, just for the sake of saying, I'm taking this, nobody else is." Although "not pleasurable" physically, Miranda found her voluntary virginity loss, with a close male friend, "enjoyable" because "it was very important for me to be in charge" and because it "kind of erased the first." Coerced sexual experiences were, in many people's minds, the one exception to the rule that virginity could be lost only once.[62] Many believed that someone who had been raped hadn't had sex, and so couldn't have "lost" her or his virginity.

Although Julie traced her feelings of impotence in later relationships to the lack of control she felt at virginity loss, I wondered whether a single sexual encounter is likely to have such lasting effects. Perhaps Julie merely used her unhappy virginity-loss experience to justify her subsequent promiscuity; perhaps she would have followed the same course regardless of Scott's behavior. Taken together, the interviews I conducted suggest that, while virginity loss need not inevitably affect future events, it can have long-term repercussions when people invest it with tremendous significance. For people who perceived virginity loss as an event of unparalleled importance, as Julie and many young Americans do, giving one's virginity to a nonreciprocating partner did appear to set in motion a series of unhappy decisions and practices which might have otherwise been avoided. (Likewise, the positive experiences of people like Kelly and Bryan may have prompted them to repeat felicitous choices in the future.) However, people who were less emotionally invested in virginity loss or who tended to view it as one of many sexual encounters—men and women who favored the process/passage metaphor, for instance—seemed to be spared from such enduring effects.

One might expect that people whose virginity-loss experiences fell short of the gift ideal would consequently reject that approach (it had, after all, left them miserable), but this did not prove to be the case. Every one of the women whose partners hadn't reciprocated continued to view virginity as a gift. I found this perplexing at first, for had these women retrospectively reinterpreted virginity as a stigma or a step in a process, they might have been able to relieve their regret at "wasting" a precious gift. Upon further reflection, I have come to believe that the gift metaphor may hold a special appeal for women who feel betrayed by their partners. Steadfastly interpreting virginity as a gift may help women like Julie maintain an image of themselves as "good girls," even though their poor choices of partners and subsequent "promiscuity" suggest otherwise. Within the gifter "worldview," they had obeyed the rules, been wronged, and responded accordingly; whereas from the standpoint of the stigma or process metaphor, they would have only themselves to blame for their misery and their ostensibly unfeminine sexual careers.[63]

"I Basically Considered Myself a Born-Again Virgin"

When people who drew on the gift metaphor were deeply disappointed with their virginity-loss experiences, they typically followed Julie's lead, resigning themselves to having given their gift unwisely and trying to make the best of their nonvirgin futures. But one man and two women in this group responded to "lost gifts" more proactively, by deciding to become born-again (or secondary) virgins. That is, they opted to refrain from the most intimate sort of sexual contact until a specified point in the future, usually marriage or committed love relationships, and to refer to their behavior as a form of renewed virginity.[64] Born-again virginity and the gift metaphor were closely linked in my study. Three of the four secondary virgins I interviewed interpreted virginity as a gift, and gifters were disproportionately likely to believe that virginity could be renewed in some sense.[65] Yet, on another level, the idea of born-again virginity is incompatible with seeing virginity as a unique and precious gift. This final profile explores these tensions.

Andrew Lin, a 19-year-old college sophomore, was born and raised in St. Louis, Missouri, where his parents had settled after emigrating from Taiwan in the 1970s. For as long as he could remember, his father and mother had been in the restaurant business, working their way up from waiting tables at a cousin's diner to owning a small chain of pizza parlors. Andrew described his parents as highly acculturated yet very Chinese. Like many East Asians, they preferred to avoid talking explicitly about sexuality—more so, he thought, than the parents of his European-American friends—but what they did say about sex echoed the sentiments of other parents he knew.[66] The one direct conversation Andrew could recall took place when he was 13. His mother had asked him, "Are you a virgin?" When he replied in the affirmative, she snapped, "Keep it that way!" He took her admonition with a grain of salt, however; he didn't think his parents *really* expected him to delay sex until he was married. Rather, "I figured that was just my mom being a mom," telling him to be careful the best way she knew how.

Like Bryan Meyers, Andrew superficially fit the stereotypical image of collegiate masculinity. He belonged to a fraternity and, like many of the brothers (most of whom were White), dressed in a tough style inspired by hip-hop performers. Yet, Andrew also surprised me by describing virginity in terms customarily linked with femininity—and identical to those used by the women in this group. To him, virginity loss meant "the emotional giving of yourself to the other person, while you're having sex also," and "falling in love with the person that you're going to be doing it with, and at least spending a long, long-term relationship."

Andrew was deeply aware that his understanding of virginity diverged from that of most of the men he knew. In his high school, boys encouraged one another to "get it over with" and received "a pat on the back" for losing their virginity, whereas girls focused on romance and had to worry that their peers might "think, 'Oh, she's easy,' or, 'Oh, now she's going to start having sex with everyone.'"[67] But Andrew found his male classmates' views less than convincing. He knew he wanted to give his virginity to a special girlfriend, as a way of showing how precious she was to him. As he put it:

[There's] a big . . . difference between just having sex with someone and losing your virginity to them. Because it's like saying that you waited for this person, rather than just, "Oh, you're one in many." Like you're one, you're special and you're, like, different than everyone else that they could've had sex with but they didn't. But they're having sex with you, because they wanted to wait for someone that was like you. That's kind of saying, "Well, you're the person I was waiting for."

When Andrew met Michelle, he knew he'd found that special girl. Attractive, smart, and fun to be around, Michelle was 17, a year older than he—"Like Mrs. Robinson or something," he laughed.[68] Andrew thought he was in love with Michelle and, although he'd never dated a girl for more than a few months, he felt certain that "this [relationship] would last for a long, long time." When they started dating, Andrew and Michelle were both virgins, a fact they discussed on several occasions. He found the possibility that they might give their virginity to one another very appealing. "We never verbalized it before, that we were going to lose our virginity to each other," he recalled. "But I think we both felt that we would. So I thought that our relationship would last a lot longer than it actually did."

In their first month together, Andrew and Michelle explored a variety of sexual activities, expanding their repertoire from kissing to caressing to fellatio and cunnilingus. Despite their mutual virginity, this degree of physical intimacy was nothing new to either of them; they'd both, in Andrew's words, "basically done everything, except have sex, with, like, five or six [different-sex partners] or so." Andrew told me that he had intentionally refrained from having vaginal sex so that he could give his virginity to someone he loved. As with Karen Lareau, this strategy seemed to help him reconcile his desire to wait for the "right" partner with the norm of sexual experimentation that prevailed among his peers.

One evening, Andrew and Michelle decided not to stop at foreplay.

We'd just gotten back from a date. And we were just upstairs in my room, hanging out, and we started fooling around, just kind of the usual, not having sex. And then we just both kind of looked at each other and I said, "Should I get a condom?" And she said, "Yes." And then we had sex.

Unfortunately, the condom broke. "I flipped out and we thought she was pregnant for a little bit," Andrew said. When the pregnancy turned out to be a false alarm, their relief was immense. Michelle wanted to continue dating, but Andrew's anxiety wouldn't fade. Nor could he get over his disappointment that giving his virginity had had exactly the opposite effect from what he'd intended. Rather than growing closer to Michelle, he felt emotionally distant and distressed. Having sex again was decidedly out of the question. "I think she mentioned it once and that kind of flipped me out even more," he said, shaking his head.

After a few weeks, Andrew regretfully ended the relationship, because "every time I looked at her . . . I automatically associated all that stress, for like, about two weeks of thinking [she] was pregnant." Knowing that the untoward turn of events had been beyond his and Michelle's control did little to relieve Andrew's misery. In retrospect, he recalled:

> It's a shame that we had that little scare, because I honestly I think our personalities were to the point where we would've gotten along really well. But, just having that mentally anguished association with her, just like, I couldn't deal with. . . . If we wouldn't have had that, I would've probably have associated it as a pretty good experience.

Andrew's decision to break up with Michelle resembles Julie's rejection of Scott. But the circumstances in which Andrew made that decision differed in one crucial respect: he felt that Michelle was willing to reciprocate his gift of virginity with emotional intimacy, whereas Julie believed that Scott was not. This knowledge apparently allowed Andrew to feel he could assert himself in his subsequent sexual relationships. Being male likely also enhanced his sense of agency, as many studies have shown that boys are socialized to take a more active and independent approach to social relations than are girls, and prevailing gender norms and structural advantages give men more power than women on average in heterosexual relationships.[69] In fact, Michelle may have interpreted Andrew's decision to break up as a failure to fulfill his obligations as the recipient of *her* virginity.

Ultimately, Andrew's anguish and disappointment prompted him to decide to refrain from vaginal sex and "wait for that special person to come around"—that is, for another girl as special as Michelle. Scholars such as Sharon Thompson have noted that many adolescents, especially girls, purposefully postpone sexual activity after disappointing virginity-loss encounters.[70] But Andrew went a step further:

I had sex once and then I stopped for a long time because my first experience was bad. . . . Well, not bad, but it just wasn't, I wasn't happy with it. And then so I said, "Fine, I'm not going to have sex until I'm sure I want to have sex with someone." And I basically considered myself a born-again virgin until about two, two months ago.

Although he believed that anyone who wanted to could reclaim his or her virginity, Andrew felt that it was relatively easy for him "because I'd only had sex once before then, and then it was with someone I had been seeing for a while." In effect, he saw himself as more like a "true" virgin than someone who'd had vaginal sex many times or who'd approached sex cavalierly in the past. The contrast with Julie Pavlicko's intentional chastity is instructive. Despite believing that a person could "emotionally . . . go through the whole process of being a virgin again . . . losing your virginity to the one really, really special person in your life," Julie didn't claim secondary virginity for herself. I suspect that she may have felt that she'd had too many sexual partners to adopt a virgin identity or that Scott's mistreatment made her too diminished to try.

Although the concept originated in conservative Christian circles, born-again virginity was for Andrew a purely secular matter. A life-long atheist (like his parents), he'd first heard the expression not in church or from a religious text, but on a risqué TV show: "I was watching *HBO Real Sex* . . . and they had, like, a whole episode on born-again virgins." Whereas religious born-again virgins told me how spiritual texts or discussions with clergy or devout peers had motivated their retreat from sex, Andrew had already abstained for a year before he discovered the term. The phrase simply struck him as the perfect shorthand for a choice he'd already made. Secondary virginity may also appeal to secular men and women because of the cultural tendency to think about sexuality in dichotomous terms.[71] Americans typically posit virginity loss as a kind of sexual off-on switch, as when public health researchers lump individuals who have had vaginal sex a single time into the same "sexually active" category as those who are currently involved with heterosexual partners. For Andrew, being an abstinent secondary virgin may have produced less psychic stress than being an abstinent *non*virgin.

Neither Andrew nor the other study participants who described themselves as born-again virgins appeared to believe that they were virgins in the same sense as people who had never had sex. Rather, they used the term as a way of indicating that their current sexual behavior was identical to their conduct as virgins and that they still valued virginity and the emotional aspects of sex. In effect, Andrew and his fellow secondary virgins saw themselves as so similar to virgins in practice that they merited an analogous designation. While the concept may seem strange or unnecessary—after all, couldn't a person just refrain from sex without invoking virginity?—it may be quite beneficial for women and men who see virginity as a precious part of the self and whose self-worth depends on making the "right" decisions about virginity loss. If, for example, Julie had been able to perceive herself as virtually a virgin, she might have felt more capable or justified in rejecting the sexual advances of men she dated after Scott.

One powerful incentive for embracing secondary virginity is the desire for a perfect virginity-loss experience—a desire shared by gifters. Another motive common to gifters stems from the power of gift exchanges to bind people together. Who, after all, would wish to be tied to someone with whom they endured an unpleasant ordeal? Styling himself as a born-again virgin eased Andrew's regrets that he'd squandered his only chance to forge a special bond with a beloved partner via a perfect encounter. He, too, could enjoy those aspects of virginity loss—albeit when he lost his *secondary* virginity. Notably, the desire to regain virginity also depends on finding virginity intrinsically valuable. Men and women who saw virginity as a stigma told me they couldn't imagine wanting to resume that shameful trait, while people who viewed it as a step in a process had a knack for framing the negative aspects of their encounters as learning experiences.

Yet, reclaiming virginity seems antithetical to the belief, so common to gifters, that virginity's value lies in its unique, nonrenewable nature. Theories of gift giving help shed light on this seeming contradiction. If gifts are *voluntary,* then an individual should be able to choose to give his (ostensibly unique) virginity when and how he wishes, including giving it a second time. The opinions of the women and men I interviewed differed depending on the nature of their own experiences. Those who lost their own virginity in nearly ideal circumstances stressed virginity's uniqueness over volition and dismissed the possibility of secondary virginity. As Bryan Meyers put it, being able to reclaim one's virginity "would, like, defeat the purpose of it. . . . It would, totally take the specialness out of it."[72] In contrast, people whose own experiences had fallen short of their expectations—Karen and Julie among them—expressed sympathy for nonvirgins who hoped to start over and *choose* a better second time.

Being a born-again virgin didn't stop Andrew from engaging in intimate sexual activities altogether. Rather, he reverted to the guidelines he'd followed before having sex with Michelle. He refrained from vaginal sex in order to preserve his secondary virginity for a future girlfriend, but felt free to do "just basically anything besides actual intercourse." (One might describe his conduct as technical secondary virginity.) As a born-again virgin, Andrew enjoyed considerable latitude when describing his sexual status to others. Although he didn't explicitly tell any of his friends that he'd lost his virginity with Michelle, not wishing to relive the trauma through the telling, he didn't try to hide his nonvirginity; nor did he take pains to inform his friends of his decision to reclaim his virginity (in contrast with the three female born-again virgins). Especially at college, where no one knew his sexual history, Andrew chose to reveal or conceal his secondary virginity according to the situation. Although he shared his story with a few close women friends, Andrew said that if any of his fraternity brothers had asked if he were a virgin, he could have honestly said "No," and declined to volunteer any further information.

Andrew didn't attribute his conduct to gender norms, but it is likely that knowing that virgin men are often derided as effeminate or gay fueled his circumspection. Indeed, two male virgins who favored the gift metaphor told me that they downplayed their virginity with all but a few good friends. Chris Albrecht, an 18-year-old White heterosexual and devout Southern Baptist, said that, if someone asked if he were a virgin,

> I would say, "Yes." I don't have problems with that. If I did, then I would . . . fix the problem [laughs]. . . . Well, it depends on the situation. I suppose if some stranger came up, I would say, "Get out of my face" or "Go away." But if, you know, I suppose, if there were a real reason, or I didn't mind, then I would say, "Yeah."

In short, although men like Andrew and Chris defied gender norms by interpreting virginity as a gift, they also took account of (and superficially complied with) social norms stigmatizing male virginity. Women who saw virginity as a gift were, in contrast, decidedly open about their virginity; a few even hoped to be taken for virgins after they'd had sex. (Karen was the only woman to intentionally misrepresent her status.) Andrew's story, like Bryan's, indicates both the attractions of the gift metaphor for young men today and the difficulty of displacing its historic association with femininity.

Andrew's Chinese American heritage also appears to have influenced his beliefs and behavior around virginity loss. Studies consistently find that Asian American youth hold more traditional attitudes about sexuality and lose their virginity at later ages on average than youth from other racial/ethnic groups.[73] Most scholars trace this pattern to Asian and Asian American parents' tendency to transmit to their children their own relatively restrictive sexual values and overall reticence about sex.[74] Although Andrew did not personally attribute his approach to virginity loss to his ethnic background, it is likely that the culturally conditioned values encouraged him to interpret virginity as a gift, a stance not typically associated with masculinity or atheism. Andrew's attitudes and conduct did, however, closely resemble those of male gifters from other racial/ethnic backgrounds.

After more than 2 years of abstinence, Andrew gave his secondary virginity to a special girlfriend, Nita. Andrew had told Nita that he was a born-again virgin, and that he was very concerned about pregnancy prevention, as soon as he realized he was falling in love with her. Andrew recalled:

> I told her I wasn't just, you know, that I didn't just have sex with anyone. Before we did it, we sat and, you know, talked about it for a while. [That] I always had bad associations with sex because of that whole first experience. And like, it really, just, we sat down and talked about it and it alleviated a lot of my stress.

Nita also reassured him that she was on the Pill and STI-free.

Much to Andrew's relief, the first time he had sex with Nita was as perfect and romantic as he had hoped his first encounter with Michelle would be. He was especially glad that Nita had known in advance how much the decision to have vaginal sex meant to him.

> I think it was a lot better . . . having her know how big of a step it was for me to do that, than to have just done [it] and said, "Oh, by the way, all this." And then she'd be like, "Oh, no . . . I did this to you!" So she knew all of it ahead of time and she accepted the responsibility and so did I. And it was pretty good. . . . Like emotionally and everything it was just healthy, I think, this time. . . . And we're still together, so I think it's fine.

By declaring himself a born-again virgin, Andrew was able to deepen his relationship with his cherished partner through a romantic first sexual encounter, even though he no longer had his true virginity to give.

Giving the Gift of Virginity: Loss and Gain, Continuity and Change

The stories recounted here leave little doubt that love and emotional reciprocation were vitally important to women and men who interpreted virginity as a gift. They described virginity as a unique and precious part of the self and believed that giving it was not only a way of expressing love but also, more crucially, a way of strengthening ongoing romantic relationships. Although few of them were strangers to physical desire, their decisions about virginity loss were motivated primarily by relational concerns. To help ensure that their gift of virginity would be reciprocated, they chose their sexual partners with the utmost care and typically took an incremental approach to sexual intimacy, most often with a single partner.

Like the people profiled in this chapter, everyone in my study who viewed virginity as a gift had been exposed to diverse understandings of virginity while growing up. Why did they come to favor the gift metaphor over the available alternatives? Gender, sexuality, and other social identities, especially religion, influenced their preferences in two ways.

First, although it is widely assumed that young people's sexual beliefs and behavior are greatly swayed by mass media, my research supports previous findings that mass media tend to reinforce beliefs fostered by family, friends, religious institutions, and schools, rather than instilling new beliefs or inspiring radical changes in perspective.[75] All of these individuals and institutions tend to encourage young people to embrace the interpretations of virginity deemed appropriate for people "like them." Traditionally, the gift metaphor has been associated with femininity and Christian morality. Not surprisingly, more young women reported being urged to perceive virginity as a gift than did young men. Devout and/or conservative Christians recalled receiving similar encouragement from clergy and fellow believers (especially family and friends). Racial/ethnic identity also appeared to shape approaches to virginity. Two of the four Latino Americans I interviewed (one man and one woman) likened virginity to a gift, a belief they personally attributed to Hispanic cultures' high regard for women's virginity and general sexual conservatism.[76] And two of the three African American women I interviewed thought of virginity as a gift, a perspective favored in Black Protestant churches (to which both women belonged) and by Black families intent on countering popular stereotypes of Black women as promiscuous.[77]

Beliefs and identity did not correspond 100 percent, however, in part because people have multiple identities that may pull them in different interpretive directions. For instance, Andrew's parents persuaded him, as a Chinese American, to interpret virginity as a gift, while his friends urged him, as a young man, to view it as a stigma. Furthermore, social changes have expanded the interpretive stances available to many social groups.[78] This expansion is particularly evident in the case of gender. The men who told me they saw virginity as a gift were disproportionately young. Second- and third-wave feminism, by promoting new models of masculinity; the HIV/AIDS crisis, by giving men a compelling reason for sexual caution (akin to women's concern with pregnancy); and the popularization of conservative Christian sexual ideology, which portrays virginity as a gift, have all contributed to the gradual loosening of the gift metaphor's association with femininity.[79] The beliefs and experiences of female and male gifters were largely similar, suggesting a weakening of the sexual double standard. Yet, I observed one gender difference that demonstrates how stubborn gender inequality can be. Several women, but no men, experienced lasting feelings of sexual disenfranchisement after giving their virginity to nonreciprocating partners—a gendered pattern resulting from a combination of the power imbalance inherent to gift relationships and gender differences in social power, which on average benefit men.

Interestingly, gifters appeared to have been exposed to more consistent messages about virginity than members of other interpretive groups. All had at least one parent who saw virginity as a gift; and, in many cases, these beliefs stemmed from their families' religious traditions.[80] Moreover, gifters tended to have close friends who not only shared their view of virginity but also behaved in accordance with their beliefs.[81] Karen's story shows how young people approaching virginity loss must negotiate discrepancies—between friends' words and actions and between personal beliefs and broader peer cultures—while Bryan's tale reveals the important role of peer support in sustaining young men who prefer a gender-atypical stance.

Young people often come to prefer the metaphors that they have learned to see as appropriate to their social identities. Yet they also select particular metaphors as ways of establishing and enacting preferred *versions* of their identities. Since women in the contemporary United States no longer need to treasure their virginity in order to remain respectably feminine (as they did before about 1970), when Kelly, Julie, and other women of their generation approach their virginity as a gift, they are constructing (more or less consciously) a conventional version of feminine, heterosexual identity. Conversely, when men of the same generation approach virginity as a gift, as did Bryan and Andrew, they are rejecting a traditional style of masculinity for a more relational, less aggressive alternative. The fact that men in this group were much more circumspect than the women when it came to disclosing their virginity suggests that it is not yet wholly acceptable for men to treat their virginity as a gift; gender unorthodoxy still carries the threat of sanctions. For women and men, the gift metaphor additionally facilitates the performance of heterosexuality, presumably because the metaphor's traditional girl-meets-boy connotation leaves little room for same-sex desire.

The interviews I conducted also indicate that interpreting virginity as a gift may help young people from devout mainstream and conservative Christian backgrounds to demonstrate the centrality of religious devotion to their identity.[82] Other researchers have suggested that men and women use virginity loss to construct their racial/ethnic identity. By choosing to approach virginity as a gift, for instance, African American women like Danice Marshall are effectively enacting a "morally upstanding Black woman" identity in contrast to the hypersexual stereotype psychologist Deborah Tolman calls the "myth of the urban girl."[83]

The patterns I observed help reveal how broader social changes affect individual lives. In addition to the gender-related changes just described, I found little support for gifters' historic claim that men and especially women should give their virginity only to their spouse. Almost everyone I spoke with believed that it was acceptable to give one's virginity to a beloved partner in a committed nonmarital relationship. Even the few who spoke of virgin marriage as an ideal, like Julie, typically conceded that few people could realistically achieve it, a concession echoing Britney Spears's about-face. This perspective—treating virginity as precious but accepting its premarital loss—has steadily grown in popularity since the 1960s, as American society has grown more secular, marriages have become less stable, and more people accept the feminist claim that women should enjoy the same sexual freedoms as men.

4

An Unendurable Stigma

One of the most curious incidents in the history of virginity loss in America took place in the summer of 1999. Late one evening in July, an unprecedented offering appeared on the Web site of Internet auction house eBay: the virginity of Francis D. Cornworth. A 17-year-old boy about to begin his senior year in high school, Francis explained his motivation for placing the advertisement succinctly: "I decided I'd like to lose my virginity. I figured with the latest eBay craze, I'd see exactly how much I could get."[1] The yearbook photo accompanying "item No. 138277430" (quantity: "one") depicted a gamely smiling White boy with a weak chin, bad overbite, dorky haircut, and unfashionably large eyeglasses.

As enticements to potential bidders, Cornworth listed his membership in the National Honor Society, presidency of his high school's computer club, proficiency as a trumpet player, and "extensive record" of community service. "I think I am desirable if I can find the right woman (or man, I'm willing to experiment)," Francis wrote. His expansive definition reflects young Americans' increasing willingness to define virginity loss as applying to encounters with same- as well as other-sex partners. He did, however, request that women and men over 60 and people known to have STIs refrain from bidding.

According to one account, the value of Cornworth's virginity rose within hours of the posting from an initial bid of $10 to $10 million.[2] If any of those bidders were in earnest, their hopes were quickly dashed. Less than 24 hours after the page appeared, eBay removed it from its site. Describing the incident as a prank, eBay spokesman Kevin Purseglove explained to reporters that the company reacted swiftly and severely both because the alleged advertiser was under age and because it is company policy to drop ads for illegal activities—including prostitution and the sale of body parts—immediately upon discovery. The hoax ultimately made the human-interest rounds in news outlets from the *New York Post* to Salon.com.[3]

In attributing potentially great worth to virginity, the attempted auction of Cornworth's bears a superficial similarity to the furor over Britney Spears's sexual status. But in every other respect, the two incidents stand in dramatic contrast, highlighting the difference between the gift and stigma metaphors. Not only can gifts by definition not be purchased—this is partly what gifters mean when they proclaim virginity to be priceless—but accepting monetary recompense for the gift of a sexual act is moreover tantamount to prostitution.[4]

The Cornworth auction, by contrast, suggests that virginity is a stigma. Sociologists consider a person to be stigmatized if he (or she) possesses a condition or attribute that, if it were known to others, would discredit him socially and change him "from a whole and usual person to a tainted, discounted one."[5] Attributes become stigmas through a social process whereby some individuals are labeled—or set apart from "normal" people—in a way that leads to loss of status and discrimination.[6] Francis Cornworth perfectly fit a stereotype seen in countless movies—*Risky Business* (1983) and *American Pie* (1999), to name but two—of an adolescent boy taking desperate measures to rid himself of his virginity before his advancing age further compounds his shame. That the hapless lad was plagued not only by his virginity but also by physical unattractiveness and social ineptitude (implied by his hobbies and academic bent) is no surprise, for one stigma tends to accompany others.[7]

Cornworth's effort to join the ranks of nonvirgins is typical of people suffering from stigmas that aren't permanent—they typically try to expunge such stigmas as soon as possible. If the poor guy was trying to make the best of an unfortunate situation by earning a bit of cash in the process, well, who could blame him for trying? In fact, the alleged Francis could even be seen as trying to downplay the intensity of his stigma by recasting his unwanted virginity as valuable enough for a stranger to purchase. Cornworth's willingness to reveal his stigma publicly is, however, rather unusual. Most stigmatized individuals try to conceal the condition that taints them, to *pass* as normal, until they are able to remove it.[8] Stigmas that are undetectable by the casual observer, such as virginity (high school folklore notwithstanding), are most easily disguised.[9] But just because a person *can* hide a stigma doesn't mean he will. Someone caught concealing a stigma may be branded deceitful and face sanctions for the stigma and deception alike. Consequently, most stigmatized people opt to share their status with a few intimates while disguising it from everyone else.[10] These tendencies point to the relative powerlessness of stigmatized women and men. A person can only make a negative designation stick to someone less powerful than himself; and having a stigma reduces a person's social status and power even more.[11] People try to resist becoming or remaining stigmatized, but they often lack the power to prevent others from identifying or exposing their stigma, sanctioning them for it, or even conferring new stigmas upon them.

Of course, not everyone interprets virginity as a stigma, nor is every case of virginity deemed equally stigmatizing. Whether a trait is stigmatized depends on social context: what is normal in one town or high school or for one type of person may be abnormal in or for another. Cornworth's gender, for instance, is crucial to understanding the eBay prank. As we have seen, Americans have historically viewed men's virginity as a stigma and women's as a gift—perceptions that undergird the sexual double standard. I therefore suspect that many who viewed Francis's advertisement automatically interpreted the boy's virginity as a stigma (or at least understood that *he* saw it that way), whereas they might have been dismayed or disturbed by a hypothetical girl "Frances" who declined to cherish her virginity. Yet we should remain leery of assuming a gender dichotomy. Although the young men I interviewed *were* considerably more likely than the women to view their own virginity as a stigma at the time they began having sex, a substantial minority of the women also felt stigmatized by their status.[12] The existence of such an "unfeminine" stance has not gone unrecognized in American popular culture—as viewers of the 1980 teen movie *Little Darlings,* in which Tatum O'Neal and Christy McNichol played two 15-year-olds competing to lose their virginity first at summer camp, can testify.

This chapter examines the beliefs and experiences of young men and women who share Francis Cornworth's vision of virginity as a stigma—or the "stigmatized," as I will call them.[13] More than the simple converse of the gift metaphor, the stigma frame gives rise to a specific and complex set of expectations, concerns, and practices, all of which are rooted in social understandings of stigmas generically. To chart this constellation of ideas and actions, I draw on theoretical and empirical research on stigma in general.[14] My analysis explores points of similarity and difference between women and men who see their virginity as a stigma and considers how virginity loss helps them fashion their identities not only as gendered beings, but also as possessors of particular sexual and racial/ethnic identities.

"Growing Up It's Always Been a Stigma, It's Always Been a Bad Thing . . . to Be a Virgin"

Kendall James tells the story of how he lost his virginity with gusto. In fact, as he confessed in our interview, it is one of his favorite personal anecdotes. At 28 years old, Kendall manages a men's clothing boutique in Philadelphia's Old City arts district. When we met, he was clad in gear from the trendy shop and sporting a thick silver nose ring, which contrasted dramatically with his mahogany complexion. Most of his ancestors had come from West Africa during the slave trade, he said, but he had some Cherokee blood as well. Kendall's had been one of the few African American families in the suburb where he grew up and one of the few supported by a single mother. Kendall's mom, a nurse's assistant, divorced her construction worker husband before Kendall started high school. He'd been happy to trade that isolating environment for the cosmopolitan city as soon as he had his diploma in hand. As a teenager, Kendall had been sexually involved with both men and women; as an adult, he identified as gay. He had lived with boyfriends twice in the past, but was currently single and "enjoying my space."

When I asked Kendall how he'd seen virginity as a boy, he explained that he and his friends first started thinking about virginity as it applied to them when they were in sixth or seventh grade. "There was a point in grade school and high school where it was a big deal to lose it," he said. "Or better yet, it was a bigger deal if you didn't lose it, if you were a virgin."

Scarcely anyone Kendall knew, himself included, had discussed sex or virginity with their parents; and the Baptist church he and his mother attended held premarital sex in such disdain that he dismissed its teachings as irrelevant. (As an adult, he rejected organized religion for interfering with his "relationship with whatever power is out there.") Instead, he and his friends gleaned what information they could from one another, older siblings and cousins, and movies like *Porky's* and *Fast Times at Ridgemont High*. Kendall recalled:

> I think almost every teenlike movie . . . was about getting laid or not getting laid, and what an idiot you were for not getting laid. And then girls, you know, hemming and hawing, "Should I put out? Should I not put out?" . . . Growing up it's always been a stigma, it's always been a bad thing, per se, to be a virgin. I'm sure I knew a lot more virgins than let on. But [you] couldn't be a virgin in public.

Although they knew that some adults, and even some kids, felt otherwise, to Kendall and his crowd, "virginity was a sign of dorkiness." Just remembering their anxious efforts to hide their sexual inexperience made him laugh: "It's funny . . . I'm sure I lied. I'm sure, you know, at ten, I was like, 'Hey, I'm not no virgin!' You know, not even knowing what the word meant, probably, at that point." In my study, such zeal for masking virginity set the stigmatized apart from people who preferred the gift and process metaphors.

By the end of elementary school, Kendall had resolved to lose his virginity as soon as he could. After all, having sex not only made you "cool," but was also supposed to feel great. Yet while Kendall was eager to experience sex, he wasn't at all interested in romance or dating. In fact, he was mystified to discover that a few of his buddies hoped to lose their virginity with girlfriends. Seeing virginity loss as an end in itself and remaining relatively aloof from love and relationships were typical of men and women who interpreted virginity as a stigma. Most of them took a pragmatic approach to choosing sexual partners. Half lost their virginity with casual partners—friends, acquaintances, or strangers—and even those who lost their virginity with boyfriends or girlfriends were seldom in love or in relationships of more than a few weeks' duration.[15] In short, they selected their virginity-loss partners on entirely different bases than gifters.

Kendall's eagerness to shed his virginity and his belief that sex was meant for personal pleasure—both characteristic of people who framed virginity as a stigma—helped determine the kinds of sexual things he did while still a virgin. Although he'd masturbated dozens of times before turning 12, Kendall had scant sexual experience with girls and none with boys. He said:

> We had like, you know, done doctor and played and fondling and stuff. But nothing like, even out of clothes. It was like, "We've got boobies," and you know, stupid stuff like that. . . . I mean, I was aware and I knew what could happen. But . . . there wasn't anybody to experiment with.

The first time he had a chance to do more than "stupid stuff," Kendall was with a girl who wanted to have sex—and he saw no reason to stop short of getting rid of his virginity and getting on with pleasure. Nor did the majority of stigmatized men and women. Two-thirds had never tried heavy petting before losing their virginity because, like Kendall, they had been able to have "real" sex right away.[16]

What happened the day 12-year-old Kendall lost his virginity took him by surprise. It was as if he'd been swept onto the set of one of the over-the-top teen movies he'd seen. Late in the afternoon, his mother had rushed off to help her sister with "some family emergency," leaving Kendall in the care of Tammy, the pretty older sister of his best friend from next door. "She could only have been three or four years older," Kendall said. Bored with the TV show they were watching, Kendall and Tammy started joking around and got into a playful wrestling match. Then: "Wrestling and erections and curiosity and. . . ." Before he knew what was happening, they were having sex on the living room floor. "It was kind of a surprise!" he exclaimed, laughing. "It was a shock and it was, it was mind-blowing."

Kendall didn't know whether Tammy had realized that he was a virgin. He certainly didn't tell her; and she never said what she thought. Because he'd been so "big for his age" at 12, even his parents tended to treat him as older than his years, and Tammy may have done the same. Kendall was relieved to have kept his secret—as 5 of 8 people who concealed their virginity from their partners had—though it is likely that, if Tammy had discovered his virginity, his extreme youth would have minimized the intensity of his stigma.

Another topic that neither Kendall nor Tammy raised was the possibility of pregnancy or STIs. "Probably because I was so young," he surmised.

> I can't remember any kind of talk about the Pill or rubbers or anything. . . . [I]t wasn't really a planned thing. But when it did happen . . . when I was in the middle of everything, it really didn't even occur to me. And . . . I didn't really have enough information about birth control. I mean, I knew that babies could come of sex. But I didn't think this was necessarily sex to begin with. And then, secondly . . . adults have babies, kids don't have babies. So it really . . . never came up.

Few people had been concerned about HIV at the time (it was 1982) and besides, he recalled with chagrin, "It was always the girl on the Pill. . . . You know, it's really sad and stupid, but that's how it was until, like, the [late] '80s." Overall, the stigmatized were much less likely to take precautions against pregnancy and STIs than people who interpreted virginity in other ways. Two-fifths practiced neither safer sex nor contraception. One reason for their disinclination was their impatience to lose their virginity, which often meant—as it did for Kendall—being unwilling to postpone sex if an opportunity arose at a time when they weren't "prepared."

Although Kendall was ecstatic to have lost his virginity, especially in such an exciting way (and without embarrassing himself), he nonetheless chose to keep his news a secret. First and foremost, he was afraid that sharing the story might get him or Tammy into trouble with their parents, or upset his friend Kevin, Tammy's brother. He was also loath to dispel the impression of nonvirginity he'd so deliberately cultivated among his peers. He explained:

> All throughout my school career, I rarely confirmed or denied any virgin or sex issues. Everyone always assumed, because I was bigger, I had a deeper voice, you know, and I was mature for my age. . . . So they always assumed. And I never said, "Oh, not until last week." . . . And I was a popular guy.

Concealing the details of virginity loss after the fact is virtually mandatory for virgins who have disguised their stigma, lest they risk being denounced as liars. Many of the people I interviewed noted that, although it would have been humiliating to have their former virginity made public, it could have been just as bad to be labeled as deceitful. Luckily for Kendall, by the time his friends asked outright about his virginity, "It was already done," *and* he'd been able to regale them with true tales of sexual encounters with girls he met after Tammy. "If I would call back all of my friends in sixth grade," he said, "I would imagine that all of them would have thought that I wasn't a virgin. And it wasn't from me saying, 'Oh yeah, Kevin's sister, blah blah blah.'"

Kendall used two common strategies for concealing the stigma of his virginity. He actively bragged that he wasn't a virgin when he actually was; and he emphasized personal traits that are typically associated with nonvirginity, like his physical maturity and popularity. Kendall further benefited from belonging to a group of friends among whom sexual bravado and reluctance to call one another's bluffs (perhaps for fear of self-exposure) were the norm.[17]

For several months after he had sex with Tammy, Kendall suffered from "the crush that wouldn't end" and found himself daydreaming about being her boyfriend. But, he said, "Tammy and I never, never spoke about it ever again. . . . There was never sex again and it was never brought up again." He could only assume that she saw their tryst as a momentary diversion or even a mistake. In fact, I spoke with only one person who lost his virginity with an acquaintance or stranger and went on to have sex with them subsequently; such is the nature of casual encounters. Since Kendall wasn't interested in dating and didn't go out of his way looking for new sexual partners, almost two years passed before he had sex of any kind again. "But," he quipped, "in that two years I became a master at masturbation."

Around the time he turned 14, Kendall decided, "I've had enough fun myself and I want to try something else." He embarked on a decade-long odyssey of sexual experimentation, trying all manner of sexual activities with all sorts of partners, which he later understood as part of the process of coming out as gay. He said:

> My first experiences were with women and my third experience was with a guy. And my fourth experience was with a girl. . . . So for a while it, you know, I tried it. And I, it was, I told myself, experimentation. You know, just being curious.

This approach to sex with casual partners differs dramatically from that taken by Julie Pavlicko and other gifters. Men and women who saw virginity as a stigma spoke of their experiences with casual sex in terms of experimentation, not promiscuity; and none of them attributed their behavior to feeling powerless to stop or refuse. Their only regrets were occasional lapses in practicing safer sex and choosing partners who, in retrospect, repelled them.

Looking back, Kendall wondered whether one of the reasons he'd been so eager to shed the stigma of virginity was the degree to which it had been mixed up with the stigma of being gay. He'd certainly *felt* sexually attracted to boys by the time he longed to lose his virginity, even if he wasn't yet comfortable admitting it to himself. In the contemporary United States, virginity, especially men's virginity, is routinely associated with homosexuality in popular culture and media, including several of the films Kendall saw as a youth (*Fast Times* and *The Breakfast Club,* to name but two). In this context, losing virginity with a different-sex partner offers young men (and women) a way of demonstrating their heterosexuality and proving—to themselves or to others—that they aren't gay.[18] All of the stigmatized who knew or suspected they were gay recalled feeling that the stigmas of virginity and homosexuality were somehow intertwined.[19]

Through virginity loss, they had sought, more or less consciously, to lose two stigmas at once. Given the conflation of these two stigmas, it is not surprising that most of the gay men in my study interpreted virginity as a stigma.[20]

Coming out in such a protracted way, coupled with the fact that vaginal sex was "not [as] mind-blowing pleasurable" as he'd expected, changed Kendall's understanding of virginity loss. He began to perceive it less as a one-time escape from a shameful trait and more as a first step in an ongoing process of learning about sex. From this new perspective, Kendall saw losing his virginity as an event that took him from "having the knowledge but not the experience" to "making them mesh together." That revelation marked the beginning of an educational journey he thought no one should forgo:

> I don't object to saving yourself until marriage, I just don't think it's smart. I think, because we're experimental animals, I think that the relationship with someone's first should be a relationship that grows and evolves and not necessarily stays sexual.

In fact, after losing their virginity, all but three of the stigmatized came to prefer other metaphors. Once relieved of their own stigmas, they felt free to reconsider virginity anew; and their own experiences suggested that sex improved with practice. Perhaps because they saw pleasure as the primary purpose of sex, virgins in this group tended to harbor unusually— and unrealistically—high expectations about the physical enjoyment to be had from first sex.[21]

Kendall's sexuality was not the only aspect of his social identity implicated in his approach to virginity loss. Historically men have been encouraged to frame virginity as a stigma; and the men in my study were more likely to favor the stigma metaphor than the women. This tendency was pronounced among the African American men I interviewed; other scholars have observed similar patterns. Sociologist Elijah Anderson's ethnographic research suggests that young urban Black men often see sex as a "game" for achieving personal aggrandizement and status among peers.[22] Benjamin Bowser's interviews with African American men reveal a similar worldview, accompanied by the tendency to begin sexual activity early, with little experimentation before first vaginal sex, followed by serial sexual relationships with relatively casual partners.[23] National surveys likewise find that Black men tend to approach sexuality in recreational terms and become sexually active at younger ages and in less-committed relationships than men from other racial/ethnic backgrounds.[24] According to Bowser, this "hypersexual" posture appeals to young African American men as a means of achieving manhood in a society where routes to economic success are often blocked by institutionalized racism.[25] From these men's perspective, virginity would undoubtedly represent a stigma; and losing it would mark the achievement of a compelling gendered and raced sexual identity. In this way, Kendall's story supports what scholars have noted about young African American men; though certainly in many ways his experiences resemble those of stigmatized men of other races.

The beliefs and experiences of the African American men I interviewed differed dramatically from those of their female counterparts, all but one of whom interpreted virginity as a gift. Danice Marshall, profiled earlier, typifies these women in her careful avoidance of becoming "one of [a player's] statistics" and her choice to give her virginity to her first long-term boyfriend because he was "different than the other guys I had . . . dated and I trusted him more." Though I interviewed only three Black women, their stories closely resemble those recorded by other researchers. Many of the African American women interviewed by anthropologist Claire Sterk-Elifson described sex as something given in "return" for love, affection, and respect; women who spoke with psychologist Gail Elizabeth Wyatt often said they'd lost their virginity to show love for a partner; the adolescent girls in Renee White's study cherished the romantic ideal of reserving sex for a loving, perfect partner even while behaving in ways that recognized a more pedestrian reality; and Elijah Anderson concluded that many poor young Black women approach sex as part of a "dream" about romance and family building.[26]

In my study, gender differences in approaches to virginity loss were considerably more pronounced among African Americans than among other racial/ethnic groups. This difference may be an artifact of the relatively small number of Blacks I interviewed; however, other researchers have found similar patterns in more extensive samples.[27] Since most young people choose same-race sexual partners, if it is true that African American men and women are strongly disposed to view virginity as a stigma and gift, respectively, then misunderstandings and distress at virginity loss may be especially common among heterosexual African Americans.[28] Virginity loss may, therefore, contribute to what various scholars have characterized as a pervasive and harmful climate of sexual mistrust between African American women and men.[29] That said, none of the Black men and women I interviewed mentioned experiencing such conflicts, whereas several White participants did.

"Is There Something Wrong with You?"

Although half of the stigmatized lost their virginity with a friend or on a one-night stand, an equal number were dating their virginity-loss partners. Twenty-six-year-old Marty Baker had been one such virgin. Marty, who is White, had grown up in a predominantly middle-class suburb, though his father was a plumber and his mother a sales clerk. He shared his parents' ambivalence toward their Presbyterian faith. His lifelong fondness for the outdoors was reflected in his career, managing a specialty camping goods store, and in the flannel shirt and well-maintained hiking boots he wore when we met. At that time, Marty had been married for 3 years and had a year-old daughter.

As a teenager, Marty had been eager to lose his virginity. When he was in high school, he said, "To be called a virgin was demeaning," for both guys and girls. Although it would have seemed "too mature to want to have sex" at age 13 or 14, by the time Marty and his friends were 15 and 16 and some of their acquaintances had become sexually active, they increasingly viewed virginity as a stigma. "Everyone was supposed to [have sex]," he explained, "and you, if you wanted to be older . . . if you were going to grow up—people were starting to, having some sex." To Marty's crowd, being a virgin after high school would have signaled a deep personal flaw, triggering questions such as: "'[W]hy are you still a virgin . . . why haven't you deflowered yourself?' So to speak. 'Is there something wrong with you?' Or, '[Are] there overbearing parents involved?' Or, 'Is there something like religious attitudes?'" Positing virginity as abnormal and in need of explanation was a common reaction among the stigmatized, as was linking virginity to other stigmatized statuses, like religious fanaticism or being tied to a parent's apron strings. Indeed, people frequently interpret one stigma as indicating the existence of another—Francis Cornworth's multiple burdens being a case in point.

Marty's conviction that nonvirginity was the normal condition for high school juniors and seniors guided his conduct around his peers.[30] He and the four boys he'd been good friends with since childhood knew who among them were virgins and who were not, but they did their best to keep that knowledge secret from others. Marty explained:

> I guess maybe in the locker room . . . if I had been in a situation where I was around people who all had [had sex], maybe I would've been put down for it. But . . . I saw it in other people, without letting on that I was or wasn't [laughs].

Needless to say, he'd looked forward to the day when he'd "stand a little bit taller" as a nonvirgin and feel relieved of "the pressure of wanting to know what it was all about, personally."

Marty's discontent intensified during his junior year, a time when many of his acquaintances (though only one close friend) lost their virginity. He had experimented sexually with half a dozen casual partners by then. He'd kissed some girls in sixth grade and, in seventh grade, "played spin the bottle and second base and . . . touched breasts." Then, at a party the summer before eighth grade, Marty and a girl he knew from school had gone to an upstairs bedroom where "I received oral sex and everything up to that, you know, touching below [the waist]." When they returned to the party, he recalled, there were

> all these people standing around drinking, [asking] "Where have you been?" questions. And your hair's all messed up, her hair was all messed up. So it was, like, obvious. . . . There was tons of pressure to spill out what it is you've done upstairs.

Although he and the girl had just been acquaintances before that night, they decided to become "boyfriend and girlfriend," an arrangement that lasted about a month. In the next 2 years, Marty "approached the same caliber of things, you know, being naked and fooling around," sometimes with girls he was dating, sometimes with more casual partners. But, he explained, "the situations were either, you know, the person wasn't willing to or it had never gotten this far." One-third of the stigmatized engaged in heavy petting with at least one partner before the person with whom they lost their virginity—the same proportion as among gifters. But where heavy-petting gifters expressly intended to maintain their virginity until they found the "perfect" partner, heavy petters in the stigma group remained virgins only because they hadn't found partners willing to go "all the way." For this reason, sexually experienced virgins in the stigma group were typically older (over 16) at virginity loss than were their inexperienced counterparts, and should be distinguished from technical virgins.[31]

The more sexual experience Marty amassed, the more intensely he wanted to lose his virginity. His ventures with foreplay suggested that vaginal sex "would feel really good" and he wanted "to find out what everyone was ranting and raving about." Indeed, almost everyone who interpreted virginity as a stigma described their quest for virginity loss as motivated not only by the desire to escape their stigma, but also, secondarily, by the incentives of physical pleasure, which they typically spoke of as an end in itself, and curiosity about sex. These latter motivations were rare among gifters, given their focus on the emotional aspects of sex, but common among people who saw virginity loss as a process.

Although Marty enjoyed dating and felt it would be nice to lose his virginity with a girlfriend, he wasn't interested in waiting until he fell in love or established a committed relationship. In fact, he confessed, if he had remained a virgin much longer, he would have sought out a casual partner for the express purpose of virginity loss. He therefore considered himself lucky that he started dating Pam when he did, in the winter of his junior year. At 18, Pam was a year older than Marty and a senior, like his three closest male friends. They had gotten to know each other at parties, said Marty, and "it wasn't really long at all, maybe three weeks' dating, before we had sex." During those weeks, Marty and Pam had quickly proceeded from kissing to genital touching to giving and receiving oral sex. They liked one another but were not in love. The nature of their relationship and the speed with which their sexual intimacy progressed were typical of people who lost the stigma of virginity with a girlfriend or boyfriend; only 2 of the 9 who had boyfriends or girlfriends had been in love with their partners and few had been dating for more than a few weeks.

Though it embarrassed him to do so, Marty told Pam that he was a virgin. He felt obliged to be honest with his girlfriend, and he knew that Pam could easily discover the truth from their mutual friends. (For these reasons, only three men in this group hid their virginity from a partner they were dating.) Happily, Pam—who was not a virgin—reacted to Marty's revelation with enthusiasm. As he put it, "She was kind of excited about it—to have her be with me, so she would be my first." On the surface, Pam's reaction to Marty's virginity is surprising: the classic responses to stigma are derision, discrimination, and social rejection. Yet, in the case of stigmas that are nearly universal or easy to identify with—as virginity likely was for a recent nonvirgin like Pam—negative reactions are often leavened with compassion.[32] Stigmas may also invoke sympathy when their possessor has positive personal traits or respects the group norms that condemn him—and Marty was an attractive teenager eager to lose his virginity. For his part, Marty saw Pam's greater sexual experience as "kind of neat, because then it wasn't a fumbling thing—she kind of knew what to do." Indeed, the majority of people who interpreted virginity as a stigma had preferred sexually experienced partners, and none of them hoped to lose their virginity with another virgin.

Marty and Pam didn't know in advance when they'd find a private space for having sex. Rather, one night when Pam's parents were spending an evening away from home, "it ended up happening, and I just kind of followed suit. So I guess maybe I was led. But it was quite all right." They used a condom, thinking primarily of pregnancy prevention. Marty laughed remembering how much he had worried about "whether or not I was going to do it right." What if he had lost his virginity only to be branded sexually incompetent? He was careful to point out, "[T]hat's my own pressure. Not by her. And not my friends." Fortunately, the encounter went smoothly. "I kind of knew what I was supposed to do," he said. "It was just, you know, the actual act. Everything else was pretty up to par." Relieved to have shed his virginity, Marty shared the news with his longtime friends. He said nothing to his newer acquaintances, however, lest he shatter the impression of nonvirginity he had worked so diligently to foster. He also wanted to protect Pam's privacy. He did, however, enjoy a newfound freedom to talk about sex without fear of having his virginity discovered.

Over the next 2 months, Marty chuckled, "We did [it] a lot. And I became fairly obsessed with it." Then, out of nowhere, Pam decided to break things off. Although their relationship hadn't been particularly deep, Marty was upset by the suddenness of Pam's decision and the tensions it produced among their mutual friends. He also regretted losing "the woman I had prospects of having sex with. I'm sure that wasn't what was in the forefront of my mind at that point, but it would have a good portion to do with it." Marty recovered quickly from the breakup, especially compared with gifters who got dumped after virginity loss, and went on to have sex with casual partners as well as serious girlfriends, the last of whom became his wife.

In retrospect, Marty declared himself wholly pleased with the way he lost his virginity, even though the encounter hadn't been as physically pleasurable as he'd hoped for. "It's been a lot better since then," he said with a laugh. "As far as like, looking back on it, I wouldn't consider that an awe-inspiring sexual encounter. But it was definitely pretty neat." This minor disappointment, combined with having been freed from his stigma, inspired Marty gradually to reevaluate his beliefs about virginity loss. By the time I interviewed him, he understood virginity loss less as a way of eliminating a stigma and more as the beginning of a lifelong process of learning about sex:

> I guess, like, losing your virginity—everything up until that point was like geared about losing it. And then after you lost it, then it was like, "Okay, now what can I do to improve what's going on?" . . . Right off the beginning, it was just being able to have done it. And then, like, you kind of knew what you were doing. . . . And then after that came exploration into ways of, types, and places. Yeah, so there's definitely a before and after.

"It Was My First Time, and . . . I Didn't Want to Look Foolish"

Where Kendall and Marty relished the stories of how they lost their virginity, Bill Gordon remembered his experience as singularly traumatic. He had scarcely shared it with anyone. For although Bill succeeded in expunging the stigma of his virginity, he failed to hide his sexual inexperience from his partner; and when she ridiculed him for it, he wound up feeling stigmatized all over again. His story illustrates how important successful concealment and avoiding further stigmas were to people in this group, and how much power they ceded to their partners by virtue of the metaphor they preferred.

When I met Bill, he was 31 years old and living in southern New Jersey, not far from the town where he grew up. The first in his family to graduate from college, Bill worked for a national tutoring service, instructing high school students in the finer points of the SATs. He wore khaki trousers and a white button-down shirt, which echoed his sandy brown hair and fair skin and seemed at odds with his bluff and blustery demeanor. He had lived with a girlfriend briefly in his late 20s, but it had-n't worked out. Since then, he had gravitated toward more casual rela-tionships, though he hoped eventually to marry and have children.

When I asked Bill what he had thought about virginity while growing up, he began by telling me about what his mother, a full-time home-maker, and father, an auto mechanic, had taught him. His mother main-tained that sex was "a gift from God that should be shared only by peo-ple who really love each other," even though she rarely managed to herd the family to their Methodist church. Especially after Bill had a steady girlfriend, "my mother made it clear that she didn't believe in premari-tal sex." The message from Bill's father was less straightforward, how-ever.

> My father asserted that . . . you shouldn't do it. But he revealed to me experiences when he was in the army. So there was a conflict there, where my mother was saying one thing. My father was supporting my mother, but also saying, "Look, I did it, too."

Despite prolonged exposure to their parents' and pastors' conservative stance on virginity, Bill and his friends found it less than persuasive, es-pecially by the time they were teenagers. To them, virginity was a cause for embarrassment, one that they intended to rid themselves of as soon as possible. People who hadn't had sex, Bill recalled, "were deemed less than the people who had." Virginity was especially demeaning for men in Bill's high school. If a guy was a virgin, he explained, "somehow they weren't man enough." But many of his friends saw women virgins in a different light:

> It would've been more embarrassing and probably would've been harder on the guy. . . . They wouldn't have made fun of the girl, but they would've made fun of the guy. Some of the guys might even be intrigued by the fact that this [girl] never had sex. . . . Being possibly the one per-son who devirginizes her.

This pattern is consistent with the sexual double standard and with pop-ular culture's tendency to eroticize women's virginity while disparaging men's. Not coincidentally, Bill and his friends were avid fans of the soft-porn magazines and videos in which this gendered vision of virginity is particularly pronounced.

And yet, Bill said, "I could never quite get with that idea. . . . I didn't want somebody who was a virgin. It would make me more uncomfortable. It would remind me of my sister." His preference for sexually experienced partners was typical, though even more pronounced than Marty's. On the surface, this predilection seems to pose a threat to these virgins' intense desire to hide or minimize the stigma of virginity. Logically speaking, sexually adept partners would be especially well equipped to identify and criticize a virgin's inexperience, a danger few virgins seemed to recognize. Theories of stigma can help unravel this apparent paradox. In addition to the negative connotations of stigma, which render virgins inherently degraded and thus undesirable as partners, the stigmatized may fear symbolic contamination from associating closely with virgins. Sociologists call this phenomenon—being stigmatized through contact with the stigmatized—*courtesy stigma*; it has been observed in all manner of stigmatizing situations.[33]

Although Bill never valued his virginity, losing it had seemed neither imperative nor practically possible to him until his peers started having sex, around the time he entered high school. From then on, Bill felt the stigma of his own virginity growing more acute with every passing year. By twelfth grade, he said, "It was assumed that no one was still a virgin." In addition to the peer culture and advancing age that heightened his sense of stigma, an experience Bill had as a boy may have given him further incentives to lose his virginity. As he put it, "I went through a *homo*sexual phase, around second grade, until like, fifth grade."

In second grade, I had anal intercourse with a friend of mine. . . . We used to go into the woods and lay a blanket down and then take down our pants and just rub our penises on top of each other in the woods. That was the first sexual experience I had. And then eventually we had anal intercourse. I penetrated him. . . . Those are my first experiences. And then [I] hit a period of like. Just, in fifth grade it started, not being interested in *guys* anymore, I just was interested in women.

Experimenting with his friend gave Bill firsthand knowledge that genital sex could feel very pleasurable. It also suggested that he might be homosexual, which may have lent a particular urgency to his desire to lose his virginity, as doing so would prove his heterosexuality. His emphatic declaration of his heterosexual identity at other points in our interview strongly supports this interpretation.

But despite his intentions, Bill remained a virgin until he was an 18-year-old college freshman. Three things had, he believed, conspired against him. First, high school sex education classes, TV specials, and news reports had left him morbidly afraid of catching an STI, particularly herpes. He had also worried about making a fool of himself the first time he had sex.[34] Most important, the girl he dated throughout high school had been reluctant to have vaginal sex.

Bill and Colleen had started dating as sophomores and, by the end of junior year, their sexual relationship had grown very intimate—they often exchanged oral sex. Bill described their emotional relationship as based less on love than on the status and social security that came with having a steady partner. But Colleen's traditional beliefs about premarital sex combined with Bill's fears about STIs and appearing inept—which were undiminished by knowing that Colleen, too, was a virgin—to keep them from going further. Bill said:

> It was never really discussed. . . . She never directly stated that she wanted to have sex. Although one time we were in a car and we were both naked and she said that she wanted me to lie on top of her, so that she could see what it was like for us to be married. So she had some idea that this couldn't be done unless we were married.

Like Marty Baker, Bill gained experience with heavy petting in part because he didn't immediately find a partner who was willing to go "all the way."

By the time he and Colleen broke up, the summer after high school, Bill felt as though he had fallen far behind his peers. He hadn't hidden his virginity from Colleen since he believed that dating necessitated honesty and because his feelings of stigma had been mitigated by their youth when they met. But with his friends, Bill did his best to keep his virginity a secret. Reluctant to lie outright, he pursued a strategy of selective silence and omission. He was particularly happy to take advantage of his friends' assumption that sex was bound to be part of any relationship as lengthy as his and Colleen's. Only in retrospect did Bill realize that, despite the scorn they all heaped upon virgins, some of his friends must have been virgins, too.

When Bill arrived at college, a state school a few hours from home, he was unattached for the first time in 3 years, determined to lose his virginity, and resigned to subterfuge until it was gone. After his frustrations with Colleen, he found the informal "hook-ups" that prevailed at his college vastly preferable to dating. And he was surprised and delighted to discover that many young women there were actually eager to have sex. In his first sexual encounters at college, fear of rejection and appearing inexperienced kept Bill from proposing vaginal sex. Then he found out that one of his partners had taken offense at his restraint. He recounted:

> When I first got into college . . . there was opportunities to have sex, but I didn't even take advantage of them because I was afraid. And one time I, a woman that I met at a party . . . spent some time rolling around the bed with her, but short of intercourse. She told her friend that she was pissed off with me because I didn't fuck her. And that's when I started thinking, like, "Oh my god, maybe these women don't like what I'm doing. Maybe I'm doing something wrong here."

Bill's self-reproach was predictable: people who can potentially remove their stigmas face considerable pressure to do so and are often harshly criticized for failing to take advantage of whatever stigma-erasing opportunities arise.[35]

Once Bill realized that having sex might be as easy as asking, he hoped to lose his virginity the next time he hooked up. Although the stigmatized harbored a slight preference for losing their virginity with girlfriends or boyfriends, they had few compunctions about doing so with casual partners. In fact, for virgins who want to keep their virginity secret, choosing a relative stranger may have distinct advantages. Strangers possess no knowledge of one another's sexual histories and are unlikely to seek any, especially in the absence of mutual friends. Nor do social norms compel people to tell strangers the complete truth about themselves.[36] Furthermore, if an unfamiliar partner did identify a virgin's secret—perhaps from a fumbling performance—the negative consequences would be relatively minor. A stranger couldn't broadcast the news of a virgin's deceit to friends she didn't know; and the shamed virgin would never need encounter his betrayer again. No wonder, then, that so many people in the stigma group were glad to lose their virginity with people they barely knew.

One Friday afternoon, Bill's dorm-mate Amy introduced him to Diane, a friend who was visiting for the weekend. When he saw Diane again that evening, Bill knew nothing about her except that she was very attractive, around his age, and from Amy's hometown. He reminisced:

> Later on that night, I was at [the] tavern and there she was, out on the dance floor dancing, and all these guys . . . were like gawking at this woman from out of town. Like, "Who's this lady, where did she come from?" And I'm, I'm staring at her, too. And the next thing I know, she stopped dancing, she comes over to me and she says, "I've had enough of this, let's get out of here and do something else." So [I] just literally walked out of the place with her, and like my friends were like, slack-jawed, you know. . . . So it was like a heroic thing, you know, it was like an ego booster.

What Diane meant by "something else" became apparent when she escorted Bill back to Amy's dorm room. When she asked for a moment to "get . . . comfortable," Bill ran to his room for a condom, hoping he hadn't misread her signals. When he got back, Diane "had taken all of her clothes off and had nice mellow music on."

Diane's obvious experience with sex, while intoxicating, aggravated Bill's anxieties about turning in a first-rate performance and steeled his determination to keep his virginity secret. Even so, he recognized that achieving the latter goal depended partly on accomplishing the former, and that worrying about ineptitude might ironically cause it. When I asked if he'd told Diane he was a virgin, Bill laughed:

> Of course not. I don't think so! "Uh, I've never done this before." . . . You know, it might've happened had she been a virgin, then it would've been maybe okay, really, learning about this for the first time. But it was so obvious to me that she wasn't, that I felt demeaned by, if I had said that.

Bill's intense desire to avoid appearing inexperienced also stopped him from insisting on using the condom he'd fetched. He recalled:

> I said, "Well, I have this condom here." And she said, "Oh, you don't need any protection, I'm okay." And because I was so nervous, it was my first time—and I would've never done this, as I got older—but I, I didn't want to look foolish, so I ended up having sex with her without any protection. And she said that she was okay, she had that taken care of. And I didn't go into any great details, I was just so nervous.

Ultimately, Diane's desirability and Bill's longing to lose his virginity outweighed his reservations. As he put it, "She was so good-looking that I said, 'This is it. This is it!'" Indeed, Bill was one of several people who eschewed contraception and safer sex *precisely because* they saw virginity as stigmatizing and believed that demanding safer sex would make them seem inexperienced or, worse, expose them for the virgins they were.

Unfortunately, Bill's worst fears came to pass. He laughed anxiously as he told the tale:

> I was so nervous, it was my first time, and . . . I didn't want to look foolish. . . . And we had sex and I didn't know anything about it. . . . I tried to do what I saw the people do in the porno movies, move my body in a certain way, and do it really fast, because that's what they seemed to do. . . . She was saying to me, "There's another person here, you know." . . . And that's like, totally, you know, kind of scared to death, feeling like, okay this is like the biggest moment of my life, this is the greatest thing ever, and . . . I ejaculated very quickly. It was like, just, interested in getting myself off and didn't even think about her. . . . And then we had sex from behind and [I] ejaculated again. And then I was ready to go. That was terrible. And one of the reasons I was ready to go was because I just felt like I was, I wasn't performing well, you know. I felt like I had really fucked this thing up. She was totally unsatisfied and I had no control, I didn't know what I was doing.

Although Diane made no effort to disguise her frustration and disappointment, she didn't accuse Bill of being a virgin—a small mercy for which he was deeply grateful.[37] Still, he felt newly stigmatized as sexually incompetent. If Diane *had* attributed Bill's awkwardness to virginity, the stigma of lying would have been added to his load.

Bill's experience with Diane demonstrates the power a sexual partner may derive from firsthand knowledge of a virgin's sexual conduct. Sexual partners are uniquely well situated to identify and publicize virgins' sexual ineptitude and, by extension, their virginity—this is doubly true in the case of experienced partners like Diane. Ironically, then, it is especially difficult and perilous to disguise virginity from precisely the kind of partners that the stigmatized preferred. Insofar as sexual experience tends to increase with age and people tend to choose partners near them in age, older virgins like Bill may find it particularly difficult to conceal their status. Indeed, the men whose partners uncovered their hidden virginity/inexperience were all 18 or older when they lost their virginity with women who were similarly aged but sexually more practiced.

As if proving himself sexually inept were not enough, Bill was also ter-rified that he'd gotten an STI. The morning after his night with Diane, he "woke up and had this big nodule on the side of my penis and I was con-vinced that I had herpes." A doctor assured him that the spot was "just a pimple," but that did little to relieve Bill's concern. Nor did the physical sensations of vaginal sex live up to his lofty expectations. "I expected it to be more . . . physically pleasurable than it was," he said, "the way I had heard it talked about. It just, my first experience in no way near matched that. I didn't feel the ecstasy." All things considered, Bill said, "It was a dreadful experience."

Bill did find some consolation in knowing that he'd lost his virginity with an extremely attractive partner and in being able to tell his friends that he'd had sex with a woman they'd all desired.

> It just felt like, "Oh my God, I've just had sex with this gorgeous woman." And it was like, it was more important that I could say that and know that and, it was much more enjoyable than the actual experi-ence itself. . . . It was like a trophy, you know. And then it was nice that my friends wanted to know what happened. And, you know, I was, it was wonderful to be able to tell them that I had sex with her.

He carefully concealed the fact that he had lost his virginity with Diane, however. "I think in later years I've talked about when I lost my virginity, who it was with," Bill explained. "But I don't think, I think a certain amount of time had to have passed. . . . I had to get some years beyond it." He prolonged his deception partly in order to hide the fact that he had been lying; but he also worried that the stigma might taint him even after it was gone (as many stigmas do).[38] Being derided for his past stigma was a very real possibility for Bill, who had, as he saw it, remained a virgin embarrassingly late in life and possibly as a result of his own shortcom-ings.

Consolations notwithstanding, Bill felt so mortified by his clumsy per-formance—and his long-standing fear of contracting an STI was magni-fied to such an extent—that when Diane propositioned him on a subse-quent visit to campus, he declined. He said:

> She came back on subsequent weekends, and wanted more of the same. I just was totally turned off by her, because of what had happened, my penis, I had a big nodule on. . . . And then she started telling me that she

thought she might be pregnant . . . and it was like, "Oh my God, so not only do I, I narrowly escaped disease and death, she's telling me she thinks she might be pregnant." So it was terrible, it was a terrible experience.

In fact, Bill swore off vaginal sex for the next 3 years, although he did continue to exchange oral sex with casual partners, a practice about which he felt "safe."[39] When he at last gave vaginal sex another try, it was with a girlfriend—not because he'd come to disapprove of casual sex, but because he felt being in a relationship insulated him from derision and disease. He said:

> The next girlfriend I had, in my senior year of college . . . was the first person that I ever engaged in a sexual relationship with where we had sex on a regular basis, not just like once or twice and that's the end of it. . . . And that was the first time that I was able to have sex and . . . have some, good feelings about it. And that to me was, that was a step in a more positive direction.

Bill's later experiences might conceivably have prompted him to revise his understanding of virginity. Yet Bill and the two other men who felt degraded by their virginity-loss experiences were the only ones in this group who did *not* ultimately reject the stigma metaphor for the passage alternative.[40] Although it is possible that they were more attached to this traditionally masculine perspective than other men who held it, it is more likely that the nature of their virginity-loss encounters served to reinforce, rather than challenge, their interpretations. Where people like Kendall felt relieved of their stigma following virginity loss, men like Bill felt just as stigmatized as before, albeit in a new way.

The very nature of stigma—which involves being labeled by more powerful persons—ensures that virgins who see themselves as stigmatized are always to some extent at the mercy of others, especially their sexual partners. Like many who shared his interpretive stance, Bill tried to protect himself from shame and ridicule by concealing his inexperience from the woman with whom he had sex. But for a variety of reasons, not least their discrepant levels of sexual experience, Diane discovered Bill's lack of expertise. To make matters worse, she reacted harshly, as people are wont to do when faced with stigmatized individuals. Her response probably would have been even more severe if she and Bill had been dating. For example, Dan Levy, a 29-year-old White heterosexual chef, believed that his girlfriend refused to continue having sex with him after he lost his virginity with her (at age 18) precisely because she surmised that he had hidden his virginity. By making fun of Bill, Diane may even have been attempting to influence their sexual encounter in one of the few ways women are "allowed" to.[41]

In retrospect, Bill believed that Diane might have responded more sympathetically if he had confessed his virginity; but he maintained that such an admission had been impossible in practice. Not only was it too embarrassing to admit he was a virgin, but what if Diane had laughed at his confession, then refused to have sex with him? He'd feel degraded and still be a virgin! As it was, Bill suffered from knowing that Diane, not he, had been in control of their encounter. Worse yet, because he (like many men) saw shedding the stigma of virginity as a way of proving his masculinity, the way he lost his virginity left him feeling distinctly unmanly.

Altogether, I interviewed three men—Bill and Dan Levy included—who were so harshly derided for their virginity or sexual ineptitude, which they had tried to conceal, that they subsequently forswore sexual relationships for a year or more.[42] That all three were men who lost their virginity with women is significant, for it suggests that, among stigmatized virgins, feeling stripped of sexual agency depends not only on the power dynamics fostered by the metaphor, but also on the genders of the virgin and the partner. Social norms positing virginity as more stigmatizing for men than women, the belief that women are sexually passive compared with men, and women's relative disinclination to engage in casual sex all increase the chances that men who see virginity as a stigma will feel disempowered at virginity loss.

"I Just Did Not Want to Be a Virgin"

Stigmatized women approached and experienced virginity loss much as men did, with one exception: women tended to be empowered by the very expectations for gender and sexuality that tended to disenfranchise the men. Emma McCabe's story reveals both dynamics in action. When I interviewed Emma she had just turned 24, but with her slight build, quirky manner, and spiky bleached-blond hair, she could have easily passed for a college junior. She was single, child free, and worked at a small publishing house, where she hoped to be promoted from assistant to full editor within the year. A few drunken kisses with women friends notwithstanding, she described herself as heterosexual.

Emma's father and mother, both of whom came from large Anglo-Catholic families, felt it was important to raise their daughter as a member of the Church. But at the same time, befitting their scientific training (in electrical engineering and psychology, respectively), they encouraged her to take a critical stance toward Catholic doctrine from her first day at parochial grammar school onward. It is perhaps not surprising, then, that in spite of the Church's prohibition of premarital sex, Emma had, as a teenager, been determined to do away with her virginity. She recalled:

> My initial perspective was [that it was] just something I wanted to get over with. I just did *not* want to be a virgin. . . . And looking back, that wasn't particularly intelligent or mature. . . . But at the same time, that was how I viewed it when I was a virgin.

From her standpoint, the embarrassment attached to virginity depended on the age of the virgin. "It's weird," she said. "Like, in my mind, 15 was a little early, 16 was on time, 17 was late, you know. . . . There wasn't much leeway as far as that." She was one of many people in this group who spoke of a "window" of time during which normal people lost their virginity.[43] Being a virgin before that age wasn't stigmatizing, but remaining a virgin afterward would be.

The Catholic Church was only one of Emma's sources for information about sexuality. Before she turned 16, Emma had seen dozens of movies that dealt with sex—she vividly remembered teen flicks like *Fast Times at Ridgemont High*—and read countless issues of *Seventeen* and *Cosmopolitan*, as well as teen novels like *Forever*. The materials she found most compelling emphasized the pleasurable aspects of sex and downplayed virginity's purported glories. Emma had no doubt that these media informed her determination not only to lose her virginity "on time," but also to cultivate her skill as a sexual partner. "I thought . . . that to be, you know, a good sexual partner was cool," she told me. "To give a good blow job was like an ego rub for me." She had also looked forward to exploring sex with a variety of partners once she was no longer a virgin. "I don't think you should just sleep with one person," she declared. Her friends had, for the most part, agreed.

During her first 3 years of high school, Emma was never at a loss for dates, but none of her relationships progressed much past friendship.

That fact didn't trouble her, but it *did* bother her that, by the summer before her senior year, her entire sexual history amounted to "basically just kissing" and "a little heavy petting maybe, but nothing that intense." Emma started to worry: "I felt not horribly, but a little later than I wanted to be." Looming beneath this concern was an even more disagreeable prospect: "I didn't want to go to college a virgin." In feeling increasingly stigmatized by virginity as she drew nearer to high school graduation, Emma was typical of people who shared her views. (It's no coincidence that Francis Cornworth's creators placed him on the cusp of his senior year.) Her vague hopes of losing her virginity with a boyfriend rapidly took a back seat to her anxiety to be free of virginity's clutches.

Fortunately, one of Emma's friendships soon turned into something more. Jonathan was 18, a year older than Emma, but also a senior. As friends, they had "a very close . . . emotional relationship," and "very strong physical chemistry, like if we were just standing next to each other." Chemistry aside, however, "Before we'd done anything sexual, he was just a friend. . . . I just didn't think about him in those ways." One afternoon, Jonathan invited Emma to join him in bed, ostensibly to take a nap. "Real smooth," she laughed, remembering. Within a few weeks, they progressed from kissing and touching to fellatio and cunnilingus. Sex wasn't on the agenda every time they met, but their exploration sessions were far from infrequent.

Emma made it clear that she wanted to take things further, but Jonathan seemed reluctant.

> I had been bugging him for a while. Like, I wanted to have sex and he didn't. 'Cause he—he was in love with somebody else, number 1. And like, the other woman was who he had lost his virginity to. So there was that kind of emotional weight going on there. . . . And . . . there's this whole weird dynamic going on, 'cause he was a really good friend of mine, and so I cared about him. But at the same time, he was not transferring the kind of emotional bond we had as friends into our physical relationship.

Because of their friendship, Emma knew about Jonathan's previous sexual exploits—in addition to the relationship in which he'd lost his virginity, he'd had oral sex with a male acquaintance—and Jonathan was aware that Emma was a virgin and hoped he'd help remedy her predicament.[44] In seeking her friend's assistance, Emma pursued a favorite strategy of people with stigmas—attempting to capitalize on the sympathy and desire to help that often accompany averse reactions to the stigmatized. She also availed herself of another resource of the stigmatized: the ability to choose compassionate, well-intentioned companions.[45]

How much sympathy people express for the stigmatized is, however, mitigated by other factors. Most notably, given prevailing gender ideals, female virgins like Emma are more apt to be regarded favorably than males. The virulence of a stigma may also be tempered by the personal characteristics of its possessor and by her acceptance of the social norms from which her stigma derives. Like Marty, Emma was physically attractive, relatively young, and eager to lose her virginity. These factors worked together to Emma's benefit such that, even though she saw her virginity as degrading, Jonathan's reaction left her feeling anything but. In retrospect, she surmised, "I think he did get off to some extent about being my first"—precisely the sentiment Bill Gordon observed among his male friends in high school.

A stigmatized person cannot, of course, attempt to capitalize on others' sympathy if they aren't aware of her stigma. This fact discouraged Emma from concealing her virginity, as did several features of the social world in which she moved. Although she would have preferred that her high school friends think she wasn't a virgin, they had known one another since childhood and therefore knew each other's romantic histories well enough to discern who had (or hadn't) had the opportunity to have sex. Since Emma wasn't willing to lie to her friends, she resigned herself to being honest, if reticent, with them. Indeed, people seldom hide stigmas that can easily be discovered or are relatively mild.[46] In less-familiar circumstances, however, Emma was happy to feign knowledge about sexual matters (as did Bill and Marty) and to hope that people would assume that a pretty, popular 17-year-old wasn't a virgin (Kendall's strategy). These were prudent decisions, for people are typically penalized more harshly for hiding stigmas from their intimates than from strangers or casual contacts.[47]

About 6 months after Emma's first encounter with Jonathan, her persistent pursuit paid off.

So I'd been bugging him for a while and, like, his body wanted to, but he was trying to control himself and stuff. There were a couple times where we came close, but he was just like, you know, "I don't have a condom, we can't do this." And then finally one night—it was around Christmas,

I think—we had gone to a movie and just went back to his house and had condoms. . . . And this is another thing. Like, thank God I didn't bleed, 'cause I lost my virginity on a white couch, in his parents' house [laughs]!

Their long friendship and openness about their sexual histories significantly reduced the disincentives to use a condom. Indeed, safer sex was the almost-universal rule among women and men who lost their virginity with friends or romantic partners who knew the truth about their stigmatizing status.

Emma kept having sex with Jonathan "off and on" for 4 or 5 more months—a time frame typical for people who lost their virginity with a friend or someone they were dating. She'd wished she could discuss this new dimension of their relationship with her friends but felt unable to do so because they were Jonathan's friends, too. As it turned out, her caution was justified. "I didn't tell anyone in my high school class until, like, a year after the fact. And people flipped out, like really . . . wigged." Further complicating matters were the changes that having sex wrought in Emma's feelings for Jonathan. Despite having initially seen him only as a friend, she became "convinced that he would wake up one day, you know, figure out that he was in love with me and all that." She laughed, "But that didn't happen." With hindsight, she traced her desire for a romance with Jonathan to the purported significance of virginity loss:

In times since . . . there are guys I've slept with, and it's just like, okay, you know, that was fun or whatever, but there's nothing . . . that kind of bond isn't the same as the first time. . . . [P]eople put more emotional weight on it . . . just because it is the first time.

Fortunately, Emma's friendship with Jonathan survived the strain of their divergent inclinations—it helped that they "went away to different colleges and got some time and space"—and they remained friends 7 years later.

Like Kendall and Marty, Emma felt overjoyed to have lost her virginity but also somewhat disappointed to discover that sex wasn't everything she'd expected. "There was just kind of like, 'Oh . . . it hurt,' and 'That was sex,'" she said. "But I wasn't a virgin anymore!" Over time, Emma too came to see virginity loss as the beginning of a learning process.

I see everything in life as kind of a process and, like, losing your virginity is kind of the start of a process. . . . I mean, maybe there are some people who had a fantastic first time . . . maybe they do exist. But in general, it's just like, the first time with anything tends to be a little awkward at best, you know. And so . . . it's just kind of the start of something that progresses.

Looking back, she wondered if she might have learned more from, and gotten more pleasure out of, losing her virginity if she had waited for a partner who was more available emotionally:

Not necessarily that it should be the love of your life or anything like that. But . . . it would be better in a lot ways if it was someone who you had an emotional bond with and you had a good communication with as well. . . . My first experience was very, just physical. . . . But if you have one that just gives more of an indication of what the possibilities are. . . . It kind of sets the stage for better experiences in the future.

Significantly, Emma valued emotional closeness for different reasons than those cited by gifters, as did the nine other stigmatized who suspected that virginity loss with a closer partner would have been more enjoyable. And, in the final analysis, she said, "I honestly don't think I would" change the way she lost her virginity, even if she could.

Emma's beliefs and experiences—and those of the three other women who interpreted virginity as a stigma—bear a striking resemblance to the beliefs and experiences of the men who favored this approach. Yet, none of the women experienced virginity loss as disempowering. In fact, Emma's tale shows how women who saw virginity as a stigma *benefited* from the sexual double standard. First, men's relatively greater willingness to have sex outside of dating relationships enabled these women to lose their virginity fairly rapidly once they wished to do so, by propositioning male friends or strangers. The women also profited from widespread social approval of feminine virginity. Their personal sentiments notwithstanding, women like Emma surmised that few people would find their virginity appalling. Lacking a strong incentive to conceal their virginity from sexual partners, Emma and two other women simply announced it, thereby freeing themselves from the possibility of discovery and ridicule. Less than half of the men did likewise. The two women in the study who did hide their virginity from male partners found that popular stereotypes of women as sexually passive worked to their advantage.[48] Whereas Bill's compulsion to play the active partner led to bumbling and accusations of sexual inexperience, these women went unchallenged—aided by the fact that they bled little during coitus.

Although Emma and the other stigmatized women didn't see themselves as setting out to challenge gendered sexual standards, by interpreting and losing their virginity the way they did, they positioned themselves as sexually unorthodox women. Not surprisingly, given the social changes that have taken place since the early 1970s, the younger women I interviewed—those who reached adolescence after the emergence of HIV/AIDS—were considerably more likely than their older sisters to have felt stigmatized.[49] The feminist movement, the fortification of liberal sexual values (in reaction to the influence of the Christian right), and the new media images of feminine sexuality all helped make the stigma metaphor seem more available and appropriate to women Emma's age than it did to women just a few years older.

It is worth noting, however, that these changes may affect women differently, depending on their racial/ethnic identity. Although the men in my study who interpreted virginity as a stigma came from diverse racial/ethnic backgrounds, all of the women who shared their perspective were White. Previous studies have suggested that young White women, while by no means free from concerns about sexual reputation, may feel relatively free to approach sexuality in gender-unorthodox ways because they have historically been stereotyped as asexual. In contrast, young women of color may feel compelled to repress or refuse to act on their sexual desires because they have been maligned as sexually promiscuous and out of control.[50]

"Part of Me Was Going, 'Yes, You Are No Longer a Virgin!' And Another Part of Me Was Saying, 'I Didn't Want That to Happen'"

Ed Winters was profoundly ambivalent about the way he lost his virginity. For although Ed had felt stigmatized as a virgin, he had not wanted to lose his virginity when and with whom he did: a female acquaintance coerced him into having sex with her when he was 16. His story, though unique, helps specify how people's sexual careers can be colored by their (in)ability to assert themselves at virginity loss. It also shows that there are limits to the circumstances under which people are willing to lose the stigma of virginity. When Ed and I met, he was 28 years old and working as a computer systems analyst. He played bass guitar in a Gothic rock band, befitting his dyed black hair, makeup-whitened skin, and wiry body clad in leather and buckles. Although most of his sexual relationships had been with women, he described himself as bisexual. He'd lived with a girlfriend for several years after college and now shared a townhouse with four platonic friends.

Shortly after I arrived at Ed's office, he told me that in the days since I'd contacted him, he'd been pondering what it was, exactly, that made virginity so significant to so many people. "Even though supposedly it's not, it is," he reflected. "Everyone's either trying to keep it or lose it, give it away or get it back. And I think a lot of the significance behind the whole concept of virginity is just how vague its essential value is. I think that causes a lot of conflict."

Ed had first glimpsed that conflict in the divergent views of his parents, who had divorced just after his birth and subsequently left the Roman Catholic Church. His mother, who was comfortable talking about sexual topics from masturbation to orgies, encouraged Ed to "go out, have fun . . . see a lot of people before you make your mind up." Her view of premarital chastity was particularly dim, as Ed recalled:

> I remember my mom saying, "Virginity is stupid." Both she and my dad were virgins when they got married. . . . And she said it was, like, the worst move she ever made in her life, you know. And if you're going to spend the rest of your life with someone, you should damn well know how to have sex with them.

Ed's father, by contrast, barely strayed from the Catholic doctrine he'd ostensibly rejected. Although he was too "embarrassed talking about sex" to say so directly, Ed's dad made it clear that he thought his teenage sons had no business being sexually active. Yet, when Ed was 21,

> my dad asked me if I was still a virgin, 'cause you see my dad thought I might be gay [laughs]. He's not too terribly far off, but. . . . That was really funny. He asked me, like, "You're not a virgin anymore are you, are you, Ed?" And I'm like, "No."

His dad's relief was palpable.

Yet another set of ideas prevailed in the high school Ed attended:

> [N]ot being a virgin was a status symbol. The younger that you did it, up to a certain age, the better. Because losing virginity implied that you had a girlfriend, and that was a really big deal. . . . You know, the people that had the car and had the money and had the girl were, like, "Well, he may be an asshole, but he's doing pretty well for himself."

The stigma of virginity was moreover associated with other stigmas, such as being "socially backwards," a designation that accurately described Ed and his Dungeons and Dragons–playing "freak" friends, or relatively poor, which he was, too. His mother, a high school graduate, made just enough money selling office equipment to afford a tiny apartment in a wealthy suburb where Ed and his brother could attend good public schools. Ed's father, a sporadically employed musician, provided little in the way of financial help. By virtue of their outcast status, Ed and his friends escaped the intense peer pressure that beset members of the popular cliques; but even they felt it increasingly urgent to lose their virginity "once we hit 16, 17."

Well before that urgency peaked, Ed had been determined to appear sexually experienced. He disguised his virginity whenever he could, sometimes going so far as to lie about it, as, he surmised, his friends did, too. Laughing, he explained:

> The whole virginity thing was like the one thing that you could lie credibly about. So. You know, and it wouldn't. I mean, it could be just the, like, "My many conquests in the Niagara Falls region." . . . Or you could, just on the sly, you know. The person that you had seen for, like, two weeks last year was actually, you know, "Oh, yeah, I did her." . . . I mean, the thing is, you also have to approach . . . something that everyone seems to value so highly, you know, losing virginity, with a certain amount of matter-of-fact nonchalance. Which kind of belies how, how important a lot of people make it.

In retrospect, Ed thought it ironic that a group of friends who were all probably virgins found it so imperative to disguise their status; but "at the time . . . it's just like one of those . . . seemingly necessary lies. So you don't actually look different than the people that are your friends." Like Kendall, Ed benefited from belonging to a group in which reluctance to call others' bluffs was the norm. He compared his crowd to poker play-ers: "You're pretty sure everyone's lying, but you can't really know for sure until you see the cards."

In truth, Ed had scarcely done anything sexual before he lost his vir-ginity, not least because his lack of popularity gave him few opportunities to try. "I was . . . really, really scrawny. Really, really dorky. And really, really socially inept," he explained. "Back in high school, that was not a combination that attracted women." Prior to the day he lost his virginity, Ed said, "I think I kissed like maybe two, three people. . . . And a little, like, fooling around, you know, petting through fabric. . . . But nothing . . . that I would consider . . . serious."

Shortly after Ed turned 16, he, his older brother, and their father were invited to spend a week skiing with wealthy family friends. From the mo-ment they arrived at the resort, Angela, the friends' 19-year-old daughter, began to pursue Ed sexually. He and she knew one another from similar vacations over the years and, while not close, got along "well enough" as a rule. Though flattered, Ed tried to deflect Angela's advances at first. He said:

> It was just one of those things where like from the very beginning she said, "You!" And I was really scared . . . because, friend of the family, someone I know. . . . So for the first two days . . . I was doing that . . . "I want to, but I can't" sort of thing. You know, we'd kiss and we'd flirt . . . but I'd always just be like, "No, no, no." 'Cause, you know, I was terrified that my dad would find out. Also terrified that her father would find out.

But Angela refused to take Ed's "no's" for an answer. They were sharing a chair lift up the mountain when she said, "Ed, you have a choice. You can either have sex with me or I'll just tell everyone you already did. And, more to the point, I'll say that you made me have sex with you." At the time, Ed could see no way out of Angela's trap. Who would believe that a girl had forced a guy to have sex with her, rather than the other way around? He thought about telling Angela that he was a virgin, but he was afraid that she might see that as a challenge rather than a defect. Looking back, he said:

> I realize that she said a lot of things . . . just to get a reaction out of peo-ple, and no one would have believed her. But, you know, I didn't know, I didn't know squat. I was not, not very worldly at the age of 16.

When their lift reached the top of the slope, Angela pulled Ed into a small supply shed and repeated her demand. Feeling utterly unable to escape, Ed dropped his ski pants to his ankles and fumbled around until his penis was in Angela's vagina. He ejaculated scant seconds later, adding to his embarrassment and confusion. He had been too stunned to say anything about birth control or safer sex. If Angela surmised his virginity from his awkward performance—he thought she might well have —she gave no outward sign; nor did she tease him about his lack of dexterity.

Immediately afterward, Ed didn't know what to feel or think. He was delighted not to be a virgin anymore, but profoundly upset about being coerced into sex.

> All I know is that I was put in a situation where I, saying no would have been much worse than saying yes. . . . It was one of those things where after it happened it was like, "Huh? What just happened?" And part of me was going like, "Yes, Ed, you are no longer a virgin!" And another part of me was saying, like, "I didn't want that to happen."

As shameful as virginity seems to the stigmatized, it is not so shameful that they would willingly lose their virginity/stigma through nonconsensual sex.

Ed's experience differs from Bill's in instructive ways. Like Bill, Ed felt that he'd had no control over what happened when he lost his virginity. But where Bill blamed himself for that lack of control, Ed found fault exclusively with Angela. Ed also escaped the shame and sense of being newly stigmatized that haunted Bill, for Angela had neither poked fun at his inexperience nor intimated that he was a virgin. Although many rape victims report feeling stigmatized, Ed didn't at first think of himself as having been raped.[51] Later, when he discovered the concept of acquaintance rape, that seemed like the right thing to call his experience. But sometimes Ed wasn't sure, especially since he'd had an erection.

> I wasn't raped by a guy. It was by a woman. And a lot of people say that can't happen. And to tell the truth, I don't know if it can happen even myself. You know, it depends on what you call rape. All I know is that I was put in a situation where . . . saying no would have been much worse than saying yes. And so I don't know . . . if what happened was actually rape, but in my mind, it kind of did and kind of didn't.

From this new perspective, his belief that coerced sex isn't the victim's fault helped to minimize his feelings of stigma. Thus, although Ed was very unhappy with his virginity-loss experience, his unhappiness resulted from having been raped, not from decisions he made because he interpreted virginity as a stigma (as was the case for Bill).

In their remaining days at the ski resort, Angela hinted that she'd like another tryst. But Ed, his anger and bitterness mounting, couldn't stomach the idea of having sex again with someone who had manipulated him that way. Many months passed before he, a once inveterate masturbator, could muster any sexual desire. As he explained, "After I . . . started realizing what had happened . . . I pretty much didn't have sex until . . . after I graduated from high school."

Two days after commencement, one of Ed's friendships took a romantic turn. He had by then recovered his interest in sex, and he and his now-girlfriend "had sex all the time. We were like, three or four times a day. And it was pretty darn all right!" From that relationship up to the present, Ed told me, he enjoyed sex immensely. And yet, he was rarely able to ejaculate—a dysfunction he traced to Angela's offense. He was also deeply uncomfortable with the prospect of ever having sex with a virgin. "I don't want . . . anyone else go through that," he said.

Because of the manner in which he'd lost his virginity, and because he had been passing as a nonvirgin, Ed didn't tell his friends about his change in status. He sketched his rationale:

While on the inside [you] may be wanting to jump up and down and scream, like, "I'm not a virgin, I got laid!" [laughs] . . . [I]f you did, they'd all know that up to that point you were a virgin. So everything else that you might have said before that time was a complete lie and you can't get caught in the lie. So even if you did lose your virginity and it was your first time and it was, like, fantastic, all you could really do is say, like, "Oh, yeah, I did her. I, you know, it was okay."

In fact, he confided only in his brother—"He was just sort of like, 'Fine, whatever,' 'cause he was still a virgin"—and his friend Kathleen. Lest he appear deceitful or newly initiated, "With everyone else I was still like, you know, 'Oh, yeah, I've been having sex for, you know, years now.'"

Intensely disappointed with sex and virginity loss, Ed, like almost everyone in this group, gradually began to reenvision virginity as a step in a process. Later turning points in his sexual career—most notably, dating a woman who introduced him to the pleasures of rough sex and recognizing that he was sexually attracted to some men—reinforced his new perspective.[52] By the time of our interview, Ed believed that "virginity is a state of mind more than anything else," and its loss a "moving from one state, of childhood, to a more adult state." Ed had also come to exclude coerced sex from his definition of virginity loss. But, interestingly, he did not apply this new definition retrospectively to himself, perhaps because doing so would have necessitated revising the way he had understood his sexual history for several years—a disorienting experience at best.[53] The same was true of Miranda Rivera, who also lost her virginity through acquaintance rape.

Ed also felt that it would be a mistake to imbue virginity loss with more significance than any single event could realistically bear. When people lose their virginity, he explained:

> They suddenly do something that is supposed to be this major event in their lives. . . . And they go through it, and it's not that. Some of them freak out, I think, because everything's the same afterwards. Nothing's really changed. You're still the exact same person you were before. . . . I think that's why people freak out, because they haven't changed, they, their lives haven't been turned around. They're not suddenly Men, with capital M's, and Women with capital W's. They're still, same people, same fears, same everything that they had going into it, but now they have the added burden of thinking that somehow this is all supposed to be different.

It would be more sensible, he thought, to recognize that, "for a lot of guys, it's just fumbling and not knowing what you're doing and thinking that you screwed up and being pretty damn sure that you sucked. And for a number of women, either being painful, unenjoyable, or just—," he trailed off. Although his own experience had left him with "a really, really, really poor opinion of the whole process of losing one's virginity," he was convinced that, if approached with subdued expectations and a modicum of care, virginity loss could be a relatively harmless step in the process of exploring one's sexuality.

Shedding a Stigma

The stigmatized shared much in common, whether they were men or women; gay, bisexual, or straight; Black or White; raised in religious or secular families.[54] Like Francis Cornworth of eBay fame, these women and men approached virginity loss above all as a means for getting rid of a shameful condition, for casting aside the sexual identity of virgin—with its attendant dorkiness, embarrassment, and social backwardness—and embracing the identity of nonvirgin, with its connotations of status, cool, and masculinity or unorthodox femininity. In short, they saw virginity loss as transforming them from one kind of person into another; as bringing their actual identities (who they really were), in sociologist Erving Goffman's terms, into line with their virtual identities (who they appeared or wished to be). The stigmatized expressed relatively little interest in romance and relationships, especially compared with people who saw virginity as a gift. They focused instead on the physical pleasures of sex and worried little, if at all, about having "perfect" virginity-loss encounters.

Given their relatively minimal expectations, the stigmatized were more easily satisfied with their virginity-loss encounters than their counterparts in the gift group. Even so, there were some conditions under which they believed virginity loss should not take place. As Bill and several other men learned from unpleasant experience, losing one's virginity with a partner who derided you for your sexual inexperience wasn't much of an improvement over retaining the stigma of virginity. Ed was adamant that being coerced into virginity loss was worse than spending a few more years hiding the stigma.

Stigmatized men and women further differed from devotees of the gift and process metaphors in the tremendous effort they put into the impressions they made on others. Every one of them reported actively or passively disguising their virginity from friends or peers on at least some occasions, and many had hidden their virginity from sexual partners as well. This distinctive bent toward concealment was the chief reason that the stigmatized were the group least likely to use birth control or practice safer sex.

Broad social changes can have a profound impact on individual lives, as the stories in this chapter demonstrate. The most obvious change concerns the gendering of the stigma metaphor. The belief that men's virginity is stigmatizing was well established in American culture before the oldest participants in my study were born. As one might predict, a larger proportion of the men I spoke with saw their virginity as a stigma than did the women. But the stigma metaphor was not rare among the women. By the time Emma and the other women in this group were nearing adolescence, the feminist movement and new media images of feminine sexuality had helped make this perspective on virginity loss available to young women.[55] The younger women I interviewed were considerably more likely than their older sisters to have interpreted virginity as a stigma. Approaching virginity as a stigma allowed them to challenge the sexual double standard and defy traditional feminine norms.

The feminist movement has also helped transform understandings of virginity loss with regard to coerced sex; Americans now recognize that such a thing as acquaintance rape exists. Ed's ultimate decision to exclude coerced encounters from his definition of virginity loss suggests that the feminist argument that rape is a form of violence, not sex, has gradually pervaded mainstream American culture.

Despite changes in the gendering of the stigma metaphor, traditional beliefs about gender and sexuality have endured, helping determine the power relations between virgins and their partners. The very nature of stigmas ensures that virgins who favor the stigma metaphor will always be somewhat beholden to their sexual partners. Yet, Bill's and Emma's stories show us how social norms about gender and sexuality interact with the less and more powerful roles of the virgin and partner, in ways that tend to empower female virgins while disempowering their male counterparts. One's gender had precisely the opposite effect among gifters, with relatively powerless gift givers suffering further disadvantages if they were women.

Examining the relationship between gender and the stigma metaphor highlights the reciprocal relationship between interpretations of virginity and social identities more generally. The people I spoke with were drawn to the metaphor in part because of their childhood sexual socialization; but they also favored it because of the kinds of social identities it allowed them to construct. Given the popular equation of virginity with homosexuality, men like Bill and Marty approached virginity loss as a public demonstration of their heterosexuality, while Kendall and others used it to test the suspicion that they might be gay.[56] For these men, losing the stigma of virginity also provided a way of claiming a traditional kind of masculinity; whereas for women like Emma, it signified achieving a liberated, sex-positive sort of femininity. Having a denigrating virginity-loss encounter like Bill's meant having one's masculinity called into question. These gendered meanings varied further depending on the virgin's racial/ethnic background. In a society where racism shapes access to resources as well as understandings of sexuality, African American men may approach shedding the stigma of virginity as a practical avenue for proving masculinity, whereas White women may view it as a means of rejecting the stereotype of sexually pure femininity. In short, despite the similar beliefs and behaviors it fosters, the stigma metaphor takes on different nuances depending on individuals' intersecting gender, sexual, and racial/ethnic identities.

A religious upbringing and identification appeared to have had little effect on the interpretive preferences of the stigmatized, especially as compared with gifters. Many of the stigmatized came from families that were not particularly devout or were actively skeptical about the religious traditions to which they belonged. Others, like Kendall, found the teachings of the churches they attended too extreme, and too different from the opinions they heard all around them, to take seriously.

Interestingly, although the men and women in the stigma group learned about different possible interpretations of virginity from the same sources as gifters—family, friends, mass media, school, and religious institutions—the stigmatized received less consistent messages about virginity. Every gifter had at least one parent who vocally supported the gift metaphor, and they typically reported that their close friends had shared their parents' beliefs. In contrast, many of the stigmatized told me that they weren't altogether sure what their parents thought about virginity. Others, like Ed and Bill, had one parent who clearly disdained virginity, even as the other framed it as precious. People in the stigma group also remembered being surrounded by friends and acquaintances who viewed virginity as shameful and embarrassing. Not surprisingly, friends' endorsements took precedence over equivocal or unknown parental beliefs. And, although both groups of young people were avid consumers of the diverse visions of virginity in the mass media, they differentially attended to the media that reinforced their preexisting interpretive inclinations. For example, Emma McCabe and Kelly Lewis (profiled in chapter 3) both consumed the same sex-themed teen movies, magazines like *Seventeen* and *Cosmopolitan*, and the novel, *Forever*. But where Kelly took to heart those images that matched her mother's and friends' vision of virginity as a gift, Emma gave credence to the messages that confirmed her and her peers' impression that virginity was stigmatizing.

The vast majority of the men and women in my study who lost their virginity, seeing it as a stigma, told me that certain experiences—disappointment with the physical aspects of sex, coming out as gay, or merely being released from their stigma—inspired them to reconceptualize virginity loss as a step in the process of growing up. Almost one-third of the people I interviewed had, however, interpreted virginity loss as a process —or rite of passage—while they were still virgins. It is to their experiences that I now turn.

5

A Natural Step

Margaret Mead's best-selling volumes on South Pacific youth, published between 1928 and 1935, and Bronislaw Malinowski's sensationally titled 1929 monograph, *The Sexual Lives of Savages,* introduced educated Americans to the concept of puberty rites—ritualized celebrations of an individual's passage from childhood to adolescence or adulthood.[1] Anthropologists noted that these transitions typically entailed a shift from relative asexuality to potential or actual sexual activity, often marked by virginity loss (customarily defined as first vaginal sex). Virginity loss accordingly came to be understood as a *rite of passage* through which boys were transformed into men and girls into women.[2] In some non-Western societies, virginity loss was closely associated with marriage, as it is in Judeo-Christian tradition; in other societies, the two passages could be separable, a fact that, at the time, many Americans and Europeans found disturbingly "uncivilized."[3]

Once Americans viewed virginity loss as a rite of passage in other cultures, it took but a small leap to train that interpretive lens on themselves. The popular reach of the passage/process metaphor is evident in any number of semiautobiographical recollections of the 1940s.[4] Although men penned the majority of these reminiscences, anthropologists applied the rite of passage concept to both female and male virginity loss; the perspective therefore offered an implicit alternative to the sexual double standard embodied in the gift and stigma metaphors.[5]

As college enrollments swelled following the Second World War, more and more young Americans had the opportunity to take anthropology courses in which they learned that virginity loss could be interpreted as a rite of passage. By the late 1950s, as the baby-boom generation began to enter adolescence, reassuring anxious parents with anthropological insights had become something of a cottage industry, with Margaret Mead at its helm.[6] It was in this context that movie director William Asher released his 1963 youth hit, *Beach Party*. Primarily a vehicle for singing stars Frankie Avalon and Annette Funicello, the romantic comedy cleverly unfurled its central love story through the eyes of a culturally tone-deaf "developmental biologist, social anthropologist, and explorer" intent on recording the sexual mores of American youth. In the film, Dr. Robert O. Sutwell (Bob Cummings) has made his name studying puberty rites (his term) in the South Pacific. But for his latest project, the bearded and bespectacled Sutwell has decided to scrutinize college-age surfers (all male) and their female friends, whom he describes as "a true subculture —they live in a society as primitive as the aborigine of New Guinea." Among the titles he's considering for his eventual book are *Post-Adolescent Surfing Subculture*, *The Behavior Pattern of the Young Adult and Its Relation to Primitive Tribes*, and, with a broad wink at Alfred Kinsey's best-selling scientific study of sexual behavior, *The Sutwell Report*.

Armed with a telescope, camera, and tape recorder, Sutwell observes the "kids" as they surf, dance, and flirt on the beach and at a local beatnik club. His attention inevitably centers on the crowd's informal leaders, Frankie (Frankie Avalon) and Dolores (Annette Funicello), whose romance wavers when Dolores's "cold feet" stop her from sharing a beach cottage with Frankie, "all alone . . . just like we're married." When Sutwell rescues Dolores from the clutches of a local biker gang, she agrees to become his "first contact" (i.e., key informant). Finding "Bob" refreshingly mature for not making sexual advances on her, Dolores confides that she intends to remain a virgin until she marries and that she hopes Frankie wises up—and rebuffs the blonde bombshell he's currently chasing—before it's too late.

In keeping with its anthropological subplot, the film frames virginity loss as a rite of passage. Sutwell's dictated field notes describe the youths' flirting, sexy dancing, and make-out sessions as puberty rites. Dolores herself likens virginity loss to a step in the process of growing up when she complains to her friend Rhonda (Valora Noland), "I want Frankie to think of me as more than just a girl." Confused, Rhonda says, "But you're not even a woman," implying sexual status as well as chronological age. Dolores clearly has the former in mind, for she snaps, "But I'm close—and I'm not getting any closer until I'm a wife!" In effect, she believes that virginity loss and marriage both transform girls into women— and that the two events should take place together. (In this respect, the movie presents women's virginity as a gift for future husbands; little is said about male sexuality beyond the suggestion that decent men don't let their lusts interfere with women's desire to postpone sex until marriage.) By the end of the film, Frankie and Dolores have joyfully reunited, with sex and marriage on hold. Meanwhile, Sutwell has undergone something of a rite of passage himself, transformed by his research and Dolores's expert tutelage from a tunnel-visioned scholar—so obtuse about sex that he is wholly unaware that his beautiful assistant, Marianne (Dorothy Malone), is heads over heels in love with him—to a clean-shaven, Bermuda shorts-wearing flirt eager to recruit Marianne to help "keep me from getting involved" on his next expedition, "with the natives, that is."

Although the women and men I interviewed were born too late to cite *Beach Party* as influencing their own understandings of virginity, one-third of them shared its perspective on the subject. These young people described virginity loss as a central step in the transition from youth to adulthood—precisely the kind of event anthropologists refer to as a rite of passage. More specifically, they likened virginity loss to a step in two interrelated processes: becoming an adult, and acquiring knowledge about sexuality.[7] Recalling discussions among her high school friends, Jessica Tanaka, a 27-year-old bisexual Japanese American from a working-class background, invoked both themes:

> I guess we sort of romanticized the whole, like, losing your virginity, like, becoming a woman, like, being grown-up kind of thing. . . . Like, we really couldn't figure out what it would be like, we'd have to go and find out on our own. . . . It was just sort of one of those things that eventually would happen, and then we would *know*. And . . . we would be really disappointed or really not disappointed [laughs].

Heather Folger, a 28-year-old heterosexual middle-class White woman, compared virginity loss to other life transitions. "[It's a] pretty big milestone in people's lives. . . . Maybe not on a par with marriage or birth or death, but it's definitely one of the things that you'll always remember." People who liken virginity loss to a learning process or to a transition between life stages are effectively saying the same thing: that virginity loss represents a rite of passage, a process of transition from sexual youth to adulthood.[8] I use the expressions *rite of passage* and *process* interchangeably, and call the metaphor's devotees "processers" for short.

Anthropologist Victor Turner compared the person undergoing a rite of passage to a "blank slate, on which is inscribed the knowledge and wisdom of the group, in those respects that pertain to the new status."[9] Because of their relative ignorance about sexual intercourse (or whatever act they see as resulting in virginity loss), virgins are potentially at the mercy of their chosen sexual partners, especially experienced ones.[10] Yet, since virginity loss is an informal passage, unregulated by formal institutions, virgins do have some control over it.[11] Virgins and their sexual partners, like all informal initiates and their "helpers," both possess some power and must negotiate with one another as the passage proceeds.

Consistent with the gender-neutral application of the concept in anthropology and popular culture, the women I interviewed were only slightly more likely than men to describe virginity loss as a step in the process of growing up.[12] Yet, although the rite of passage metaphor appears to offer an alternative to the traditionally feminine and masculine gift and stigma metaphors, it is not gender neutral. Because people tend to think in terms of becoming not just generic adults, but specifically adult *women* and *men,* when they draw on the process metaphor to guide their virginity-loss experiences they are constructing *gendered* adult identities.[13] (In a similar manner, the metaphor helps people fashion specific sexual identities.) Whether the process perspective tends to disempower male or female virgins disproportionately, as do its stigma and gift counterparts, is a central question in this chapter.

"I Was a Virgin at One Point and I . . . Never Really Thought about It"

Meghan O'Brien hadn't attached much importance to virginity while she was growing up. To her, it was a simple designation for a certain stage in life:

> I guess I never really thought of virginity as, like, a qualitative thing. It was just . . . you have not had sex, you are a virgin. It wasn't like a feeling or anything like that to me. So if someone asked me how I felt about it, I think I would just say, you know, I was a virgin at one point and I . . . never really thought about it. That was just the way it just was.

The third daughter in a large Irish-American family, Meghan had grown up on the outskirts of Boston. She had attended an exclusive private high school and now, at 22, was within months of receiving her bachelor's degree from a prestigious liberal arts college. Her father and mother had pursued fairly ordinary careers—as a private attorney and the volunteer director of a children's recreation center, respectively—but their extended families included more than a few of New England's social and political elite. Meghan's reserved manner and appearance testified to her upbringing: she wore discreetly expensive sportswear and kept her straight brown hair brushed neatly back from her well-scrubbed face. By the time I interviewed Meghan, she no longer attended mass every Sunday, as she had when living at home, but she considered Catholic worship an indispensable part of her life.

Sex was rarely discussed in Meghan's family, but when she was about ten, her parents sat her down for "The Talk." This amounted to a review of basic reproductive biology and the decree, "You're Irish Catholic and you shouldn't have sex before marriage." Meghan took the latter with a grain of salt. Having once found a packet of condoms in her parents' bedside table, she figured that while they probably felt compelled to impart Catholic doctrine, they didn't expect their daughters to follow it to the letter.

The sex education Meghan received at school was altogether different in breadth and tone. In formal health classes, sex was discussed with value-neutral candor—all consensual acts were "okay"—and when talk in the hallways and cafeteria turned to sex, as it often did, no one praised or condemned virginity or the lack thereof. Other students' sexual status was a topic of perennial interest, but Meghan recalled little if any peer pressure around sex. Typical of people who favored the process metaphor, she remembered feeling secure in the knowledge that virginity loss was an inevitable part of growing up. She didn't need to ask *whether* she would lose her virginity, though she did wonder about *when* and *with whom*—choices she saw as hers for the making. Virginity loss is, of course, not *literally* inevitable; but no one I interviewed saw lifelong celibacy as a desirable option—nor do any but a vanishingly small number of Americans.[14]

Meghan's matter-of-fact approach didn't mean that she saw decisions about sex as inconsequential. But she looked forward to virginity loss for reasons quite different from those cited by gifters and the stigmatized. Instead of valuing virginity for its power to bind a special romantic relationship or longing desperately for its absence, Meghan desired the positive changes that accompanied virginity loss—changes like being one step closer to adulthood and gaining practical knowledge about sex's role in a caring relationship. She spoke of virginity loss not as significant in itself, but as "just like a steppingstone."

Perceiving sex as a natural part of a long-term romance, Meghan expected that she'd lose her virginity with one of her first steady boyfriends. She adamantly declared that this wasn't because she disapproved of casual sex—she didn't—but because she thought she'd be more comfortable learning about sex in an ongoing relationship. For one thing, losing her virginity with a boyfriend would give her the opportunity to learn about sex in stages. She explained:

> I just think that . . . when you're young, you're not . . . so comfortable with your own body, and you don't exactly know what you want, what you need. And I think it's more safe to just kind of step into things, you know, slowly, than to just . . . to have sex very quickly.

Tellingly, no one who preferred the process metaphor considered remaining a virgin until marriage (a significant change from *Beach Party* days).

Sometimes Meghan imagined that virginity loss would be like "these mad sex scenes in movies," but more often she anticipated it being as physically awkward as other new experiences, like the first time she went skiing. Expecting some clumsiness was typical of women and men who shared her interpretation—as was the hope that one's own virginity-loss encounter might prove an exception to the rule. This stands in striking contrast with the perfect romantic scenes envisaged by most gifters and with stigmatized men's fear of awkwardness as a telltale sign of their sexual naiveté.

Meghan wasn't very experienced sexually when she started dating Rich in her freshman year in high school. "I did a lot of kissing when I was young," she recalled with a shy grin. "But, you know, innocent kissing." Rich, she said, "was the first person I did anything else with." Meghan and Rich were the same age, took many classes together, and were equally devoted to sports (tennis and track). The longer they dated, the more deeply they fell in love, and the more sexually intimate their relationship became. Meghan described their early encounters as a series of practice sessions. She said:

> I can remember lots of times like, being naked with each other. But we really wouldn't do anything, we would just kind of, like, lay around

with each other. But that was enough . . . for us at that point. And I guess sometimes we would come close, I mean, the areas would touch or something. But I don't know if we were really ever trying. We weren't, we knew, both of us knew we did not want to be having sex at that point. . . . It was just, I think we were just kind of, like, getting to know each other's bodies.

By the time they were juniors, Rich and Meghan had fondled each other to orgasm many times and she'd given him fellatio once or twice. In effect, they learned about sex through a step-by-step process that they saw as (potentially) leading up to the big step of virginity loss. Incremental approaches to physical intimacy were universal among women and men in the rite-of-passage group. Unlike gifters, for whom incremental sexual activity represented a way of testing a partner's capacity for reciprocity, Meghan and her kindred spirits spoke of their expanding sexual repertoires as a kind of education. However, unlike Meghan, the majority went through this learning process with at least one partner before the person with whom they lost their virginity.

Although Meghan didn't think about it consciously, the fact that she was heterosexual provided the framework in which she made choices about sex and sexual partners. Nine of the ten heterosexual male and female processers lost their virginity with steady romantic partners, after engaging in increasingly intimate sexual activities with them, as did both bisexual women and two lesbians who hadn't come out at the time. In contrast, the two openly lesbian women and one openly gay man in the process group had virtually no experience with same-sex partners prior to losing their virginity; all three lost their virginity with friends. What poet and scholar Adrienne Rich has called *compulsory heterosexuality* contributes to these different trajectories.[15] Whereas high school youth are virtually expected to engage in heterosexual romance, relatively few adolescents openly identify as gay. (This was especially true in the early to mid-1990s, when the participants in question lost their virginity.) Given their predominance, greater visibility, and relative freedom from social sanctions, heterosexual teens may simply have more opportunities to develop romantic relationships than their gay and lesbian counterparts.[16]

Meghan's choices were further shaped by her understanding of virginity. Processers cared considerably more about who their partners were than did the stigmatized, and they were far more likely to lose their virginity with someone they were dating. But they did not speak of waiting for the "right" or "perfect" partner, as did gifters, nor did they insist on being in love, although about half of them, like Meghan, were. Rather, they described romantic relationships as the context best suited for satisfying in stages their curiosity about sex.

Meghan and Rich had both been virgins when they started dating, a fact they discussed with increasing frequency the longer they remained a couple. "We had talked about it a lot, like a *lot*," Meghan laughed. "I mean, I think, like, my junior year it was kind of like this obsession we had, you know?" In framing virginity and nonvirginity as normal stages in an inevitable process, rather than as causes for shame or pride, she exemplifies the process frame. All but two processers told their partners that they were virgins.[17] Half of the partners were virgins themselves. But even after Meghan and Rich decided that they wanted to lose their virginity together, when it came to actually having sex, "We were both very nervous." Under the circumstances, Meghan felt their mutual virginity had been an advantage:

> I think if one of us had been more experienced than the other, it would have been kind of like a, more of a pressure about, well, "You know what you're doing and I don't," kind of thing. So, neither of us knew what we were doing and, you know, we figured it out just fine. . . . I think that it was better like that.

Her concerns about nonvirgin partners weren't unique; several others also wondered whether nonvirgins might try to capitalize on their greater knowledge.

In the fall of their senior year, when both of them were 18, Meghan and Rich were poised to take what she called the "natural" next step in their sexual relationship. When Rich's parents announced they were going away for a weekend, he and Meghan hastened to prepare. While Rich bought condoms, Meghan got her parents' permission to spend the night at a girlfriend's. But things didn't go according to plan.

> This was the weekend we were going to have sex, like, it was so dramatic! . . . And all of a sudden both of us were just really scared or nervous or something. . . . And he had a big track meet the next day or something. And, you know, we're up real late because neither of us wanted to just, like, initiate, you know what I mean? And . . . I was so

nervous that it probably wouldn't have worked anyway, because I mean, I just wasn't enjoying myself. He probably wasn't enjoying himself. . . . I think it was because we had planned it that it didn't work. So we were like, "Forget it," you know. "We'll do this another time."

Just a few weeks later, they found themselves together under less contrived circumstances:

We didn't know we were going to be staying in the same place, we didn't know we were going to be in the same bed, and we ended up together. And it just kind of happened. You know, we were just kind of kissing, fooling around, and then one thing led to another and it was like, neither of us knew it was going to hap— [trails off]. Well, we probably did in the back of our minds somewhere, but it wasn't like this rigid or set plan, like it had been before. And it just happened naturally, so that was nice. Unprotected, though.

Not using a condom, even though they had planned to, was the one thing Meghan regretted about the encounter. "I didn't even think about protection at that point," she said, "because we didn't realize it was going to happen. And then it did. . . . It was very short because of, because we didn't have protection." Seeing virginity loss as a step in a process, ironically, contributed to their lapse. Meghan was one of four people in this group who, despite discussing safer sex with their partners and planning to use condoms, wound up losing their virginity when "one thing led to another" in a place and time where a condom wasn't available. (In contrast, when the stigmatized declined to practice safer sex, it was because they feared exposing their virginity.) Since Meghan and Rich both expected that they would continue having sex, she soon went on the Pill, alleviating their worries about unprotected encounters in the future.

Meghan found virginity loss emotionally "very enjoyable" but physically unremarkable, especially compared with the times she'd reached climax in other ways. Both the brevity of the act and their mutual inexperience with vaginal sex were, she felt, to blame. "Neither of us orgasmed," she explained. "I'd say it was just more that we were trying it out." Physically mediocre or even uncomfortable virginity-loss encounters were quite common among women who lost their virginity with men, due to the discomfort women often experience the first time inserting a penis into the vagina.

Like most who favored the passage metaphor, Meghan felt that her vision of virginity loss as a natural, if critical, step in learning about sex was confirmed by what happened when she lost her virginity, as well as by the experimentation that had gone before:

> Like, "That was it?" You know, like, "That's done? That was what we were waiting for, for so long?" 'Cause it's, I think it's a pretty natural thing, and once you do it, it's, I don't know. You, like, from what you see, you know, these mad sex scenes in movies, that was kind of like, "Oh, well, it wasn't quite like that." But that was also because it was our first time and everything.

Subsequent encounters bolstered Meghan's impression of taking part in an ongoing transformation. At first, "we didn't have sex a lot. And then . . . by the end of senior year and starting college, it was like, you know, we had sex more often. . . . I think it was just kind of like a natural progression." Happily, she found vaginal sex more physically pleasurable over time. This was a common trajectory: two-thirds of the processers continued to explore sex with their virginity-loss partners after virginity loss, for about 8 months on average. (Comparable figures for the stigmatized and gifters are 6 months and 2 years, respectively.) Looking back, Meghan described losing her virginity as a learning experience par excellence. "[It] just made me more aware of my sexuality," she said. "I mean, once . . . we had kind of decided that was where our relationship was going, we were more sexually experimenting." In short, virginity loss brought the enlightening changes she'd hoped for.

Pleased to have made the transition from virgin to nonvirgin, Meghan told her closest friends the news, inviting them to help celebrate this new stage in her life. Her parents were another story, however. A few months after she lost her virginity, Meghan's father chanced across "this whole letter [from a friend] . . . about me having sex." She recalled:

> He didn't say anything for about two days, to anyone. . . . Then finally he says . . . , "I need to have [a] talk with you." And he cried, he was so upset. He was so upset he just. I think . . . he was worried. I was in high school. I was, you know, I think he thought that this was just going to lead to trouble. That maybe I'd get pregnant or something bad would happen. . . . It was horrible, he was just so angry. And then I got upset and . . . He was like, "I really hope you stop this." And he never asked

me again, but I think he honestly thought that we had stopped after that.[18]

Such intensely negative reactions were unusual among the parents of this group—a number of them had, in fact, helped their children obtain birth control or condoms—and was probably due in part to the O'Briens' devout Catholicism. Clearly, Meghan misinterpreted her parents' flexibility on this point of religious doctrine.

Meghan's frankness with her friends and partners throughout her sexual career was also typical. Overall, processers were much less concerned with others' impressions of their sexual status, before *and* after virginity loss, than gifters or the stigmatized. Seeing virginity and nonvirginity as inevitable stages, rather than as causes for shame or pride, they felt neither compelled to conceal their virginity or boast of its absence, nor tempted to brag about it or hide its loss. No one in this group tried to pass as nonvirgin; nor were they ashamed of having recently been virgins.

Meghan and Rich dated until they were juniors in college, when Meghan decided she wanted to see other people. Their relationship, which lasted a total of 8 years, was unusual in its duration before and after virginity loss. Deciding to have sex with a subsequent boyfriend, Rob, struck Meghan as another learning process. She explained:

I think the first time I had sex with somebody else was . . . a really big deal to me because I had that same sense of, like, nervousness. . . . It wasn't about the act, it was more just being with this other person and, you know, it's going to be different. . . . It was funny, it was the same type of thing, like, "Well, I don't want to have sex until, you know, we're clear-cut and know what's going on." . . . It was a different kind of waiting period, but it was the same thing.

Three-fourths of processers followed a similar pattern. Moreover, Meghan's reaction to first sex with Rob highlights the significance of first times. Many rites of passage center on events that are first of their kind; as anthropologist Arnold van Gennep noted, the idea that "only the *first time* counts . . . is truly universal and . . . is everywhere expressed to some extent through special rites."[19] While virginity loss may represent the ultimate sexual first time, each sexual relationship offers the possibility of its own first time.

Meghan's beliefs and experiences were shaped by her gender and sexual identity. In American culture, it is acceptable for women and men to approach virginity loss as a rite of passage; overall, the women I interviewed were somewhat more likely to have done so. For women, the process metaphor offers an alternative to the traditional understanding of virginity as a gift, but one which carries less risk of being branded as promiscuous or unfeminine than treating virginity as a stigma. When women in this group lost their virginity, they constructed an identity as sexually "liberated," but not truly unorthodox, adult women. For those who lost their virginity with men, as Meghan did, the act offered a way of establishing a heterosexual identity, although only the women who subsequently came out as lesbians explicitly described it as such. The heterosexual women in my study were, in fact, less apt to see their own virginity loss as a step in a process than were the lesbians and bisexual women, a difference stemming from the fact that lesbian and bisexual women experienced the process of coming out as intertwined with virginity loss.

Meghan's beliefs and experiences may also have been influenced in subtle ways by her racial/ethnic background. Comparatively few women of color took this gender-atypical stance; being White probably made it easier for Meghan to do so.[20] (Stigmatized women were also disproportionately White.) Previous studies have suggested that African American women and Latinas may feel pressured not to reject traditional ideals for feminine virginity, because doing so reinforces popular stereotypes of women of color as promiscuous.[21] Young Asian American women, for their part, may feel caught between the sexual stereotypes of the submissive "lotus blossom" and the sexually predatory "dragon lady"; treating virginity loss as a rite of passage may offer a welcome alternative to both images (whereas the gift and stigma metaphors, respectively, would help confirm them).[22]

How gender and sexual identity shape, and are shaped by, virginity loss as seen through the rite-of-passage lens becomes even clearer when we explore the story of a gay man who shared Meghan's perspective.

"I Think Awkward's a Good Word to Describe It"

Tom Hansen hadn't started thinking of virginity loss as a rite of passage until he was in his early twenties. He'd lost his virginity at 23, just a year before our interview. Closely intertwined with both changes in Tom's life was his gradual recognition that he was gay, which had prompted him in turn to question certain aspects of the evangelical Christian tradition in which he'd been raised. The box office manager of a repertory theater, Tom came from Scandinavian German heritage; he had fly-away blond hair, a round face, and a contagious smile. His father ran a bookstore and his mother taught preschool in suburban Pittsburgh, where Tom had grown up.

As a youth, Tom had agreed wholeheartedly with his parents' understanding of virginity, which was endorsed by their independent Christian church.

> When I was younger, I guess I followed my parents. . . . They never told me it was wrong to lose my virginity—like if I were, I'd go to hell or anything. You know, that's not the way they worked. . . . But then I sort of respected them and respected their wishes. . . . So I considered that it would probably be better to wait until I got married. . . . In high school, I guess even through college, I was pretty, I was proud of it, the fact that I hadn't lost my virginity.

In effect, he had interpreted virginity as a gift. Such sentiments weren't particularly popular among his high school classmates, boys or girls; but Tom knew he wasn't entirely alone in feeling—or behaving—as he did. He recalled a conversation with one of his closest friends:

> At our graduation party we sat down with the yearbook and looked through all the pictures of our graduating class. And we decided who was sleeping with whom. You know, "Remember this guy, when he was with this girl?" and, you know, whatever. And out of the 419, we found that amongst us knew twelve to be confirmed virgins. And two girls were in wheelchairs. So [chagrin filled his voice]. . . . I used to tell that as a joke, but it's not as funny now. But I was one of the twelve, in high school. And so were, like, three or four of my friends. Not a lot of them, a lot of my friends were not virgins. But like three or four other kids that I knew and had grown up with . . . I knew that they were.

That knowledge had strengthened his convictions—he'd never wanted to hide his virginity from people who saw things differently—as did his parents' own example:

It wasn't that they ever said, "No, and don't, because of this." But it was, you know, almost an expectation. "Oh, you wouldn't do that because you'll want to wait until you're married, because it's better that way." And I always assumed that they had, too.

What worked for them, he reasoned, would work for him.

But a series of events, beginning in college, spurred Tom to rethink his views on virginity.[23] Chief among them was his growing recognition that he was sexually and romantically attracted to men. He'd felt the first inklings in high school and had attempted—unsuccessfully—to "protect" himself by choosing to attend a conservative Christian college. Since "one doesn't get married if one is gay," he said, "I . . . quickly realiz[ed] that it was not going to be a possibility for me to wait until I was married."[24] Tom's beliefs were further shaken by what he saw around him at school. Some of his evangelical peers flouted their nonvirginity, while others interpreted the biblical ban on premarital sex in extremely broad terms, seeing oral sex with multiple partners as compatible with maintaining their virginity. One day, a friend from Tom's dorm confided that, just before he left for school, his mother had instructed him: "Before you marry a girl, sleep with her. 'Cause if you don't like it, don't marry her. Then she's not the one. . . . You have to make sure you're compatible." Tom wasn't sure he agreed, but his friend's remark gave him another possibility to ponder.

If all that were not enough, when Tom was a senior in college, his father—on the brink of a divorce—vindictively announced that he and Tom's mother hadn't practiced what they'd preached. Tom said:

> I was clueless, completely clueless that . . . my parents had slept together before they were married. . . . My mom was 16, and he was 18. You know, they were still in high school! And I just thought, "Oh my God, what am *I* waiting for?" I was 22 years old, 23 years old, I'm like, "What a fool I am!" Because I had held their model as sort of like, "Okay, that seemed to work for them, so." . . . Not that I regret anything . . . and not afterwards did I think, "Oh, now I'd better go lose my virginity now because I've wasted all this time." But I think I was more open to it after that.

Gradually, Tom's conviction that virginity should be a special gift exchanged between spouses gave way to a new perspective, centered on learning and personal change:

I didn't hold it against people if they had [lost their virginity], but I was sort of a little frightened, because I hadn't. . . . Because I felt like I was in a different, like, class of knowledge. That was sort of scary because they were so much further ahead than I was. So I was—I guess intimidated is a good word—by it. But I think my view was [not] that I had to wait, I just chose to. Just because I thought it was a good idea. Not religiously . . . I wasn't afraid of, you know, doing something wrong religiously. I wasn't ready and I didn't really find anyone that I wanted to sleep with.

He made a point of distinguishing himself from people who saw virginity as a stigma: "I don't think it's something that you want to do just, you know . . . to prove to yourself that you can do it, or prove to your friends that you've done it." In short, while he was still a virgin, Tom reinterpreted virginity loss, coming to see it as a step in a process. His recognition that he was gay, accompanied by his church's disapproval of homosexuality, his exposure to dissenting opinions and hypocrisy at school, and his parents' failings as role models all motivated this shift in beliefs.

Ever practical, Tom resolved "that I would have to lose my virginity. . . . I'm not going to go until I'm, like, 50 years old and decide, 'Oh, I'm going to have sex,' and then no one wants you," he said. Furthermore, before he met someone who might become a life partner, "I wanted to know what I was doing; I wanted to have a little bit of experience at least." Like Meghan, Tom worried that a nonvirgin partner might try to take advantage of his novice status: "Of course there's the fear of the other person, who's had a ton of sexual experience, and you're like, 'I'm a blithering idiot, I don't know what I'm doing.'" Such caution, despite the desire to make the transition, is typical of irrevocable transitions.[25]

In high school, Tom had dated a number of women, but—fortunately, he said—he "wasn't in that group where you had to be sleeping together to be considered to be dating." He'd had lots of women friends in college, some of whom he had kissed, but never a girlfriend. Those friendships had, he believed, helped him pass as straight. Six months after college graduation, at which point he "had kissed . . . maybe 20 girls probably total in my life," Tom's friend Amy tried to seduce him. Despite knowing that he was gay, he felt he should give sex with women one last chance: "I thought, all right, this is a shot. . . . So I tried. And nothing happened. The equipment did not function. . . . [We were] like, buck naked, fooling around and—nothing." With Tom unable to sustain an erection, they forwent vaginal intercourse.

Then, a week later, Amy confessed that she was now sure that she was a lesbian. She told Tom, "I just never felt it was right, but you were the closest thing I could think of as right. And it was better, but it wasn't what I wanted." When Amy asked if he thought *he* might be gay, Tom answered, "Yes." Their mutual relief was palpable. "The next week, she went out and found a girlfriend. . . . And," he added ruefully, "I waited until September [i.e., several months], because I was foolish." In approaching sexual encounters with girls as a way of "testing" his sexual identity, Tom resembled many of the gay and bisexual boys anthropologist Gilbert Herdt and psychologist Andrew Boxer observed in their ethnography of a Chicago center for lesbigay youth.[26] Also consistent with Herdt and Boxer's findings, the younger generation of gay men and lesbians in my study (born 1973–1980) came out at younger ages on average and were more likely to lose their virginity with same-sex partners than their slightly older counterparts (regardless of how they interpreted virginity).

Tom had come out to a few friends before Amy, but after talking with her, he accelerated the process.[27] He hoped that doing so would pave the way to virginity loss with another man. Once his closest friends knew about his sexual identity, Tom felt he could safely come out to Kent, "the only other gay [man] I had ever met and been friends with." The specter of sexual contact hovered in his mind when he told Kent that he, too, was gay:

> Because he was the one I was attracted to. And as my first opportunity, after all these years of being completely, you know, away from everybody else and safe. . . . And I was old enough and responsible enough, I figured I would, you know, take a chance. So that was the first time I ever said anything [to Kent], and then. Losing my virginity was much later. I said [that I was gay], and nothing happened between us until a good while later.

Tom was not alone in choosing a same-sex friend as a first sexual partner; the two lesbians in this group who had come out while they were virgins did likewise. In contrast, all but one of the heterosexual and bisexual processers lost their virginity with girlfriends or boyfriends. This is not to suggest that gay men and lesbians are less selective than their heterosexual counterparts; plenty of heterosexuals in the gift and stigma groups lost their virginity with friends or casual partners, after all. Rather, given the lack of openly gay people, especially at younger ages, some may opt to expand their sexual opportunities by including platonic friends among their prospective partners.[28] The ability to meet same-sex romantic partners also depends on where people live and the social circles in which they move. As a gay man living in a suburb well outside of Pittsburgh, with mostly conservative Christian acquaintances, Tom found meeting potential partners more difficult than did someone like Kendall James, who spent his adolescence just minutes from Philadelphia, a huge city with a thriving and highly visible lesbigay community.

After coming out to Kent, Tom tried several times to orchestrate a situation in which they would be alone. But "every time I made plans, it didn't work." Finally, more than a year after graduating from college, Tom invited Kent to join him and some college friends on a road trip to a concert in Cleveland. When they arrived,

> there were enough tickets for everybody but two people. So I of course volunteered not to go. . . . We went to see a movie, had dinner, whatever, and just went back to the house [of their former-classmate host]. . . . And she had a hot tub outside. So . . . I had just gotten into the hot tub, and he's like, "Can I kiss you?" And I said, "Sure." And that was it. He whipped off his clothes so quickly [laughs]! I was like, "Oh my God" [laughs]. I had no. I mean, I had *zero* experience at that point. . . . I mean, I never had any sexual experience whatsoever with another guy.

Nor had Kent, as Tom knew. When Tom had come out to his friend, they'd talked about being virgins—with men as well as women—and agreed that virginity loss between men meant giving or receiving anal sex.

Tom's sexual identity and interpretation of virginity intertwined to influence his early sexual career. Suppressing his attraction to men, passing as straight, and trying to convince himself that he was had given Tom plenty of reasons and opportunities to experiment sexually with women, albeit not sufficient motivation to lose his virginity with one. In fact, the gay men and lesbians who told me they saw virginity loss as a process—and who were openly gay as virgins—typically had as much experience with other-sex partners as their heterosexual counterparts, even though they'd had little if any intimate contact with same-sex partners prior to virginity loss.

After exchanging fellatio and attempting anal penetration—"which doesn't work in the hot tub, ever," Tom quipped, not to mention (he rolled his eyes) that "we were both new at this whole thing"—they made their way to the guest bedroom they'd been assigned.

> That pretty much ended the whole virginity thing. But I had conveniently packed condoms and lubricant and anything else that I could possibly think of that I'd need. . . . I always plan. . . . So I just. Yeah, I knew what I wanted, but I didn't know what was going to happen. So I just, I bought them maybe a month beforehand. . . . I just bought them hoping that I'd use them some day.

Tom's concern with safer sex was typical of people who saw virginity as a rite of passage. Two-thirds of them practiced safer sex during virginity loss, a rate comparable to that of gifters. Viewing virginity loss as a step in a process had encouraged these women and men to lose their virginity in ongoing romantic relationships or friendships, in which they were comfortable talking about condoms and/or contraception. Furthermore, perceiving sexual inexperience as a natural stage in life, rather than as a stigma, they felt no need to try to conceal their virginity by rejecting protective measures. (Lesbians who lost their virginity with other women were an exception, as I discuss below.)

Virginity loss was everything Tom had hoped for—and yet at the same time it wasn't.

> I expected more out of it. . . . I didn't regret it. At the same time I didn't think it was something super incredible. I mean, I was nervous [laughs]. I was very nervous. . . . First of all, I was fooling around in somebody else's hot tub not knowing when they would be home. . . . I think, given a little bit more freedom at the time . . . I would have been happier. . . . I mean . . . since then I've kissed . . . a couple other [men] who are much better kissers. . . . And at the same time, thinking, "Wow!" I mean, we were just fumbling around like idiots. But I knew I was old enough and, you know, I was ready.

In all, he said, "I think awkward's a good word to describe it." Though this awkwardness came as something of a surprise, Tom easily accepted it—not least because he thought it might have been inevitable given the physiology of receptive anal sex. Having a clumsy first time also confirmed his impression that virginity loss was a step in a longer process. As

he put it, "I don't think my viewpoint has changed any, except for 'practice makes perfect'—maybe there's that adage added to it." Men and
women who favored the process metaphor were far better prepared for
"imperfect" or physically unremarkable encounters, and reacted to them
with much greater aplomb, than people who saw virginity as a gift or
stigma. They believed they still had a lot to learn about sex, and they had
more reasonable expectations about physical sexual pleasure; few expected first sex to be intensely enjoyable. In contrast, gifters felt deeply let
down by less-than-perfect partners and encounters, while the stigmatized
typically worried that clumsiness betrayed their inexperience and/or that
they'd missed out on the immense physical joy they'd expected.

Tom also found sex with Kent enlightening because it confirmed, in a
very tangible way, his perception of himself as gay.

> For the first time I just felt right. . . . It was the first time that I actually
> kissed somebody and actually didn't think it was, you know, boring. It
> was like, "Wow!" This is what I'm supposed to be doing . . . this is actu-
> ally going through with things I feel, rather than what I'm supposed to
> do. So I didn't feel obligated or, you know, that this was the right thing
> to do or this was what my parents would have me do.

Tom didn't feel transformed overnight. Rather, losing his virginity had
been the final step in a decade-long process changing him from an inexperienced boy unsure of his sexual identity into an openly and actively
gay man. In most respects, however, processers' expectations and experiences of virginity loss differed very little by sexual identity.

Although Tom was happy not to be a virgin, he remained circumspect
about revealing his new status. One disincentive was the fact that he and
Kent moved in the same social circle, and it seemed inappropriate for two
of the group to be sexually involved. Moreover, he feared that his more
conservative (or less intimate) friends would be offended to learn he was
gay. With them, as with his parents, with whom he was still closeted when
I met him, Tom took the path of least resistance:

> I would have to tell them lies, so I just avoid the question. My dad asked
> if I was a virgin. I said, "I'm 24 years old, what do you think?" And that
> gave him an answer and it didn't give him a necessarily truthful answer,
> or an untruthful [one] . . . and he didn't have to ask anymore.

Like Meghan and others who shared their view of virginity, Tom wanted to be frank with his friends, and even his parents, but felt it prudent to tailor his disclosures according to social context.

Status passages often occur simultaneously, and almost all of the gay and bisexual male and female processers spoke of virginity loss as inextricably intertwined with the process of coming out. This sense of undergoing two linked processes at once was, I believe, the chief reason that the lesbigay individuals I interviewed subscribed to the process metaphor in greater proportions than did their heterosexual counterparts.[29] Tom's story shows how concurrent rites of passage may complicate one another.[30] On the one hand, he felt that if he had been able to come out earlier, it would have been easier to lose his virginity:

> I would've dated girls, I would have dated guys, and started a lot earlier. . . . I probably wouldn't have had sex at the young age, still. I think that's something I was really way into being ready for. But if I had been more aware of what I was doing and dating and, like, hanging out with guys and, you know, fooling around, just getting more experience. Then I would have progressed faster.

On the other hand, being raised to see sex and virginity loss as a part of marriage—and thus reserved for heterosexuals—had made it more difficult for him to come out.

Not long after Tom and Kent lost their virginity together, Tom was lured away from Pittsburgh by a job offer from a theater in Philadelphia. He and Kent still visited one another 5 months later and, following Tom's new "practice makes perfect" adage, were continuing to explore sex together. This was unusual for someone who lost his virginity with a friend. Neither Tom nor Kent expected their relationship to blossom into anything more. "I'm not the type that will just have sex with anyone," Tom said, adding that he looked forward to discovering what it would be like to have sex with a man he loved.

Before I left Tom's house, I asked what he would do if he could go back in time. Although he admitted wishing that he'd lost his virginity under "more romantic" circumstances—the Florentine setting of *A Room with a View* came to mind—Tom's retrospective desires centered on the years and events preceding that momentous step.

I wish that I could go back and just be as wise about the world, as aware of things, as [I am now]. Because I've learned so much from being very foolish and making stupid mistakes and, you know, not being bold enough to tell everybody. . . . If I were 16 now, I think it would be a lot easier to go out and be out in high school. Just because, first of all, you'd be cool. And you know, then you['d] have Ellen [DeGeneres] to back you up.[31]

His comment deftly captures two levels of change: the increasing visibility of and tolerance for lesbigay people in American society over the past few decades, and Tom's personal journey from seeing virginity as a gift to viewing virginity loss as one aspect of learning about sexual and romantic relationships.

"I Felt Different Afterwards, but I Didn't Feel Like I Had Crossed over Some Great Line"

Feminist theorists often remark that lesbians' lives take distinctive shape from the ways their gender and sexual identities affect one another, or what theorists would term their intersection, such that their experiences cannot be simply equated with those of gay men or heterosexual women.[32] Abby Rosen's virginity-loss story is a case in point. When I interviewed her, Abby was 33 and had just embarked on a new career as a science librarian, much to the delight of her biologist father and librarian mother. She described her family as culturally Jewish but not particularly religious. A tall, athletic redhead, Abby had played soccer throughout high school and college and now coached a local girls' club team in her spare time. For the past 10 years, she identified herself as a lesbian. When I arrived at their house, she introduced her live-in partner as her wife. Neither woman had yet had children, although they hoped to in the future.

By her own account, Abby had never felt proud or ashamed of her virginity (or, later, her lack thereof). In the junior high and high schools she'd attended, virginity loss "was a big deal." But whereas many of her friends had perceived virginity loss as possessing "a significance beyond a physical act," Abby herself "just never had that much significance attached to one particular event." Instead, she had seen virginity loss "in terms of growing up, getting more experiences in life in general." Thinking that it would be unrealistic to expect "stars shooting in the skies and violins playing and everything else," Abby had instead hoped that losing her virginity would be a learning experience. In fact, she said, "I would hate to think of someone hanging, like, this is going to be it for the rest of my life, on this one event, because almost no one I know is still with the same person that they had sex with."

Why had Abby come to interpret virginity loss so differently from her peers? She thought being Jewish among mostly Christian classmates had something to do with it; plus she had been a careful student of human behavior. She recalled her youthful reasoning:

> I knew that some kids in their religious classes were . . . told, "Don't have sex." So I knew that message was out there, I knew that certain people thought it was only . . . for marriage and not for beforehand. But . . . I was smart enough to figure out that perhaps the message wasn't an entirely accurate one. . . . I just knew it was out there and I knew it wasn't true.

On a less conscious level, Abby may have gravitated toward the process metaphor because she was going through the transition of coming out—first as bisexual and later as a lesbian—at the same time as she was becoming sexually active. As with gay men, the lesbians and bisexual women I interviewed were substantially more likely to have seen their own virginity loss as a step in a process than were their heterosexual counterparts.

Looking back, Abby believed that her nascent sexual identity had influenced the sexual decisions she made as a teenager, even though she hadn't been aware of it at the time. Before she recognized that she was sexually attracted to women, Abby hadn't really been interested in having sex or losing her virginity—both of which she had been taught to equate with vaginal intercourse. During high school, she had engaged in heavy petting, cunnilingus, and fellatio with several young men, but never seriously contemplated doing anything more. She explained:

> I don't think it was ever a conscious thing. I just . . . never did anything that I was uncomfortable with . . . and I never did any more than I wanted to. So I guess if I had wanted to, I would have, but I hadn't. And

I was in the . . . very long process of figuring out my own sexuality, so that might have been part of it.

Other scholars have likewise found that lesbian and bisexual girls tend to see sexual experimentation with boys as a matter of course, rather than as a way of "testing" their sexual identity.[33]

By the time she came out as bisexual, as a 20-year-old college sophomore, Abby knew she wanted to have sex with a woman. Once she did, she reasoned (having revised her definition of sex since high school), she would no longer be a virgin. Abby looked forward to having romantic relationships, but her desire to satisfy her curiosity about sex was stronger than her inclination to lose her virginity with a girlfriend. She would be happy, she thought, if her first lesbian encounter was "trusting and caring and responsible." Among the women Abby trusted and liked "a whole lot" was Tara, a soccer teammate with whom she had been friends for several months. They had shared their sexual histories as friends, so Tara knew that Abby was a virgin and Abby knew that Tara was not. "[Tara] was actually straight," Abby explained with a laugh, "but had slept with both men and women before." Despite finding Tara attractive, Abby hadn't expected their relationship to take a sexual turn. They had never touched one another sexually before the spontaneous encounter in which they gave each other oral sex. "It was the kind of thing where one night it just happened," she recalled. "No great planning ahead of time." Pregnancy wasn't a possibility and STIs didn't cross their minds, so they didn't practice safer sex. In this, they were typical of the women I interviewed who lost their virginity with other women, but an exception among processers.[34]

Abby found sex with Tara physically and emotionally pleasurable. She was one of the few women in this group who described her virginity-loss encounter as very enjoyable physically; this may well be because she lost her virginity through cunnilingus, rather than penetrative vaginal sex, which many women find uncomfortable or even painful at first.

Abby also felt that the experience had enlightened and transformed her in small but meaningful ways. Having already given and received oral sex, albeit with men, she hadn't expected to learn anything new about sex per se from virginity loss. As she put it, "It wasn't like, 'Now I know what's it's like,' because I had actually done all those things before." Abby stood out in this interpretive group for expecting virginity loss *not* to be physically awkward, probably because she was one of the few not making the leap from oral to vaginal or anal sex. Having sex with a woman did, however, reinforce Abby's understanding that she wasn't heterosexual; and she felt subtly changed by virginity loss, in a way that confirmed her sense that it was part of a process.

> I felt different afterwards, but I didn't feel like I had crossed over some great line, that I was, you know, forever changed or any of those things [laughs]. [It was] more coming to terms with my sexuality and finally doing something that I had wanted to do, than any physical change in myself or any, you know, "I am a woman now," kind of thing [laughs]. . . . So I, I felt different because I had done something I had never done before. And I had, you know, been coming out to myself, coming out to friends, coming out wherever, but. This was sort of, I felt, another step in that process.

By laughing at the notion that virginity loss suddenly turns girls into women, Abby was poking fun at popular media depictions, like *Beach Party,* even as she agreed with their basic interpretation of virginity loss.

Her curiosity sated and her sexual interest in women confirmed, Abby knew that most of her future romantic and sexual partners would be women. She had sensed from the outset that Tara was ambivalent about sex with women, and therefore correctly assumed that while they would continue to be friends, their sexual encounter would remain an isolated incident. "[She] wasn't the person I was going to spend the rest of my life [with]," Abby explained. "I had no thought that [she] would be. So [virginity loss] wasn't any of that other stuff . . . that I guess some folks attach to it." When Abby had sex again, it was with her first girlfriend, Kris, whom she met several months after her night with Tara. Making love with Kris felt like just as much of a sexual turning point as losing her virginity had, Abby told me, because it had been her first sexual experience with someone she loved. Coming out had felt even more significant, for it involved "dealing with my own sexuality, and, you know, going through all that in my head was a lot more changing than . . . any specific act. Because that really had to do more with who I was." In short, Abby saw virginity loss, coming out, and having sex with a beloved partner as interrelated steps in the process of growing up and learning about sexuality.

Abby was, on the whole, pleased with the way she lost her virginity and said that she wouldn't change anything "at all." Unlike Tom and

Meghan, who were glad to have lost their virginity with fellow virgins—people who knew as little about sex as they did—Abby hadn't given her partner's status much thought. Although knowledge is a source of power in a rite of passage, Tara hadn't abused her greater familiarity with sex; Abby had felt that she was in control of their encounter and that Tara had treated her as an equal. Was the encounter equitable because Abby and Tara were both women? We have, after all, seen that gender differences in power exacerbate the disadvantages faced by virgins who favor the gift and stigma metaphors (if they lose their virginity with an other-sex partner). Considering the story of a woman who lost her virginity with a non-virgin man will help establish whether the process frame allows for more equitable virginity-loss experiences, regardless of the partners' genders.

"Emotional Pleasure, Sure. But Physical Pleasure, the First Time, No"

Jennifer Gonzales felt she'd learned a lot from the process of losing her virginity, even though her own experience had been physically very painful. When I arrived at Jennifer's apartment, she had just gotten home from the inner-city high school where she taught English as a second language. After changing into sweatpants and a T-shirt, which accentuated her curvy figure, Jennifer made a pot of tea to share while we talked. Now 25, she had spent her youth shuttling between her mother's house in northern Virginia, where she attended school, and her paternal grandparents' home in San Juan, Puerto Rico. Her parents, who shared little besides their Puerto Rican heritage and distaste for Roman Catholicism, had divorced when Jennifer was 8. Her father, a public accountant, remarried a few years later and moved to New York, while her mother, a dental technician, stayed in Virginia with Jennifer and her siblings. Jennifer had been married for 2 years when I met her, and she was looking forward to starting a family—as soon as she could convince her husband, who wasn't Latino, that their future children should carry *her* last name as a public emblem of their ethnicity.

Twirling a strand of wavy dark hair around her finger, Jennifer explained that she saw virginity loss as one of many experiences through which people learned about sex. "There's not, like, one epiphanic moment," she declared. "It's part of a process, even." Yet, she had expected that the first time she had vaginal sex—the moment she lost her virginity

—would be a uniquely memorable episode in that long and gradual journey.[35] "I think you always remember the first time you have sex," she said.

Virginity loss was a central theme in many of the movies Jennifer saw as a teenager, such as *The Breakfast Club, Sixteen Candles,* and *Halloween,* and in the novels she'd read, especially *Forever.*[36] But the source of information about sex that Jennifer valued most, especially as a young girl, was her mother. Jennifer's mom brought home "all the books" about puberty and was open and comfortable talking about sex, which she said could and should be a source of great pleasure. Yet she also encouraged Jennifer to wait to have sex until she was at least 18. Jennifer suspects her mother's views were motivated not by any vestigial disapproval of premarital sex, her mother having repudiated the teachings of the Roman Catholic Church, but by concern for Jennifer's emotional maturity and, later, reluctance to acknowledge that her "little girl" was growing up.

Jennifer found the sex education she received in public school far less helpful, not least because, as she remembered it, the teachers were forbidden to mention birth control, much less illuminate specific aspects of sexual practice.[37] She remembered in particular an incident from fifth or sixth grade, when she and her girlfriends had eagerly brought permission slips from home, only to discover that the "big sex ed talk" wasn't about sex at all, but about tampons and personal hygiene. By the time her ninth-grade biology teacher covered sexual reproduction, Jennifer was already well informed about "the basics," though she said she did learn some interesting, if trivial, facts.

From conversations with her mother and the films and fiction she devoured, Jennifer got the impression that all sex felt wonderful, even if the first time hurt a little or brought some blood. But she'd also heard, especially from more-experienced peers, that virginity loss could be boring, bumbling, or truly painful. As she put it:

> You always see in the movies, this beautiful scene. . . . I mean, I knew that it could be painful, I knew it could really [trails off]. So I didn't have as many expectations. But you know, I saw all the movies and, you know, the first time you want to be one of total pleasure.

She prepared herself for the worst, even while hoping that her own experience would be an exception.

Knowing that the first time could be disappointing as well as joyful kept Jennifer and her friends from feeling any particular urgency to lose their virginity, even as they looked forward to doing so. Nor did they feel much pressure from classmates who, as a rule, neither celebrated nor disparaged virginity. She recalled:

> My peers didn't really care one way or another. . . . If I had gone to college as a virgin, I think I would have felt pressure. I know my friends who were virgins felt pressure constantly. . . . If I were friends with a group of people who, everybody had sex but me, maybe then I would've felt pressure in high school. But that wasn't the case.

All in all, Jennifer approached virginity loss as inevitable but firmly in her command.

She didn't deliberately set out to abide by her mother's wishes; but as it turned out, Jennifer had scant opportunities to become sexually active during high school. She wasn't looking for the "perfect" partner, but none of the boys she dated piqued her interest in pursuing a relationship or in doing anything "more interesting" than kissing. Casual trysts were out of the question, because she wanted to work her way up to sex with a single partner. So Jennifer was still a virgin when she turned 18. She explained:

> I took outside classes and dancing and I had a job and I babysat Saturday nights, so I was really busy. I think I kept myself busy because the boys weren't exactly knocking on my door. Which, you know, fine, whatever, I'll find other things to do. And I didn't actually have a boyfriend until I was a senior anyway.

Many of the people I interviewed saw the transitions from virginity to nonvirginity and from high school to college (or work) as closely linked.[38] For the stigmatized, these links were a source of anxiety and urgency, whereas processers like Jennifer tended to view them as a matter of fact. As Matt Bergquist, a 24-year-old White heterosexual engineer, put it, virginity loss was "just like one of the many changes when I was a senior and graduating high school. I don't think that it seemed that much more of a change than moving or going off to college."

Jennifer's romantic prospects took a turn for the better in December of her senior year, when she started spending time with Andy. Also 18, Andy was funny, smart, and kind—and Jennifer felt sexually attracted to him in a way she never had before. Within a month, they started to fall in love. They also began acting on their mutual attraction, starting with petting above the waist, then below, then experimenting with oral sex. Cunnilingus was simple enough—Andy had given it to his previous girlfriend, and Jennifer enjoyed receiving it—but Jennifer's first attempt to reciprocate was nothing short of comic. When she was younger, Jennifer had learned that fellatio was sometimes called a blow job, "but not that it didn't involve blowing." So during one intimate encounter, Jennifer took Andy's penis in her mouth and blew. He was confused at first, then laughed, then explained how fellatio usually worked in a way that, miraculously, kept her from feeling utterly embarrassed. Whereas people who saw virginity as a stigma felt deeply ashamed by beginners' mistakes, Jennifer quickly regained her composure and lost none of her interest in sex.

Andy knew that Jennifer was a virgin—she'd told him that well before the fellatio incident—and he'd only had sex with one girl before. Without belaboring the details, he let Jennifer know that he and his previous girlfriend, who had also been a virgin, had figured out what they liked to do through a process of trial and error (getting pleasure from vaginal sex had been particularly tricky for his girlfriend), and he imagined that he and Jennifer would do the same. Jennifer firmly believed that Andy's previous experience had prepared him to take the incremental approach to sex that she preferred. "We worked up to it," she quipped. "We'd get into it and we'd even get naked, but we wouldn't [have sex]." Rather than worry that Andy's greater experience would give him power over her, Jennifer was glad that he could help guide her. She said, "He was so patient, so understanding. It wasn't . . . that big of a deal that we couldn't wait another month." Likewise, most processers who were dating nonvirgin partners expressed gratitude for their partners' greater knowledge.

As the weeks passed and their emotional and physical intimacy intensified, Jennifer grew increasingly certain that she would lose her virginity with Andy. With her mother's grudging approval, she made an appointment with a gynecologist to get a prescription for the Pill.[39] "I was on the Pill for two or three months before," she explained with a laugh. "But I could just . . . see it coming, so I wanted to be prepared. And I figured, well, you know, it regulates my period anyway." Altogether, two-thirds of people who viewed virginity loss as a rite of passage practiced some form of safer sex or birth control at virginity loss, a rate similar to that among women and men who saw virginity as a gift.

Andy and Jennifer had been dating about 5 months when they took the step from oral to vaginal sex.

I don't think we actually made a conscious decision. Up to the point where we did it, we'd been messing around in his dad's house one day. You know, doing the regular thing and you say, "Okay," you know?

Jennifer liked the way sex with Andy made her feel emotionally; but unfortunately, that was the *only* part she liked. "Emotional pleasure, sure," she said. "But, physical pleasure, the first time, no. Physical pleasure the second time, no. The third, fourth—it took a while for me." Andy climaxed very quickly their first time together, and vaginal sex was much more painful than Jennifer had ever imagined it could be—so much so, in fact, that she had no desire to try it again. But the emotional pleasure she did feel, combined with Andy's empathy and reassurance, convinced her that it would be worth seeing if the physical side of sex might improve over time. She recalled, "I really didn't want to have sex at all again. It made me think, 'Boy, that's really not fun and not cool, let's not do it again.'" When I asked her if she'd told him that, she exclaimed: "Yeah! I told him, 'That's it?' He's like, 'Isn't that enough?' And I said, 'No!' He's like, 'We-e-ll-lll,' you know." In effect, Jennifer decided to interpret the physical pain of that first encounter as part of the process of learning about sex, rather than as a final verdict on vaginal intercourse. Later, she made a point of warning her still-virgin friends that sex got a lot better with patient practice, hoping that they could benefit from her experience. Indeed, people often feel obliged to help someone making a desirable passage overcome the obstacles in their way.[40]

The physical pain Jennifer experienced is not unrelated to the fact that she lost her virginity through receptive vaginal intercourse. Women often feel some pain or discomfort the first time they have vaginal sex—though seldom as intense as Jennifer's.[41] More common are physically mediocre "first times" like Meghan's. Because gender and sexual identity determine which sexual practices individuals engage in, they effectively, if indirectly, help determine how physically enjoyable virginity loss is, on average, for members of different social groups. Heterosexual women like Jennifer and Meghan, and gay men who equate virginity loss with receptive anal intercourse like Tom, get the short end of the pleasure stick.

At the end of summer, faced with the prospect of attending colleges hundreds of miles apart, Jennifer and Andy decided to break up. Ironically, Jennifer said, "[Sex] got better right around the time I left." Around that time she experienced her first orgasm, which seemed to mark the next big step in her ongoing education about sex.

All things considered, Jennifer was happy with the way she lost her virginity. Its physical shortcomings notwithstanding, the experience brought her emotional pleasure and, more important, paved the way for her greater understanding and enjoyment of sex later on.[42] In anthropologist Victor Turner's terms, virginity loss proved to be the passage of *status elevation* that she expected it to be.[43] She had no regrets. Indeed, none of the processers I interviewed regretted losing their virginity when, how, or with whom they did.

In approaching virginity loss as a rite of passage, Jennifer, like Meghan, adopted a stance that, while generally thought to be appropriate for women, is also somewhat unorthodox. Her heterosexuality shaped her expectations and experiences (and vice versa) in similar ways as well. But if Jennifer's interpretation of virginity was nontraditional for a woman, it was all the more so considering her Puerto Rican heritage. Latin American cultures, diverse as they are, typically revere unmarried women's virginity while allowing young men considerable latitude; U.S. Latinos and Latinas therefore tend to place a higher value on female virginity than do non-Hispanic Whites and African Americans.[44] Jennifer's beliefs about virginity clearly diverged from this traditional model. Yet, her personal conduct—losing her virginity relatively late and in a committed love relationship—*was* fairly typical of Latinas residing in the continental United States.[45]

Jennifer's family history provides a clue to her "mixed" stance. Her parents had abandoned the Catholic Church, along with its teachings about premarital sex, and become highly acculturated to Anglo America when Jennifer was just a child. Yet, Jennifer observed, they never wholly shook off the moral teachings of their conventional Puerto Rican families. Indeed, her grandparents did their best to indoctrinate her in traditional beliefs about women's sexuality during her many summers on the island. By refusing to see her virginity as a precious gift to be given in marriage, but waiting to lose it until she was 18 and in love, Jennifer managed to conform to her family's (admittedly ambivalent) teachings and to fashion herself as a sexually liberated heterosexual woman who was also authentically Puerto Rican.

Jennifer's virginity-loss experience differed from those of Meghan, Tom, and Abby in two key respects. It was physically unpleasant—rather than unremarkable or enjoyable—and her partner was a nonvirgin of the other gender. Since knowledge represents a source of power in status passages, we might predict that a sexually experienced partner would try to take advantage of a virgin, especially if that partner enjoyed additional clout on the basis of his gender. But Jennifer felt that she'd been in charge of how and when she lost her virginity. In fact, none of the women who saw their loss of virginity as a step in a process had felt sexually disempowered, regardless of their partner's gender or level of experience; nor did they feel that their gender had worked to their special benefit. The contrast with women who interpreted virginity as a gift or as a stigma is dramatic. Jennifer's story therefore raises additional questions about people who favored the rite of passage metaphor: What kinds of power dynamics did *men* in this group face if they lost their virginity with women? And how did virgins whose experiences were unpleasant physically *and* emotionally react to the "lesson" that sex could be so disappointing?

"It Seemed Like It Should Be Really Easy to Do and It Wasn't Working"

Although Jennifer experienced an unusual degree of physical discomfort at virginity loss, she was not alone in trying to reconcile the unpleasant aspects of her experience with the conviction that virginity loss represents a desirable transition. Jason Cantor faced an even more formidable task, for he was one of six people in this group whose virginity-loss encounters fell short emotionally as well as physically.

Tall and rangy, Jason had lively brown eyes, dark wiry hair, and a subtle wit. Though only 24, he ran his own Web site design company. Jason came from a prosperous suburb of Wilmington, Delaware, where his father worked in investment banking and his mother taught art in afterschool and summer programs. He had been active in the youth group at his parents' reform temple while growing up, and being Jewish had remained a central part of his identity. While he felt in no hurry to marry or have children, he looked forward to raising a family in the tradition he'd found so meaningful.

When Jason was a teenager, he had been eager to lose his virginity not because it embarrassed him, but because he had wanted to learn about sex. "I thought it [sex] would be pleasant," he said wryly, "and I guess I thought there would be a very intense feeling of closeness and things like that." Virginity loss in particular had seemed to represent "sort of the year zero in between the part of life before sexual activity and then, the one after . . . the moment between having never had sex and having had it." Jason had imagined that moment as an instant of supreme enlightenment, which he described now in retrospect:

> It's sort of like trying to unlearn something. It's like . . . the drawing of the woman where if you look at it one way it's a young woman in a hat and if you look at it the other way it's an old, older woman with a shawl over her head. . . . Once, once you see them both you can't unsee one of them. And once you've sort of, once you've ventured down that road, you've ventured down it and you can't turn around and pretend you haven't.

He expected the knowledge he'd gain through virginity loss to transform him profoundly.

Jason's curiosity about sex wasn't so intense that he felt compelled to seek out opportunities to lose his virginity. Rather, he figured, a chance would arise soon enough in the natural course of things. He and his friends had seen lots of movies in which peer pressure to have sex figured prominently—*Losing It* and *The Last American Virgin* among them—but his own high school career was marked by an absence of such pressures, as well as by a liberal, value-neutral sex education curriculum. By the time he turned 17, Jason had experienced kissing and "petting, fondling, [and having] manual sex, oral sex, things like that," with a dozen girls he dated casually or "knew generally at parties." Although Jason enjoyed these casual liaisons immensely, he wanted to be in "a positive, pretty solid emotional relationship" when he lost his virginity. This wasn't because he felt that virginity loss would be meaningless if it weren't an expression of love and commitment, as gifters did, but rather because he thought that virginity loss was an experience "you're not going to forget. So the fewer bad memories you have stored in your bank, the better probably. So it's nice if it can at least be, the person can be a good memory."

Jason was a senior in high school when he fell in love for the first time. Fifteen-year-old Melissa's parents had just joined his family's synagogue, and they hit it off right away. After a few dates to movies and concerts, Melissa and Jason decided to see each other exclusively. In the weeks that followed, they engaged in "sex play at varying levels," from kissing to oral sex—the typical pattern for heterosexuals in this interpretive group. They discussed their mutual virginity; but neither gave it much thought beyond taking it for granted that, if they dated long enough, they would probably have vaginal sex. Eventually, the question was *when* they would lose their virginity together. Jason recounted:

> There were plenty of opportunities before it happened. I think it was more just timing. . . . At the time when it happened, I think it seemed like something that we both wanted to do. Whereas previous to that, I remember at least one, I remember specifically one instance before that, where I had brought up, you know, "Do you want to have sex now?" and she had said, "No, not now." And we let that lie. So it, it was sort of a timing thing.

They'd been a couple for almost 5 months when mutual interest and opportunity coincided. When a mandatory school play rehearsal prevented Jason from joining his family on a weekend trip, he invited Melissa to stay with him overnight. He made sure to change his sheets and have plenty of condoms on hand, just in case. But even careful planning didn't prepare them for the debacle that ensued. Jason recalled:

> We spent a good twenty minutes just trying to, to penetrate and eventually I just, it just wasn't happening. So we stopped trying and went out and got some food or whatever, and I think we tried again later that day and it worked. So. And that was just—by the time it actually worked, it was, it turned into sort of a frustration thing. You know, 'cause it was something, it seemed like it should be really easy to do and it wasn't working. And I know, I know that she felt . . . pain when it actually worked. . . . And I was frustrated, so it was not very pleasant at all.

Despite the circumstances, Jason had an orgasm; Melissa did not.

Rather than renounce sex after such a fiasco, Jason and Melissa decided to give it another try. Like Jennifer and Andy, they took encouragement from the strength of their relationship and from their enjoyment of earlier sexual encounters. Happily, their persistence was rewarded. "After the first time," Jason said, "when we went back and did it more, it was actually good, it was actually very pleasant. So I'd kind of had this idea that sex is something pleasant, and it panned out that way." In this way, they made their mutual transition to nonvirginity "stick."[46] And, even though Jason's virginity-loss experience was more unpleasant than Jennifer's, and his frustration magnified by his preconception of first vaginal sex as "easy," he too came to value it for bringing him a step closer to a complete and fulfilling sexual life. In retrospect, he said the only thing he would change was as follows:

> I would've tried to make the time when it actually did happen . . . a little more nice. A little more pleasant. It was just. You know, when we first tried, it was in bed and naked and all that, and the second time it was on the floor of the living room, pants down. You know, it was just like, "Damn it, this should be working," and so I would probably get the one that worked to be more like the first try.

Jason and Melissa continued to date and to have sex for almost 2 years. He let his friends surmise that he wasn't a virgin anymore, but didn't broadcast his new status, since he wanted to maintain some semblance of privacy. The pair broke up after a frustrating year of dating long distance—while Melissa was a high school senior, Jason attended college 300 miles from home. When he was 21, Jason became involved in "another very serious relationship that went on for about a year." That romance reinforced his understanding of sex as a process in which virginity loss represented just one step:

> I think it was the first time where I really thought I was having sex that was pointedly good. And that my partner was contributing something unique and specific to the activity, you know . . . that she had skills and knowledge of how to do different things, to get different kinds of pleasure. And I remember . . . with this person that sex seemed a little more expansive then, there was more to it.

Jason's gender inevitably, if subtly, influenced his beliefs and experiences. For men, interpreting virginity loss as a step in a process served as a somewhat unorthodox compromise—acceptably masculine, according to popular opinion, but less extreme than the tradition equating men's virginity with stigma. (Jason's privileged sexual, racial, and class identities may have made it easier for him to reject the stigma metaphor.) Yet, Jason did not experience virginity loss as gender neutral; he saw this rite of passage as transforming him from a boy into a man (at least in a sexual sense). Being male did not, however, appear to affect Jason's sense of sexual agency; he felt neither as though he'd been out of control nor that he'd been at Melissa's mercy. Similarly, the other male processers also felt that they'd remained in control.

Becoming Women and Men

Women and men who viewed virginity loss as a step in a process were, by and large, exposed to the same ideas about virginity as people who preferred other interpretations. But while they were aware that virginity could be seen as a stigma or as a gift, these approaches did not appeal to them. Different patterns of sexual socialization provide a partial explanation for the groups' different interpretive inclinations. Although individuals from working- and middle-class families were equally likely to have ever viewed virginity loss as a rite of passage, middle-class youth were overrepresented among those who drew on that metaphor at the time of their own virginity loss—that is, fairly early in life.[47] Since the metaphor derives from anthropological studies that are a staple of college curricula but are seldom taught in secondary school, it may be that college-educated parents are better situated to share this perspective with their children. In general, the parents of men and women in the process group tended to hold fairly permissive attitudes about adolescent sexuality, typically taking it for granted that their offspring would have sex before marriage (though most parents frowned on virginity loss in early adolescence or with casual partners). With the exception of Tom, no one in the process group grew up in a conservative Protestant and/or devoutly religious family. Few recalled being exposed to, much less influenced by, religious teachings about virginity loss. Processers were also disproportionately likely to have participated in value-neutral comprehensive sex education programs, such as those described by Meghan and Jason. Possibly for this reason, they described their peers as nonjudgmental more often than did members of the stigma and gift groups—even when those peers disagreed with their beliefs—and reported experiencing little if any peer pressure around sexual activity.

Beyond their sexual socialization, processers were acutely aware of the possibility of constructing their identities through virginity loss—trading one social status for another being precisely what their interpretation of that event entails. They invariably spoke of virginity loss as a signal event in their transformation from relatively naive adolescents to sexually knowing adults. Many moreover described this transformation in gendered terms, as a process of becoming women or men. Because the rite of passage metaphor is seen as an appropriate, but not especially traditional, option for men and women in American culture, it provided the people in my study with a vehicle for challenging the sexual double standard by rejecting rather than reversing it (as when a man views virginity as a gift). In this sense, viewing virginity loss as a step in a process helps young people to establish a truly unorthodox adult masculine or feminine self through virginity loss. More than half of processers had done "everything but" lose their virginity with at least one casual partner. By contrast, sex play with casual partners was exceedingly rare among gifters and seen as a kind of consolation prize by the stigmatized.

The passage metaphor also helps people to fashion sexual identities. Tom, Abby, and the other gay, lesbian, and bisexual women and men in this group experienced virginity loss as intertwined with the process of coming out. Losing virginity with a same-sex partner enables individuals to "prove" their lesbigay sexual identity to themselves and others. In fact, the two lesbians who lost their virginity with men before they came out noted that those experiences contributed to their growing sense that they weren't heterosexual. Heterosexual women and men likewise demonstrated their sexual identities through virginity loss, although they were typically less conscious of doing so. If the men and women in my study used the passage frame to construct or perform other aspects of social identity, they did so in ways that I did not discern. For example, although being raised in mainstream religious traditions and/or nondevout families probably reduced the likelihood of being encouraged to view virginity as a gift, neither participants' words nor their behavior suggested that they preferred the process metaphor because it helped them construct themselves as relatively secular beings.

Taken together, the interviews I conducted help illuminate the complex ways through which young Americans come to favor one understanding of virginity loss over another. What youth learn about virginity and sexuality from their parents, peers, schools, religious institutions, and mass media—lessons that are patterned by gender, sexuality, race/ethnicity, social class, and religion—shapes their preferences; as do the specific social contexts through which they move. But traditional links between social identity and interpretations of virginity loss are weaker today than in the past, as the unconventional preferences of many of my study participants reveal. Broad social changes, especially those brought about by the feminist, gay rights, and civil rights movements, have opened new avenues, new ways of being men and women, gay and heterosexual, racially or ethnically identified, and so forth. Young women and men are, consequently, able to choose specific approaches to virginity loss based on the versions of social identity that those approaches will help them achieve.

6

Abstinence

The student workbook for Sex Respect, one of the most widely used sex education curricula in the United States, gives pride of place to a teen-written "rap" declaring:

> Love and sex
> Sex and love
> Both are gifts from up above
> One is good
> The other is great
> They would both be greater
> If you WAIT.[1]

In addition to learning that virginity is a gift, students are given the impression that the only alternative—adopted by foolish youth—is to think of virginity as a stigma. For example, the SR-produced videotape, "Dating: Predator or Partner," promises to demonstrate that

> on dates there are only two types of people . . . predators or partners. . . . Derek Wiersma grew up as a sexual predator who began having pre-marital sex at 13. Derek was interested in "the hunt" and "getting as much out of a girl as he could." . . . After college, Derek realized that preying on women was wrong and he stopped.[2]

Traditional beliefs about gender differences in sexuality permeate Sex Respect and other similar curricula that share its only-abstinence-until-marriage perspective, as does the assumption that "normal" people are heterosexual.[3] Claiming that "many things about the male and female gender . . . are opposite," the SR student workbook suggests that, "because they generally become physically aroused less easily, girls are still in a good position to slow down the young man."[4] Yet, at the same time, Sex Respect insists on a single, chaste standard for both genders: "It is equally important for both young men and women to abstain from sex outside of marriage. The time of the double standard is over."[5]

The Debate over Sex Education in America

The proportion of U.S. public school districts providing formal sex education increased substantially over the course of the 1980s and 1990s, such that more American youth are schooled in sex-related matters today than ever before.[6] But the ideals and advice imparted in sex education programs varies dramatically from one school district to another depending on the curricula they adopt. Sex education programs fall into three broad types: *comprehensive,* which present abstinence and contraception as similarly effective and morally equivalent options for preventing pregnancy and sexually transmitted infections (STIs); *abstinence-plus,* which portray abstinence as the best option for adolescents, but also discuss birth control/safer sex as an effective alternative; and *abstinence-only,* which depict sexual chastity as the only moral and effective option outside of marriage, either omitting information about contraception or emphasizing its limitations.[7]

Over the course of the 1990s, the proportion of U.S. public schools offering comprehensive sex education programs shrank significantly, while the proportion teaching abstinence-only and abstinence-plus curricula increased.[8] In 1998, of public school districts requiring sex education, 14 percent mandated comprehensive programs, 51 percent offered abstinence-plus curricula, and 35 percent provided abstinence-only education.[9] Sex Respect alone grew from a several-school pilot program in 1985 to a slick multimedia curriculum used by 1,600 school districts in 1991 and over 3,000 in 2001.[10]

The expansion of abstinence-focused sex education has dramatically altered what information students learn about methods for preventing pregnancy and STIs. In 1988, only 2 percent of secondary school sex education teachers presented abstinence until marriage as the *only* means of protecting against pregnancy and STIs; by 1999, this figure had increased tenfold, to 23 percent.[11] Conversely, the proportion of teachers depicting condoms as effective against HIV fell from 87 percent in 1988 to 59 percent in 1999.[12] But official changes in policy don't tell the whole story. In many school districts, self-censorship has left comprehensive sex education programs closely resembling their abstinence-only counterparts.[13] Tellingly, over one-third of students in nominally comprehensive programs report receiving little if any information about how and where to use and obtain contraception.[14]

One might assume that abstinence-only sex education came to the fore so rapidly because of scientific evidence demonstrating its superior effectiveness in preventing unintended pregnancies and STIs—but virtually no reliable evidence suggests that this is the case. Nor is abstinence-only education's success due to widespread opposition to comprehensive programs on the part of the American public. Indeed, the vast majority of U.S. parents are in favor of teaching children about contraception and safer sex in addition to abstinence.[15]

Rather, the nationwide shift from comprehensive to abstinence-focused sex education appears to have been motivated chiefly by federal-level funding structures put into place by moral conservatives starting in the early 1980s.[16] The U.S. government supports sex education programs through three major channels—the Adolescent Family Life Act (AFLA) of 1981, Title V of the Social Security Act of 1996, and the Special Project of Regional and National Significance–Community Based Abstinence Education (SPRANS-CBAE) of 2001—all of which require state recipients to promote sexual abstinence until marriage as "the expected standard of sexual activity."[17] Few states can afford to decline the monies provided through these programs; at most, three states have done so in any given year.[18]

To qualify for federal support, sex education programs must conform to an eight-point definition of "abstinence education," spelled out in Title V as an educational or motivational program that (emphasis added)[19]

A. has as its exclusive purpose teaching the social, psychological, and health gains to be realized by abstaining from sexual activity;

B. teaches abstinence from sexual activity outside marriage as the expected standard for all school-age children;

C. teaches that *abstinence* from sexual activity *is the only certain way to avoid* out-of-wedlock pregnancy, sexually transmitted diseases, and other associated health problems;

D. teaches that a *mutually faithful monogamous relationship in the context of marriage* is the *expected standard of sexual activity*;

E. teaches that *sexual activity outside of the context of marriage is likely to have harmful psychological and physical effects*;

F. teaches that bearing children out-of-wedlock is likely to have harmful consequences for the child, the child's parents, and society;

G. teaches young people how to reject sexual advances and how alcohol and drug use increase vulnerability to sexual advances, and

H. teaches the importance of attaining self-sufficiency before engaging in sexual activity.

Implicit in this definition is the version of sexual morality favored by conservative Christians.

None of the metaphors for virginity employed by the women and men in my study are inherently incompatible with the criteria stipulated in Title V. A person could, for instance, interpret virginity as a stigma to be endured until marriage. But, in practice, the sex education curricula that have been developed according to the federal guidelines tend to present virginity as a gift intended for a person's (heterosexual) spouse. Sex Respect, one of the first abstinence-only curricula developed with AFLA funding, exemplifies this pattern. Comprehensive sex education programs, in contrast, tend to describe early sexual encounters as steps in the process of growing up: "Young people develop their values about sexuality as part of becoming adults. Young people explore their sexuality as a natural process of achieving sexual maturity."[20] (Abstinence-plus programs vary, with some drawing on the process metaphor and others favoring the gift metaphor.) Comprehensive curricula also tend to be gender neutral and lesbigay inclusive.

Interestingly, the gift metaphor as presented in Sex Respect and its kin diverges from popular expressions in a key respect. Scarcely any of the gifters I interviewed believed that sexual activity was appropriate only in marriage. This discrepancy between the curricular and popular versions of the gift metaphor supports critics' claim that the current federal policy represents a response to the demands of a vocal moral/religious conservative minority rather than to the wishes of the relatively secular moderate majority.[21]

At the same time that public schools, spurred by federal monies, began adopting (ostensibly) secular abstinence-until-marriage curricula, conservative Christian organizations were busy developing explicitly religious sex education programs for their own youth.[22] Many of these programs, including the widely publicized True Love Waits (TLW), which was founded in 1993 with the support of the Southern Baptist Convention, conform closely to Title V requirements. As the TLW Web site succinctly puts it, "No one doubts that sexual activity in the new millennium is physically, emotionally, and socially dangerous."[23] Although the overt religiosity of these curricula prohibits their use in public schools, thousands of youth have been exposed to TLW and its cousins through church youth groups, Sunday schools, and the like. By 2000, the TLW campaign claimed to have inspired 2 million youth to sign pledges of premarital sexual purity, reading, "Believing that true love waits, I make a commitment to God, myself, my family, my friends, my future mate, and my future children to be sexually abstinent from this day until the day I enter a biblical marriage relationship."[24] Like their secular counterparts, Christian sex education programs tend to describe virginity as a gift. In a tips-for-parents column for the TLW Web site, LifeWay Christian Resources/Student Ministry Publishing editor David Crim described a family conversation on his daughter's thirteenth birthday:

> I explained . . . that, just as her mom and I had waited until just the right moment to give her the birthstone ring, we wanted her to wait until just the right moment [marriage] to give the gift of sexual intimacy to a man.[25]

Christian sex education programs also present a fourth metaphor—distinct from the gift, stigma, and rite of passage perspectives—positing premarital virginity as an act of worship. In pride of place on TLW's list of the "Top 10 Risks of Having Sex before Marriage" are the following (emphasis in original):

> *The risk of permanently damaging your testimony as a Christian.* You'll never be able to honestly say, "I was a virgin before I was married." You'll never be able to live as an example of committed purity.
> *The risk of shame.* Premarital sex imputes a spiritual state of shame that becomes a major weapon of Satan. God forgives you, but . . . you'll still be vulnerable to Satan's whispering accusations on your worth as a person and your value as an active Christian.[26]

Although the act-of-worship perspective shares the gift metaphor's roots in Christian thought, specifically the belief that virginity is a gift from

God, and its emphasis on love and relationship, it is in many ways unique. In light of these differences and current social trends—namely, rising membership in evangelical and fundamentalist Christian churches and moral conservatives' considerable influence over national and local sex education policy—it is worth exploring this fourth perspective on virginity in more detail.[27]

"It's a Really Great Way to Honor God"

In the course of my research, I interviewed two young women, both devout born-again Christians, who described maintaining their virginity until marriage as a way of worshiping God. The younger of the two women was Carrie Matthews, a 20-year-old White nursing student. A self-described heterosexual virgin, Carrie dressed in loose-fitting garments that emphasized her plumpness. A bright smile illuminated her makeup-free face. Growing up in a deeply religious Protestant family had profoundly shaped Carrie's perspective on virginity. Although her father earned most of his income as a counselor for recovering drug addicts, he had found his true calling as the pastor of a small independent evangelical church. Her mother, a housewife, volunteered many hours for the church and numerous local charities. Carrie had chosen to attend a college near home, partly so that she could remain active in her family's church.

No less immersed in popular culture than others her age, Carrie was well aware that American beliefs about virginity are diverse. But for her, she said, there was no question that

> [virginity is] the way that I want to live until I'm married. . . . I think that it's a really great way to honor God, in a sense of knowing that, like, whatever He has for me is going to be better than the things that I can pursue on my own. And . . . relationships . . . if they're not drawn out of a commitment, it *is* kind of pursuing it on my own and not trusting that He has something that's really good for me.

As further incentives, she cited virginity's health benefits—"I mean, I'm the lowest [risk] group of anyone for sexually transmitted diseases"—and its effects on her interpersonal relationships:

> I know that I'm being relationally responsible. . . . Not that I think that
> sex is automatically relationally irresponsible, but . . . [remaining a vir-
> gin is] going to be able to help me to love a person in a way that isn't
> limited or isn't bound by what's physical. It will help me to really con-
> centrate on the other parts of a relationship.

To ensure that she didn't confuse love and physical desire, Carrie rarely
dated and planned to avoid almost all sexual intimacy before marriage.
At 20, she had romantically kissed only two men. She did, however, look
forward to sex within marriage as "an opportunity . . . to get emotionally
and physically and spiritually, all sorts of connected, in a very unique
way." Despite being adamant about "stick[ing] to" her own "set of . . .
morals," Carrie made a point of telling me that she didn't view people
who have sex before marriage "as strange, evil, awful people."[28] She did,
however, think that some—like a friend who'd discovered that sex "was-
n't the thing that completed her"—could benefit from becoming born-
again virgins. Carrie didn't believe that a person could resume her or his
virginity "in the physiological sense," but she described nonvirgins who
make "the decision to be chaste" as "awesome, I respect that a lot."

Kate O'Connor, in contrast, had not always seen premarital virginity
as an act of faith. Raised in a not-very-devout Roman Catholic family,
Kate grew disenchanted with Catholicism during college and joined an
evangelical church when she was 20. She wanted to embrace her new
church's teaching that sex should be reserved for marriage, but she had
lost her virginity at age 16 and been sexually active with most of her subsequent boyfriends. She resolved this thorny dilemma when she was 22
by becoming a secondary virgin.

When I met Kate, she was 24 years old and worked as a producer for
a Philadelphia-area radio station. Descended from Irish and Dutch ancestors, she had light blue eyes and a heart-shaped face framed by auburn
hair. Kate's father had recently retired from his career as a corporate executive; her mother had stayed at home when their children were young,
then gone to work part time in retail sales when Kate's younger sister
started high school. Kate was heterosexual and had never been married
nor lived with a man.

Before Kate became a born-again Christian, she took a pragmatic approach to sex. In high school and college, she and her friends had shared
what she described as, "The typical view of . . . sex. Which is just, quote,
'Be responsible about it, but it doesn't really matter [morally].'" Virgin-

ity loss represented a significant, if value neutral, "turning point." Kate explained:

> I expected [virginity loss] to be a big deal in the sense of. . . . You're not married one day and you're married the next day, and it's this whole huge life change. . . . You are one thing one day and all of a sudden you can never say that you're that thing again. . . . To me, in my mind, that was a very big deal. Not because it was a moral thing to do or an immoral thing, but just because that's what. . . . People talked about it as being such a big deal.

In short, she saw virginity loss as a rite of passage.

Not surprisingly, Kate's early sexual history resembles that of other women and men who favored the process metaphor. She had been curious about sex, but not in such a hurry that she couldn't wait for a partner who mattered to her. "The first person should be someone you care about and then after that, you can kind of do whatever you want—that's what I used to think," she said. Starting in the summer between seventh and eighth grades, Kate had a handful of "short-lived boyfriend-girlfriend relationship things" in which sexual contact was confined to "kissing and like, you know, having a guy like feel you up." She laughed recalling the terms she and her friends had used: "First base and second base—that's what we called it then."

Kate had just turned 16 when she started dating Jack, the "first boyfriend [whom] I had for a long enough time that [genital petting] . . . happened more than once." Although Jack was a year younger than Kate, he had lost his virginity with a previous girlfriend. He told Kate that he'd like to have sex with her, too, but did not pressure her. After they'd seen each other for "a couple of months—that's like dog years in high school," Kate decided she really liked Jack and was ready to lose her virginity. Looking back, she said, "I don't think we had a wonderful relationship. I thought we did at the time. It was probably an okay one, for high school." The pair spent weeks preparing for the night they'd first have sex, discussing everything from details, "like . . . how the room would be, or how the music would be," to Kate's insistence on safer sex. "Besides, like, just getting pregnant and having sex, I was thinking about stuff like AIDS. . . . It was understood that he would wear a condom," she said.

One weekend, when Jack's parents "went away . . . and I said I was sleeping at my girlfriend's house," Kate and he had sex. Kate found vaginal penetration "horribly painful," which she attributed in retrospect to their mutual inexperience and the tension of trying something new.

> I was . . . tense and maybe nervous. And also the fact that I don't think he really knew what he was doing enough to get a woman aroused, where it wouldn't be painful. Because, you know, he's a young kid.

Virginity loss both was and wasn't the "big deal" Kate had anticipated. "I didn't feel like I had changed," she said, "but I felt like everyone knew." Her overall approach to sex also changed. "I think that made it kind of a given then, if you did it once, that you were going to do it in all your relationships after," she explained.

Kate and Jack's relationship lasted 6 months in all. They had sex only a few more times "because of . . . being in high school and when would you do it?" By the end of her freshman year in college, Kate had had sex with 3 or 4 more boyfriends and had started thinking of sex as "more of a pleasurable experience and not just practice. Which I think was probably all it was in high school, because it wasn't ever good." Discovering pleasure was not, however, to be the last, or even the biggest, turning point in Kate's sexual career.

The summer after her junior year in college, Kate found herself "thinking a lot about God." Not wanting to remain in the Roman Catholic Church, in which she'd "always felt kind of alienated," Kate wound up joining what she later discovered was a Pentecostal congregation. Her newfound faith didn't affect her sexual life at first. She explained:

> I was still dating the guy that I dated [before joining the church] . . . and [our] behavior didn't change at all. . . . I didn't even really know that the Bible says that . . . sex is a sin before marriage, because I never read it. . . . I didn't have any other Christians to talk about this with. That might have said, you know, "Maybe you should think about what you're doing," or, "Here is the scripture that says this."

Kate broke up with that boyfriend shortly before college graduation. Later that summer, she had lunch with a man she had dated in high school. In the intervening years, Keith had also become a born-again Christian and he was concerned about Kate's lax approach to sex. He told her, "You know, Kate, you shouldn't be having sex. . . . God doesn't want you to," and explained that *he* wasn't having sex. Kate was half shocked, half dismissive.

> I was like, "No way, you? You are not!" And he's like, "No, I'm not, I'm not doing it anymore." And I was like, "Right." And so he tried to tell me about . . . what he believed is God's plan for his life and how he should . . . live his life as far as dealing with women. And basically . . . what he believed was that God would lead him to whomever he was supposed to marry. And that he wouldn't have to go around dating the entire world by process of elimination to try to find the, quote, "One."

Keith called his decision "born-again virginity." Kate had heard the term once before, from a similar source as Andrew Lin: "that really dumb show" on MTV. One of the episodes featured "a girl who was a born-again virgin," but at the time, Kate said, "I think that kind of went in one ear and out the other."

Even after she heard Keith's story, and knew that the Bible forbade sex before marriage, Kate said, "The whole not having sex thing seemed totally ridiculous to me." But, over the course of the next year or so, Kate began talking with people at her church—many of whom shared Keith's beliefs about virginity—and gradually began to think that she ought to change her ways. She recounted:

> So finally I said, "All right God, if you don't want me to do it, then . . . you have to keep me from doing it and I can't do that, because I don't want to. . . ." And He did. . . . Like my, the way I viewed [sex] and the way I felt about it changed in a dramatic but kind of slow way. And got to the point where I didn't want to do it anymore, and I didn't miss it and I didn't think, "I'm missing out," or . . . I wouldn't go out with a guy and be like, you know, "Well that would be really great." It didn't even come to my mind. . . . I had been totally and completely changed.

Like Keith, Kate referred to her new mode of behavior as born-again virginity. Though she knew she couldn't be a "true" virgin when she married, she said: "My intent is . . . not to have sex again until I am married and . . . I guess that would be considered losing your second virginity."

For about a year after undergoing this change, Kate continued to date but limited sexual intimacies to kissing and petting above the waist. Yet, she increasingly found herself pondering God's instructions for "not just sex, but dating in general." She explained:

> [I]f God wants you to get married . . . He's chosen someone for you and you don't need to go through this process of elimination. . . . [Keith] was so committed to his future wife that he didn't want to cheat on her now. And I was like, "What? You're not even married. You don't even know her." And he's like, "Yeah, but she's, right now, she's my wife, wherever she is. . . . So anybody I go out with, it's almost like cheating on her and she the same for me."

By the time I interviewed Kate, she was intent on applying these principles in her own life. "I don't date anybody now," she said, "and that's so—like, to be a born-again virgin is almost, like, ancillary. . . . It's not even the point really, for me now." She admits to having "thoughts about [sex], because I think that's human nature," but intends not to kiss any man except her eventual husband. Like Carrie, Kate now believes that physical intimacy hinders a person's ability to develop a truly lasting relationship. As she put it:

> [M]y goal is not just to go out with a guy and not have sex. My goal is to find the person that I want to marry and then have a relationship that's not based on sex, but that's based on friendship and love and a commitment to God, and not just emotional and physical things. . . . I know I don't want my marriage to be based on something that fleeting.

I felt almost cruel when I asked Kate whether she would do things differently if she could go back in time. But she refused to berate herself for choices she couldn't undo. On the one hand, she felt:

> It would be even nicer if I never kissed a guy . . . 'Cause then, when I got married, everything I experienced with my husband would be just him. And there would be nothing to compare it to . . . he would never have to imagine me with someone else.

But at the same time, she said, "Everything I've done is, kind of made me the way I am today. And . . . by not doing that, I would never get to . . . experience God's grace in that way" or develop as much "compassion . . . for other people."

Since the virginity-as-worship perspective shares the gift metaphor's emphasis on love and relationship, it is not surprising that Carrie and Kate, the only study participants who saw their virginity in these religious terms, are both women. Other researchers and I have found women more inclined than men to view virginity as a gift, and also to hold premarital virginity as an ideal.[29] Both inclinations are fostered by traditional gender beliefs and serve as ways for young women to enact traditionally feminine identities.[30] Not coincidentally, many evangelical and fundamentalist Christian churches advocate the pursuit of traditional gender roles in all realms of life, including the sexual.[31]

Nor is it surprising that the two who saw virginity as an act of worship are both devout and active members of evangelical churches, for conservative Christian institutions are the chief proponents of this perspective. None of the other former or current conservative Protestants I interviewed had personally thought of their virginity in these terms, however, though a few mentioned knowing people who did.[32] To the extent that my respondents are broadly representative of evangelical and fundamentalist Americans, this finding could suggest that relatively few conservative Christians find the act-of-worship frame appealing. Alternatively, given Kate and Carrie's relative youth, it may be that future generations of conservative Christians will adopt the virginity-as-worship perspective in greater numbers.[33]

Whether the act-of-worship metaphor will gain currency outside the community in which it originated remains to be seen. Conservative Protestant denominations rank among the fastest-growing religious groups in America, and moral conservatives currently enjoy a great deal of influence over national, state, and local sex education policy.[34] If these trends persist, an increasing number of young men and women from all religious backgrounds will be exposed to the belief that virginity is an act of worship. It is possible that, as people discover the metaphor, they will adopt it as their own. Something of the sort appears to have taken place with secondary virginity during the early 1990s. Yet, Andrew Lin's secular account of becoming a born-again virgin suggests that nondevout and/or non-Christian youth are liable to adapt "Christian" sexual concepts to their own circumstances and belief systems. Andrew decided to retain his secondary virginity not until marriage but until he was in a committed love relationship. Likewise, a young person might opt to honor God with her virginity until graduating from parochial school or falling in love with a fellow believer, rather than until marriage.

Moreover, American society has been growing steadily more secular since the 1960s, the revival of Christian conservatism notwithstanding; and a majority of American adults believe that sex before marriage is acceptable, for young adults if not adolescents.[35] Secular adults are not likely to encourage young people to view their virginity as an act of worship (although they may promote approaching it as a gift); and those who approve of premarital sex are not likely to advocate preserving virginity until marriage (though they may applaud maintaining it until late adolescence or early adulthood). Also arguing against a wholesale future shift toward the act-of-worship and gift perspectives is my finding that a majority of men and women who lose their own virginity thinking of it as a stigma subsequently reject that metaphor in favor of the process/passage alternative. Such people, as adults, may encourage their children to interpret virginity loss from the start as a step in the process of growing up.

In short, my research reveals the contradictory influence of two trends —ongoing secularization and the expansion of conservative Christianity —on virginity loss in the United States today. With the exception of active conservative Protestants and devout Christians of other denominations (who tended to favor the gift metaphor), the majority of women and men in my study did not attribute their beliefs about virginity to religious training they received as youths; nor did they appear to favor certain metaphors as a way of enacting their religious identities. When people from different religious backgrounds shared an interpretation of virginity, they reported very similar beliefs and experiences (with the partial exception, among gifters, of devout/conservative Christians' greater propensity to describe virginity at marriage as ideal).[36] Other scholars have likewise observed a diminishing association between religiosity and sexual beliefs and behavior, except among conservative-religious and/or very devout youth.[37]

Given that only a minority of Americans hold such religious beliefs, it is disturbing that federal policies for sex education are tailored to religious conservatives. Shouldn't our sex education policies be appropriate for the majority of our youth? It is even more disturbing in light of what scientific studies tell us about the relative effectiveness of abstinence-only versus comprehensive sex education programs.

Evaluating Different Approaches to Sex Education

To date, few abstinence-only sex education curricula have been evaluated using scientifically sound methods.[38] Quality assessments of such leading programs as Sex Respect, Teen-Aid, and Human Sexuality: Values and Choices—all of which depict virginity as a gift—have largely failed to support advocates' claim that program participants delay first intercourse significantly longer than nonparticipants (much less postpone sex until marriage) or are less likely to become pregnant during adolescence.[39] Because the majority of teens, regardless of their experiences with sex education, have vaginal sex before they graduate high school, abstinence-only programs' policy of ignoring condoms and contraception, or of focusing on (and even exaggerating) their failure rates, pose particular problems.[40] As a report by the Centers for Disease Control notes, "[P]eople who are skeptical about condoms aren't as likely to use them—but that doesn't mean they won't have sex."[41]

In contrast, dozens of scientifically sound studies have demonstrated that sex education programs that include information about abstinence *and* contraception and STI prevention do result in participants' delaying first sex, having fewer sexual partners, and using condoms and other forms of contraception at significantly higher rates than nonparticipants —all behaviors associated with lower rates of pregnancy and STIs.[42] That's right, talking about contraception and STIs *delays* virginity loss and *promotes* safer sex. These programs, especially those that take a truly comprehensive approach to sex (e.g., curricula developed around Sexuality Information and Education Council of the United States [SIECUS] guidelines) tend to present virginity as a step in the process of growing up. Notably, none of the sex education curricula judged to reduce "sexual risk behaviors" by the CDC's Research to Classroom Project, a project commissioned to identify sex education programs shown to be effective in scientific studies, uses an abstinence-only approach.[43] That said, an increasing number of abstinence-only curricula are now undergoing rigorous evaluations; it remains to be seen if any will be found effective.

Cross-national studies also point toward the effectiveness of comprehensive sex education and of framing virginity loss as a step in a learning process. In comparing the United States to similar societies, we find that American and western European adolescents become sexually active at similar ages on average; however, pregnancy, birth, and abortion rates are significantly lower among European teens, as are STI rates.[44]

This disparity stems in part from European teens' greater propensity to use condoms and other forms of contraception, a propensity enhanced by national health insurance systems (as opposed to the private, for-profit system in the United States).[45] But cross-national differences in adolescent sexual outcomes can further be traced to broad cultural attitudes about sexuality in general, and adolescent sexuality in particular. American sexual culture is rife with ambivalence, whereas western Europeans exhibit a sex-positive pragmatism. For example, there is an openness about sexuality in Europe that is absent in the United States, evidenced by nudity in mainstream magazines and television, nudity on public beaches, and sales of sexually explicit literature. Condoms are advertised more widely in European media; in fact, condom ads have only recently been permitted on American TV. Compared with 36 developed countries, the U.S. ranks low on openness and has the highest level of teen pregnancy by far.[46] In American popular culture there is a lot of sex, but sexual themes are often depicted as secret and "dirty," especially when teenagers are involved. Although few U.S. adults reject premarital sex per se, a majority believe teenagers should abstain. Parents typically perceive teens as too immature to engage in sex responsibly and teens, in turn, usually seek to conceal their sexual activity.[47] By contrast, European mass media regularly examine sexuality, and few adults disapprove of premarital sex, even among teens. Parents tend to treat sexual activity as a normal part of healthy adolescent development—that is, as a learning process or a rite of passage—and many teens inform their parents of their sexual activity (at least if it is heterosexual).[48] These broad cultural outlooks have had profound effects on public policy, with the United States favoring policies that seek to restrict all sexual activity and western European countries promoting education about, and provision of, contraception and instilling a sense of responsibility for its use.[49]

It is more difficult to assess the effects of abstinence-only and comprehensive models of sex education on young people's emotional and psychological well-being. Although federally funded sex education programs are required to teach "that sexual activity outside . . . marriage is likely to have harmful psychological . . . effects," there is virtually no scientific evidence that this is true.[50] In the words of a joint report by Advocates for Youth and SIECUS, published in 2001:

> It is true that unprotected sexual activity can lead to unplanned pregnancies, STDs [sexually transmitted diseases], and HIV. It is also true that

intimate relationships can be harmful for some people. However, the reality is that the majority of people have had sexual relationships prior to marriage with no negative repercussions.[51]

The claim that premarital virginity loss often causes emotional harm seems predicated on the belief that virginity is a precious gift intended *for a spouse* or an act of religious faith. As we have seen, these beliefs are by no means universal among Americans today.

Furthermore, given the emotional and physical harm that we know can come from unplanned pregnancy, STIs, and HIV/AIDS, it behooves us to face the facts about virginity loss among American youth. If we can provide them with information and guidance in keeping with the reality of their lives, then we can help ease their way into adulthood and healthy sexual lives.

7

Virginity Lost

Physical health and emotional well-being represent central components of sexual health, according to the World Health Organization (WHO), former U.S. surgeon general David Satcher, and other leading authorities. As defined by the WHO in 2002:

> Sexual health is a state of physical, emotional, mental and social well-being related to sexuality; it is not merely the absence of disease, dysfunction or infirmity. Sexual health requires a positive and respectful approach to sexuality and sexual relationships, as well as the possibility of having pleasurable and safe sexual experiences, free of coercion, discrimination and violence.[1]

This definition informs my comparative analysis of the four metaphors through which people in my study made sense of virginity loss. By addressing approaches to virginity loss in terms of their effects on sexual health, I am moreover interrogating the assumption, codified in the federal government's guidelines for sex education funding, that all sexual activity outside of marriage is likely (equally likely, it is implied) to cause physical and psychological damage, irrespective of a person's understanding of sexuality or virginity.

As it turns out, the vast majority of the people I interviewed lost their virginity with few, if any, ill effects. All of the nonvirgins had lost their virginity before marriage; 2 of the 5 virgins were planning to wait until their wedding nights.[2] Whether they interpreted virginity as a gift, stigma, step in a process, or act of worship, on balance most men and women described their experiences as satisfying, even enjoyable, and avoided unintended pregnancy and STIs (a few scares notwithstanding). They also felt as though they had been in control and treated fairly by their partners. My research therefore represents an empirically based challenge to the claim that virginity loss before marriage, or during adolescence, inevitably causes physical and psychological harm.

In itself, this is an important finding. But, in light of the distinctive constellations of sexual beliefs and behaviors fostered by different metaphors for virginity, it is also crucial to consider whether specific understandings of virginity loss enhanced or diminished the physical and emotional well-being of the individuals who subscribed to them. Moreover, it is worth asking whether these metaphors perpetuate or disrupt prevailing patterns of gender inequality, especially in heterosexual relationships. Because the major models of sex education currently vying for dominance tend to promote different understandings of virginity loss, my findings can also help inform the national debate about sex education policy in the United States.

Unequal Effects

Of the four interpretive groups identified in my study, the gifters were the most likely to practice birth control or safer sex at virginity loss (and during the "close calls" that often preceded it). The close relationships these young people had with their sexual partners made it easier and more acceptable for them to protect their physical health in this manner. Close relationships could also heighten feelings of emotional well-being. But because reciprocation is the linchpin of gift relationships, virgins who favored this metaphor effectively ceded substantial control to their partners. Women and men who gave their virginity to loving, reciprocating partners—the majority in my study—pronounced themselves satisfied with their virginity-loss experiences; Kelly Lewis and Bryan Meyers's warm recollections of relationships strengthened through the mutual exchange of gifts were typical.

However, gifters whose partners did not reciprocate felt not only disappointed, even devastated, but also deprived of sexual agency. This was especially the case for heterosexual women, given their lack of power relative to men. Julie Pavlicko and the other women whose male partners did not return their gifts felt disenfranchised at virginity loss *and* in subsequent relationships. Their distress was magnified by the exceptional significance accorded to virginity loss when virginity is framed as a precious, unique gift. The gift metaphor's emphasis on reciprocation had other ill effects as well: Danielle Rice and a few other women told me that they would have left abusive or unworthy partners earlier had they not given those partners a precious part of themselves. In sum, approaching virginity as a gift facilitates behavior that protects physical health and has the potential for enhancing emotional well-being; but it also sets the stage for possible emotional devastation and the loss of agency, for women in particular.

People who favored the stigma metaphor measured their experiences against less stringent criteria, by comparison. Every man and woman who avoided coercive encounters and having new stigmas imposed upon them spoke of their virginity-loss experiences in positive terms. Some, like Marty Baker, basked in the pleasures of engaging in a new sexual activity and being stigma free; others, like Kendall James, relished the titillating stories they were able to tell. On the downside, however, the intensity with which most members of this group wished to conceal their sexual inexperience, along with the unanticipated circumstances and casual relationships in which many lost their virginity, resulted in the lowest rates of contraception and safer sex in my study. Men especially viewed concealment as imperative, given the cultural equation of masculinity with sexual experience. That imperative was aggravated by the relative powerlessness of stigmatized people, such that men in this group were especially vulnerable to humiliation and disempowerment at the hands of female partners. Derided as virgins or sexual incompetents, Bill Gordon and two other men felt such shame that they avoided sex long after losing their virginity. Gender expectations worked to the advantage of women like Emma McCabe, however, sparing them from the perils of concealment and enhancing their ability to dictate the terms and timing of virginity loss. Thus, although seeing virginity as a stigma is conducive to emotional well-being in general, it increases men's risk of emotional distress and loss of sexual agency; and it tends to discourage safer sex. The partners of the stigmatized may also fare poorly, to the extent that they are treated as a means to achieving the end of virginity loss.

Women and men who interpreted virginity loss as a rite of passage were not ensured of physically and emotionally positive virginity-loss encounters. But they were better equipped than members of other interpretive groups for dealing constructively with the awkward and unpleasant aspects of an often-imperfect experience. Some found the process of virginity loss quite enjoyable—Abby Rosen for one—while others, like Jennifer Gonzales, spoke of extracting kernels of good from largely unpleasant encounters. In a sense, it was virtually impossible for people who drew on the passage metaphor *not* to achieve what they saw as the chief goal of virginity loss—learning something—no matter what went "wrong" in the process. The fact that learning is largely an internal accomplishment moreover helped them maintain a sense of agency during and after virginity loss, regardless of their partners' level of experience, and whatever their gender or sexual identity.

Processers practiced birth control or safer sex almost as often as gifters. Prompted by their understanding of virginity, they chose partners they knew well, either romantically or as a friend, in hopes that doing so would facilitate gradual sexual exploration, greater knowledge, or heightened pleasure. Ironically, however, the belief that virginity loss was a "natural" step in a process also resulted in a few failures to use birth control/safer sex. (These failures were exceptions, not the rule.) All in all, viewing virginity loss as a step in a process tends to enhance physical and emotional well-being, and to sustain sexual agency, for women and men alike.

Although two interviews are too few to permit a definitive assessment of the act-of-worship perspective, a brief discussion of its possible effects is warranted. My conversations with Kate O'Connor and Carrie Matthews suggest that people whose religious beliefs encourage them to treat premarital virginity as an expression of faith do reap spiritual benefits from doing so. If they realize their intentions—eschewing sexual intercourse and most other sexual contact before marriage—they will be well protected against unintended pregnancies and STIs. Yet, research shows that the vast majority of teenagers who pledge to remain virgins until marriage wind up breaking their pledges; and when they do, they are significantly less likely than nonpledgers to practice safer sex.[3] Other studies, drawing on in-depth interviews, find that adolescent women who intend to remain chaste are less likely to take precautions when they do have sex.[4] Moreover, women and men who see premarital virginity as an act of worship but fail to live up to their own high standards may suffer guilt and emotional distress.[5]

That said, my cautious prediction is that young people who adopt the act-of-worship metaphor out of deep religious convictions are likely—provided they have peers, parents, and schools that support their goals—to enjoy physically and emotionally positive virginity-loss experiences, possibly on their wedding nights. But youth who lack spiritual incentives to embrace this stance are unlikely to benefit to the same degree. Indeed, it is difficult to imagine them doing more than going through the motions

—and they would have little motivation for doing even that, especially when other, possibly more appealing, interpretive alternatives are available. Notably, until same-sex marriage is a viable option, lesbigay youth are left out of the act-of-worship equation entirely.

Comparing the differential effects of the gift, stigma, passage/process, and act-of-worship metaphors, as experienced by the people I interviewed, suggests that viewing virginity loss as a rite of passage is, on balance, most conducive to physical health, emotional well-being, and the exercise of sexual agency—for men and women alike. Parents, policy makers, sex educators, and others who wish to enhance the sexual health and well-being of future generations would, therefore, do well to encourage young Americans, one-on-one and through public policies, to approach virginity loss as a step in a process.

Insofar as certain metaphors for virginity are emphasized by different models of sex education, I recommend a turn away from abstinence-only curricula and urge a move toward comprehensive education. Abstinence-only programs tend to frame virginity as a gift or as an act of worship, presenting the stigma metaphor as the implicit alternative, whereas comprehensive curricula tend to depict virginity loss as a step in a learning process. The gift metaphor, while encouraging contraception and safer sex, potentially diminishes women's emotional well-being and agency; the stigma metaphor discourages safer sex and potentially distresses and disenfranchises men. Further study may reveal that the act-of-worship frame promotes well-being and a sense of agency for young people who share its religious worldview; but there are compelling reasons to believe that it will have different effects on less- or otherwise-religious youth.

It would, of course, be possible to develop sex education programs that combine an understanding of virginity as a rite of passage with an emphasis on sexual abstinence until marriage (or lesbigay commitment ceremony). Yet several factors argue against doing so. Used consistently and correctly, condoms and oral contraceptives are virtually as effective in preventing STIs and pregnancy, respectively, as sexual abstinence is assumed to be. Data from western Europe indicate that 16- and 17-year-olds are capable of having sex without getting pregnant or contracting STIs. And when chastity-minded teens do have sex, they are much less likely to practice safer sex than peers who foresee sex in their futures. Furthermore, studies have repeatedly demonstrated that comprehensive sex education programs are effective in changing teens' conduct in ways that reduce rates of pregnancy and STIs, while abstinence-only curricula have not been shown to have similar effects.

In addition, lacking spiritual incentives to postpone sex until marriage, young men and women who forgo responsible sexual activity before (or instead of) marriage merely seem to lose an opportunity to benefit from the emotional and intellectual growth that sexual relationships can bring.[6] With the exception of Kate O'Conner and Linda Jenkins (a devout Presbyterian who saw virginity as a gift), none of the nonvirgins in my study suggested that it would have been advantageous to postpone sex past mid- to late adolescence. In fact, it seems likely that encouraging young people to remain virgins until marriage would promote early marriage—teens who take virginity pledges are twice as likely to be married by age 23 as their nonpledging counterparts, for example. Early marriages are undesirable for several reasons, not least that, other factors being equal, they are disproportionately likely to end in divorce.[7]

In sum, a comprehensive approach to sex education, in which virginity is framed as a step in the process of growing up, appears likely to benefit a majority of young women and men, whereas an abstinence-only approach, in which virginity is depicted as a gift or act of worship, is likely to be detrimental on balance. Putting this recommendation into practice may be easier said than done, however.

Rethinking Sex Education

Abstinence-based sex education has become well entrenched in American public policy since its (re)emergence in the early 1980s.[8] Even during the moderate Clinton administration, moral conservatives won major victories in their struggle to transform sex education, most notably the expansion of federal funding and other structural supports that were put in place under Presidents Reagan and George H. W. Bush. Abstinence-only sex education has received even stronger support from George W. Bush, who promised in 2000 to "elevate abstinence education from an afterthought to an urgent policy," and whose Office of Faith-Based and Community Initiatives is poised to channel even more federal monies toward the development of sex education programs by religious organizations.[9] The Bush administration has been harshly criticized by the Union of Concerned Scientists for "distort[ing] science-based performance measures to test whether abstinence-only programs were proving effective" and for ignoring, even suppressing, the scientific evidence in support of comprehensive sex education.[10] Several high-ranking scientists at the Centers for Disease Control resigned in protest over a trend toward "promot[ing] condoms as ineffective in preventing disease" and "omit[ting] information about contraception on web sites."[11] With Bush winning a second term in office, abstinence advocates are well placed to capitalize further on their successes thus far.[12]

It remains difficult for Americans to talk about sexuality in the sex-positive pragmatic terms favored by our western European cousins. Moral conservatives have been able to capitalize on a historic legacy of framing sexuality, particularly nonmarital sexuality, as inherently immoral, stigmatizing, and negative, such that they control the terms of debate around sexuality and virginity in the United States today.[13] Parents, teachers, and policy makers who have publicly opposed strict abstinence-only measures have been branded "perverts" and suffered damage to their reputations and even careers. Perhaps the best-known case of this involves former U.S. surgeon general Jocelyn Elders, who was fired in part for suggesting that public school boards *consider* including the topic of masturbation in sex education curricula.[14] The ability of the moderate mainstream to disrupt moral conservatives' dominance and have their own voices heard depends in part on developing new ways of speaking about sexuality.

Unfortunately, research findings about the comparative effectiveness of sex education programs are not likely to sway parties that favor particular stances toward virginity on the grounds of their moral superiority, nor, in all likelihood, are my findings about the relative merits of different popular metaphors for virginity. Notably, moral conservatives are increasingly framing their advocacy of abstinence education in terms of health and well-being, rather than moral/religious superiority, a move presumably intended to influence secular opinion in their favor. And yet, moral-religious conservatives represent only a minority of American parents and the general public. Opinion polls routinely find that the vast majority of U.S. adults approve of sex education programs in public schools and want them to include information about abstinence *and* about birth control and safer sex.[15] Although most American adults disapprove of sex among teenagers, especially young teens, relatively few condemn consensual sex between unmarried adults.[16] Indeed, starting with the baby-boom generation, most Americans lost their virginity before marriage, typically while they were adolescents. Furthermore, decades of high divorce rates have left many people skeptical about the viability of youthful marriage.[17] Together, these opinion trends suggest that a majority of American parents would support sex education programs that promote virginity until late adolescence or young adulthood, but not until marriage.

Advocates of comprehensive sex education express frustration that people who agree with their position remain aloof from the fray, such that the minority control the policy agenda. However, free speech activists, led by the National Coalition Against Censorship (NCAC), have joined the debate on sex education, arguing that the federal abstinence-only guidelines represent an unacceptable bounding of teachers' speech.[18] Parents in several states have filed—and won—lawsuits against abstinence-only curricula on the grounds of medical inaccuracy.[19] In late 2004, U.S. Representative Henry Waxman released a report demonstrating that the majority of federally funded abstinence-only curricula "contain false, misleading, or distorted information about reproductive health"; it received heavy press coverage and prompted numerous calls for critical examinations of current sex education policy.[20] The ACLU has argued that Sex Respect textbooks treat gender and marriage in ways that violate state laws prohibiting discrimination "based on gender, marital status, sexual orientation and religion."[21] And a wide variety of public health and medical organizations, including the American Academy of Pediatrics, American Medical Association, and American Public Health Association, have voiced support for comprehensive sex education in public schools.[22]

Additional challenges to the ascendancy of abstinence-only sex education come from new developments in media and information technology. Teen magazines have offered a source of accurate and increasingly nonjudgmental information about birth control and safer sex since the 1980s.[23] More recently, nonprofit organizations and media producers have formed partnerships to incorporate sexual health-related themes into top-rated teen television programs like *Dawson's Creek* and *Felicity*.[24] Less formally, a growing number of pop, hip-hop, and R&B performers have been touting the benefits of condom use in their songs, as when Jay-Z raps, "I wrapped the rubber tighter." Perhaps most important, the Internet and rapid expansion of personal computers have not only enabled people to access all manner of sexuality-related material from virtually any geographic location, but have also inspired a steady stream of new content, such as personal Web pages and 'zines in which teenage girls semipublicly share their experiences of wrestling with complex sexual issues.[25]

Why Virginity Loss Is Significant Today

My analysis of virginity loss in contemporary America would not be complete without a closer examination of the significance currently attributed to virginity loss by youth, parents, laypeople, and policy makers alike. Specifically, it is worth asking whether treating virginity loss as one of the most important sexual experiences of a person's life—a tendency that is particularly pronounced when virginity is framed as a gift or stigma—ultimately works to young people's advantage or disadvantage. I recognize the apparent irony of concluding a book devoted to virginity loss with a critique of the tendency to endow virginity loss with significance. Yet, I believe that it is possible—even necessary—to mount such a critique, not least because understanding the potential benefits and costs of this tendency can help American parents, educators, and policy makers guide youth more effectively through their early sexual careers.

Throughout this book, I have shown how many of the factors that historically lent great significance to virginity have lost much of their salience, due to extensive changes in social and sexual life. One of the most notable changes for a large segment of the populace has been the diminishing appeal of religious reasons for preserving virginity until marriage, brought about by the steady secularization of American society. The development of effective birth control methods—and tremendous expansion of their availability—has also had a considerable impact, by reducing the danger that virginity loss (or subsequent sexual encounters) might result in unintended pregnancy.

When, in the 1960s and 1970s, it became widely apparent that American understandings and experiences of virginity loss were undergoing radical changes, many predicted that virginity loss would soon mean little to young women and men. In fact, premarital virginity did lose much of its allure as an ideal, and it has not regained widespread favor since, the Virgin Cool trend of the 1990s and early 2000s notwithstanding. Yet, as is clear from the stories of the men and women here, young Americans from a wide range of social backgrounds still see virginity loss as an especially important life event.

One reason that virginity loss is significant today is that, thanks to the multiple meanings it carries, it offers young men and women a flexible vehicle for constructing particular versions of gender, sexual, racial/ethnic, and religious identities.[26] For instance, young men who are attached to traditional ideas about masculinity may favor the stigma metaphor as a way of enacting their understanding of manhood; conversely, young men less invested in machismo may prefer the process or gift metaphor. Virginity loss also is significant because it represents one of the few steps in the transition from youth to adulthood over which young people enjoy almost complete control. In recent decades, the American life course has grown increasingly varied and unpredictable. Many people do not experience the life events traditionally associated with adulthood until they are in their late twenties or older, much less do they experience those events in the "traditional" order.[27] Where a majority of young men and women once followed a fairly predictable path from school to paid work to marriage and parenthood, many now combine or alternate between school and paid labor, have children before or without marrying, or delay marriage long after completing their education. The people who took part in my study were no exception. At an average age of 25, they were indisputably adults, but only one-fifth of them had ever been married (of course, lesbigay participants could not legally marry) and even fewer had children; some had yet to begin their "real" careers, while others had left jobs to continue their education. Beyond being unpredictable, many aspects of the passage from youth to adulthood lie largely outside of individual control.[28] Institutional rules and financial resources govern high school and college graduation; broad economic processes determine the timing and conditions of employment; and legal statutes regulate voting, driving, and the purchase of cigarettes and alcoholic beverages.

Virginity loss, by contrast, represents a step from youth to adulthood that individuals can accomplish fairly early in life and with the assistance of just a single partner. In my study, men and women who favored the rite of passage metaphor were the most explicitly attuned to this aspect of virginity loss; but those who followed other approaches mentioned it as well. Hannah Cooper, a 29-year-old White heterosexual sign-language interpreter, who had seen her virginity as a stigma, recalled, "I think when I lost it, I decided I was an adult. Which was really stupid. . . . I thought I was grown up." In semicontrast, Danielle Rice, who interpreted virginity as a gift, said:

I felt like it was like I entered into womanhood. . . . It wasn't the [first menstrual] period that made me feel like a woman. It was sex. Like, I've done it. And I was ahead of certain . . . friends. . . . So I was like, "I've done it and I can tell you all about it."

Similarly, Carlos Rodriguez, a 28-year-old gay Latino nurse practitioner, who had seen virginity as irrelevant to his own experience, said:

I do remember stories of some friends telling me that . . . when it's time, their dads would take the[m] to some kind of brothel . . . so they would lose their virginity. I remember thinking about that when I was younger and [laughs], "I hope my father doesn't do this to me." . . . I guess . . . it meant to them some kind of reaching of manhood, you know, losing your virginity.

Growing up in a context of uncertainty, diversity, and change, American youth benefit from being able to understand virginity loss in ways that help them to fashion specific social identities and that bring them one step closer to adulthood. In fact, if the possibilities for social identities and life course trajectories continue to expand—as well they may— young Americans may invest virginity loss with even more meaning than currently is the case. Given these benefits, it makes sense to treat virginity loss as a significant and important life event.

But my research suggests that treating virginity loss as one of the most important sexual experiences of a person's life carries real costs as well. Consider, for example, the stories of Julie Pavlicko, who saw virginity as a gift, and Bill Gordon, who viewed it as a stigma. Their divergent stances notwithstanding, Julie and Bill both approached virginity loss as an event that had an unsurpassed power to determine what they would do, and who they would become, as sexual beings. Julie's distress when her boyfriend failed to reciprocate her gift of virginity was magnified and prolonged because she saw virginity loss as the best-but-irreplaceable way of bonding with a life partner. By a similar token, the humiliation and inadequacy Bill felt when Diane jeered at his inexperience were all the more intense and long-lasting because he gave the distinction between virgins and nonvirgins so much weight.

Less severe troubles also result from investing virginity loss with paramount importance. A number of men and women told me that, had they not been so worried about maintaining or eradicating their virginity per se, they would have had sex with another, earlier partner or waited for a later one. Marcy Goldberg, a 27-year-old Jewish heterosexual therapist who saw virginity as a gift, said that, had she been able to put virginity in better perspective, she would have given hers to her first boyfriend, whom she really loved, rather than the boyfriend with whom she did first have sex.

> I would've definitely had sex with Michael. . . . Not that that would make me a happier person, but I'd have more things to compare, not even compare to . . . just more experience. . . . 'Cause now I only have Chuck and my husband. And Chuck wasn't all that good [laughs]. And, you know, my husband's great, but, you know.

Conversely, Marty Baker surmised that, had he felt less pressure to shed his virginity, he might have waited for a girlfriend with whom he was really close, thereby gaining even more from the experience.

> Not to say that there was anything wrong with [my virginity-loss encounter]. Just like, personally . . . I would have chosen to have a different, this other person. . . . Just because the [virginity-loss] relationship wasn't as strong and the second one was definitely a better, like, I considered myself in a very tangible friendship with her.

In short, men and women who view virginity loss as the most significant event of their sexual careers may be more likely to experience adverse outcomes than people who do not see virginity loss as uniquely important. For this reason, it might be wise to temper the importance that American cultural and social institutions grant to virginity loss. Several of the women and men in my study reached the same conclusion. In the words of Lisa Orlofksy, a 35-year-old Jewish lesbian who worked as a school administrator:

> By focusing on [virginity loss], we put too much attention to it, which can . . . I think, sort of encourage people to lose it before they're ready. Or they hold on to it while they do other things that could be considered sex.

In Conclusion

Although virginity loss represents an important turning point in sexual life, surprisingly little was known about young Americans' definitions, interpretations, and experiences of virginity loss before I began my research. Through my interviews, I have been able to develop a four-faceted model for understanding virginity loss today, based on the metaphors of the gift, the stigma, the rite of passage, and the act of worship. Because specific metaphors give rise to distinctive expectations and desires, my model provides a way to understand a person's decisions and behavior, before, during, and after virginity loss. Moreover, since my model derives from people's own understandings of virginity loss, it remains faithful to their beliefs and experiences in a way that a model deduced from previous studies or my own cultural assumptions cannot.

How people interpret virginity loss depends in large part on their social identities—both the ones they already possess, like being male or female, and the identities they wish to have, like being cool or unconventional. Throughout the preceding chapters, I have shown how youth are encouraged—by parents, peers, and popular culture—to interpret virginity loss in ways that are deemed appropriate for individuals of their gender, racial/ethnic background, religion, and so forth. Thus, young women are typically urged to view virginity as a gift, while men are encouraged to see it as a stigma. Yet, because social identities are more flexible today than ever before, young Americans can also draw on different interpretations of virginity to construct themselves as the kinds of people they'd like to be. For instance, by interpreting her loss of virginity as a rite of passage, a young woman can establish a somewhat unorthodox feminine identity, whereas the gift and stigma frames respectively imply traditional femininity and a wholesale rejection thereof. In this sense, virginity loss can transform one type of person into another.

Social identities are not the only factor implicated in the processes whereby young people come to prefer one understanding of virginity loss over another. Women and men learn about virginity loss from parents, peers, popular culture, schools, and religious institutions. When these sources of information disagree about the meaning of virginity loss, what close friends or other peers believe typically outweighs the attitudes of other sources, parents included. Contrary to common assumptions, popular culture tends to reinforce, rather than determine, beliefs. Although people are exposed to diverse understandings of virginity through mass media, they selectively attend to the messages that match their current inclinations. For example, Kelly Lewis and Emma McCabe learned about virginity loss from the same movies, magazines, and especially the teen novel, *Forever*; but Kelly focused on images that framed virginity as a gift, while Emma concentrated on those that treated virginity as a stigma.

Generational differences are also very important. The resurgence of moral conservatism, the HIV/AIDS epidemic, the growing visibility of lesbigay communities, and second- and third-wave feminism all helped to transform Americans' approaches to virginity loss. My research reveals clear differences by generation, with younger men being more likely than older men to interpret virginity as a gift, and younger people of all sexual identities being more likely than their "elders" to define virginity loss in same-sex inclusive ways. Younger-generation lesbigay people are also more likely to come out at earlier ages, to eschew heterosexual "experimentation," and to insist on applying a uniform definition to virginity loss with same- and other-sex partners. Given the likelihood that lesbigay youth will become increasingly visible, moral conservatives' efforts notwithstanding, it is likely that definitions of sex and sexual acts, virginity included, will continue to change, even broaden, in the years ahead.

Several decades have passed since premarital virginity was the all-but-undisputed ideal of the land. American society has changed tremendously in that time, such that proposals to turn back the clock are altogether unrealistic.[29] Indeed, a great many Americans would not wish to return to bygone views of virginity loss. It is important that young women and men feel able to embrace virginity, if and when they wish to do so. But attempts to declare a new era of Virgin Cool and refusals to provide accurate information about sexual health are no more likely to prevent teenagers from having sex today than they were in the 1950s, when a majority of Americans had sex before marriage. Rather, we would do well to give teenagers the tools to help make their virginity-loss experiences as healthy, safe, and happy as possible.

Methodological Appendix

Telling Truths about Virginity Loss

One of the questions I've often been asked about this project is, "How can you be sure that the people you interviewed told the truth?" Study participants' truthfulness is of perennial concern of all social scientists; and this concern is magnified by the private nature of sexuality in American culture. Beyond the possibility that participants may lie outright, researchers must confront the fact that accounts of any event inevitably entail a certain degree of interpretation. When people share stories about their experiences, they frequently highlight different things depending on their audience, their reason for telling, and even their mood at the time. Sometimes these choices are conscious, sometimes not. People may also reinterpret their experiences over time; what they see as the truth about their lives at one point in time may differ from what they understand to be true at another juncture. Drawing on postmodernist theorists' insights about the nature of reality and representation, Norman Denzin, Catherine Riessman, and other experts in qualitative sociological methodology recommend that researchers accept that the same story can be told in different truthful ways, rather than struggling in vain to uncover the one single "Truth" about a given event.[1] Truth, in this singular sense, does not exist; but a scholar who recognizes the multiplicity of truth, and the inevitability of (re)interpretation, can learn a great deal about the meanings and purposes of specific accounts told under particular circumstances. This is not to suggest that accounts can never be false. For instance, one would be wise to doubt the truthfulness of a person who claimed to have lost her virginity on the planet Mars.

Ultimately, although the women and men in my study undoubtedly highlighted some aspects of their experiences and downplayed others, I feel relatively confident that the stories they told me reflected the basic contours of their experiences, as they currently understood and interpreted them. Merely agreeing to participate in such a study implies a certain willingness to share details of one's sexual history. Moreover, I informed everyone I interviewed that they could decline to answer any of my questions. Very few exercised this option; in fact, many of them shared extremely unpleasant stories and some cast their own behavior in profoundly unflattering light. A few even appeared to recall events spontaneously as we conversed. The fact that most of the interviews took place several years or more after virginity loss may have enhanced participants' willingness to reveal the less savory aspects of their experiences. I also asked everyone with whom I spoke to consider whether, and how, their understandings of virginity loss had changed over time. The format of the interviews may have encouraged candor as well, since it is difficult consistently to misrepresent one's beliefs and experiences over the course of a one- to three-hour conversation. This is not to suggest, however, that the men and women with whom I spoke would not have told a different version of their stories to a friend, parent, or another interviewer, or at another point in time.

In my analysis, I describe the various ways that people in my study had interpreted and reinterpreted their experiences up to the time of our interviews. These women and men will undoubtedly continue to reinterpret their experiences as time goes on; indeed, some appeared to begin reinterpreting virginity loss during the interview itself.

Interviewing Style: A Feminist Partnership

One of my goals as a researcher was to make the interviews as much like conversations as possible. Conversational interviews enhance rapport, making it easier for people to share the intimate details of their lives. They also help to counteract the inequality that too often characterizes scholars' relationships with their informants. Almost by definition, researchers enjoy a position of power vis-à-vis the people whose lives they study. They decide which issues should be studied and determine what information is to be revealed, when, and by whom. In most studies, information flows solely from participant to researcher. Scholars who prefer to keep their disclosures to a minimum while data are being collected do so for several reasons. Not least, they fear (quite reasonably) that revealing the guiding hypotheses or preliminary findings of a study will encourage study participants to respond in ways intended to "please" the interviewer.

Yet many ethnographers and feminist scholars contend that researchers who refuse to share information—for example, declining to answer direct questions during an interview—are taking advantage of their more powerful position vis-à-vis the people on whose participation their investigations depend.[2] Sharing this concern with inequity, I decided to conclude every interview by inviting participants to ask me questions and to respond to midinterview queries as best I could (the semistructured interview format I used tends to encourage such queries). Many of the women and men I spoke with did ask questions. Most common were inquiries about what kinds of encounters or beliefs were "normal" and questions about my own virginity-loss experience. I answered the first type of question by stressing the extent of variation I saw among study participants, and replied to the latter type of question as honestly as possible, but with a minimum of detail. People who asked me questions during the interview often seemed to be "testing" my trustworthiness and receptivity to their experiences. For example, after I spoke with Lavinia Thompson, a 30-year-old, heterosexual, African American paralegal, I wrote the following note:

> Although she answered me when I asked how old she'd been when she lost her virginity, she really opened up after I answered her question about how old I was—and it turned out we'd been the same age.

I believe that my willingness to respond frankly to such questions enhanced, rather than compromised, the quality of my research. When it came to sharing my own *opinions* with women and men whose beliefs appeared to differ substantially from mine, I confess that I was less forthcoming—without lying outright—for fear that being entirely open would "poison" the interview and destroy my rapport with the respondent.

I include here a table summarizing key aspects of study participants' backgrounds and current lives, as well as three tables showing how interpretations of virginity were patterned by gender, sexual identity, and generation.

TABLE 1 *Profiles of Study Participants*

Name	Age	Gender	Sexual Identity[a]	Race/ Ethnicity	Religion[b]	Social Class[c]
Chris Albrecht	18	M	heterosexual	White	Southern Baptist	middle
Ettrick Anderson	19	M	gay	African American	various Protestant	working
Marty Baker	26	M	heterosexual	White	Presbyterian	working
Matt Bergquist	24	M	heterosexual	White	Roman Catholic	middle
Missy Blum	24	F	bisexual	White	Jewish	middle
Charlotte Brandt	28	F	heterosexual	White	none	middle
Jason Cantor	24	M	heterosexual	White	Jewish	middle
Kevin Cleary	22	M	heterosexual	White	Roman Catholic	middle
Hannah Cooper	29	F	heterosexual	White	mainline Protestant	middle
Don Coulter	32	M	heterosexual	White	Presbyterian	working
Tim Davis	18	M	heterosexual	White	Roman Catholic	middle
Terence Deluca	27	M	heterosexual	White	Roman Catholic	working
Paul Duval	25	M	heterosexual	Haitian American	Roman Catholic	working
Alyssa Edwards	21	F	heterosexual	White	Lutheran	middle
Sean Farris	29	M	gay	White	Roman Catholic	middle
Heather Folger	28	F	heterosexual	White	Unitarian	middle
Fernando Garcia	21	M	gay	Cuban American	Roman Catholic	middle
Marcy Goldberg	27	F	heterosexual	White	Jewish	working
Jennifer Gonzales	25	F	heterosexual	Latina	none	middle
Bill Gordon	31	M	heterosexual	White	Methodist	working
Dana Hagy	30	F	heterosexual	White	(Lutheran) evangelical	middle
Tony Halloran	21	M	heterosexual	White	Roman Catholic	working
Tom Hansen	24	M	gay	White	evangelical Protestant	middle
Wendy Hargrave	18	F	heterosexual	White	Roman Catholic	working
Tessa Hauser	32	F	lesbian	White	Episcopalian	middle
Kendall James	28	M	gay	African American	Baptist	middle
Dave Jeffries	26	M	heterosexual	White	Lutheran	middle
Linda Jenkins	26	F	heterosexual	White	Presbyterian	middle
Juliette Jordan	19	F	lesbian	African American	Baptist/Roman Catholic	middle
Jay Karoulis	18	M	bisexual	White	Greek Orthodox	working
Brenda Kim	25	F	bisexual	Korean American	Presbyterian	working
Karen Lareau	21	F	heterosexual	White	Episcopalian	middle
Jon Laumann	27	M	heterosexual	White	Lutheran	middle

[a] At time of interview.
[b] At time of interview, if unchanged; if changed, religion during youth is in parentheses.
[c] While growing up.

Where from?	Current Occupation	Family Status, Kids	Age at VL	Interp. (before) at VL	Current Interp.
TX	student	single, none	virgin	n/a	gift
MD	student	single, none	14	stigma	process
NJ	retail manager	married, 1 child	17	stigma	process
SD	engineer	married, 1 child	17	process	process
PA	nonprofit assistant	single, none	17	gift	gift
VT	fundraiser	single, none	17, V2 @ 22	gift	gift
DE	website designer	single, none	17	process	process
PA	student	single, none	16	stigma	process
OH	sign-language interpreter	divorced, cohabiting, none	13	(gift) stigma	process
TX	architect	cohabiting, none	18	stigma	process
MI	student	single, none	15	stigma	process
MA	HVAC mechanic	married, 2 kids	13	process	process
NY	bookstore clerk	single, none	17	stigma	stigma
PA	student	single, none	17	gift	gift
CT	financial analyst	single, none	15	stigma	process
DC	office worker	single, none	17	process	process
FL	theater student	single, none	virgin	n/a	gift
PA	therapist	married, none	18	gift	gift
VA/PR	teacher	married, none	18	process	process
NJ	tutor	ex-cohabiter, none	18	stigma	stigma
IL	homemaker	married, 3 kids	17	gift	gift
PA	food service	single, none	20	stigma	stigma/gift
PA	box office manager	single, none	23	(gift) process	process
PA	student	single, none	14	gift	gift
OH	nurse practitioner	life partner, stepson	18	process	process
PA	retail manager	ex-cohabiter, none	12	stigma	process
MN	computer programmer	single, none	18	(gift) stigma	process
CA	registered nurse	married, none	20, V2 @ 25	gift	gift
PA	student	single, none	16	process	process
PA	student	single, none	15	gift	gift
NJ	accountant	ex-cohabiter, none	19	(gift) process	process
NC/TX	student	single, none	20	gift	gift
NC	travel agent	ex-cohabiter, none	16	process	process

TABLE 1 *Profiles of Study Participants (Continued)*

Name	Age	Gender	Sexual Identity[a]	Race/ Ethnicity	Religion[b]	Social Class[c]
Daniel Levy	29	M	heterosexual	White	Jewish	middle
Kelly Lewis	24	F	heterosexual	White	Lutheran	middle
Andrew Lin	19	M	heterosexual	Chinese American	atheist	middle
Scott Lindstrom	25	M	heterosexual	White	(Baptist) none	working
Danice Marshall	28	F	heterosexual	African American	evangelical Protestant	middle
Carrie Matthews	20	F	heterosexual	White	evangelical Protestant	middle
Emma McCabe	24	F	heterosexual	White	Roman Catholic	middle
Bryan Meyers	18	M	heterosexual	White	Methodist	middle
Meghan O'Brien	22	F	heterosexual	White	Roman Catholic	middle
Kate O'Connor	24	F	heterosexual	White	(Roman Catholic) evangelical Protestant	middle
Lisa Orlofsky	35	F	lesbian	White	Jewish	middle
Cindy Passmore	32	F	heterosexual	White	Roman Catholic	working
Greg Passoli	23	M	gay	White	Roman Catholic	middle
Julie Pavlicko	25	F	heterosexual	White	fundamentalist Protestant	working
Rachel Prokopy	18	F	bisexual	White	Jewish	middle
Danielle Rice	27	F	heterosexual	White	Lutheran	middle
Miranda Rivera	29	F	lesbian	Puerto Rican	(various Protestant) Episcopalian	middle
Carlos Rodriguez	28	M	gay	Peruvian American	Roman Catholic	working
Abby Rosen	33	F	lesbian	White	Jewish	middle
Geoff Seaton	30	M	gay	White	Methodist	middle
Deborah Sherman	29	F	lesbian	White	(Unitarian) Jewish	middle
Seth Silber	19	M	gay	White	Jewish	middle
Amy Solon	20	F	lesbian	White	none	middle
Jessica Tanaka	27	F	bisexual	Japanese American	atheist	working
Lavinia Thompson	30	F	heterosexual	African American	evangelical Protestant	working
Tricia Watson	20	F	heterosexual	White	Roman Catholic	working
Ed Winters	28	M	bisexual	White	Roman Catholic	working
Susan Vigliotti	32	F	heterosexual	White	none	middle

[a] At time of interview.
[b] At time of interview, if unchanged; if changed, religion during youth is in parentheses.
[c] While growing up.

Where from?	Current Occupation	Family Status, Kids	Age at VL	Interp. (before) at VL	Current Interp.
NJ	chef	single, none	18	stigma	stigma
PA	office assistant	cohabiting, none	15	gift	gift
MO	student	single, none	16, V2 @ 19	gift	gift
MI	veterinary student	married, none	19	(gift) stigma	process
PA	nurse practitioner	cohabiting, none	16	gift	gift
PA	student	single, none	virgin	n/a	act of worship
MD	assistant editor	single, none	17	stigma	process
NY	student	single, none	16	gift	gift
MA	student	single, none	18	process	process
NJ	radio producer	single, none	16, now V2	process	act of worship (as V2)
PA	school administrator	life partner, pregnant	22	stigma	process
DE	bookkeeper	married, 2 kids	15	stigma	gift
NY/OH	nonprofit director	single, none	9	irrelevant	process
PA	counselor	single, none	15	gift	gift
SC	student	single, none	virgin	n/a	(gift) process
MD	telecommunications technician	married, 2 kids	14	gift	gift
PR	teacher	ex-cohabiter, none	21 (rape)	gift	gift
NY	nurse practitioner	ex-cohabiter, none	14	irrelevant	irrelevant
NJ	science librarian	life partner, none	20	process	process
NJ	hairdresser	cohabiting, none	5 (w/boy), 12 (w/girl)	irrelevant	irrelevant
MD	audiologist	life partner, none	19	(gift) process	process
PA	student	single, none	15	stigma	process
NY	student	single, none	virgin	n/a	(gift, stigma) process
CA	videographer	cohabiting, none	14	process	process
PA	paralegal	single, none	15	gift	gift
RI	student	single, none	13	process	process
CT	computer systems analyst	ex-cohabiter, none	16 (rape)	stigma	process
NY	psychologist	married, none	17	process	process

TABLE 2

Interpretations of Virginity at Time of Virginity Loss and Ever, by Gender

Interpretations of Virginity

	At Time of Virginity Loss[a]			Ever		
	Women	Men	Total	Women	Men	Total
Gift	42% (14)	18% (5)	31% (19)	61% (20)	36% (10)	49% (30)
Stigma	12% (4)	54% (15)	31% (19)	21% (7)	57% (16)	38% (23)
Process	42% (14)	18% (5)	31% (19)	52% (17)	61% (17)	56% (34)
Other[b]	3% (1)	11% (3)	7% (4)	6% (2)	11% (3)	8% (5)
Total[c]	99% (33)	101% (28)	100% (61)	140% (33)	165% (28)	151% (61)

[a] Figures include virgins' beliefs at time of interview.
[b] "Virginity is irrelevant" and "virginity as an act of worship."
[c] Percentages total more than 100 because some participants reinterpreted virginity over time.

TABLE 3

Interpretations of Virginity at Time of Virginity Loss and Ever,
by Sexual Identity *

Interpretations of Virginity

	At Time of Virginity Loss[a]				Ever			
	Hetero-sexual	Lesbian/Gay	Bisexual	Total	Hetero-sexual	Lesbian/Gay	Bisexual	Total[c]
Gift	38% (15)	13% (2)	33% (2)	31% (19)	54% (21)	31% (5)	67% (4)	49% (30)
Stigma	33% (13)	38% (6)	17% (1)	33% (20)	38% (15)	38% (6)	33% (2)	38% (23)
Process	27% (10)	31% (5)	50% (3)	30% (18)	46% (18)	73% (12)	67% (4)	56% (34)
Other[b]	3% (1)	19% (3)	0% (0)	7% (4)	5% (2)	19% (3)	0% (0)	8% (5)
Total[c]	101% (39)	101% (16)	100% (6)	101% (61)	143% (39)	161% (16)	167% (6)	151% (61)

* Sexual identity at time of interview.
[a] Figures include virgins' beliefs at time of interview.
[b] "Virginity is irrelevant" and "virginity as an act of worship."
[c] Percentages total more than 100 because some participants reinterpreted virginity over time.

TABLE 4

Interpretation of Virginity Ever, by Gender and Age Group

	Younger (ages 18 to 25)		Older (ages 26 to 35)	
	Women	Men	Women	Men
Gift	56% (9)	56% (9)	65% (11)	8% (1)
Stigma	25% (4)	56% (9)	18% (3)	58% (7)
Process	56% (9)	63% (10)	47% (8)	58% (7)
Total[a]	137% (16)	175% (16)	130% (17)	124% (12)

[a] Percentages total more than 100 because some participants reinterpreted virginity over time.

Notes

NOTES TO THE INTRODUCTION

1. Bernstein, 2004. Headlines cited: Jeff Barker, "A Is for Abstinence," *Baltimore Sun,* July 26, 2001; Lorraine Ali and Jule Scelfo, "Choosing Virginity," *Newsweek,* December 9, 2002; Alex Tresniowski, Shermakaye Bass, Vicki Bane, and John Slania, "Like a Virgin (Sort Of)," *People,* September 9, 2002; Tamar Lewin, "More in High School Are Virgins, Study Finds," *New York Times,* September 29, 2002; Tamar Lewin, "1 in 5 Teenagers Has Sex before 15, Study Finds," *New York Times,* May 20, 2003; Michelle Tauber et al., "Young Teens and Sex," *People,* January 31, 2005.

2. Ingrassia 1994, 59.

3. Ingrassia 1994, 64.

4. "Conservative Christian" is an umbrella term referring to conservative Protestants—denominations with evangelical and fundamentalist worldviews (e.g., Southern Baptists, Pentecostals) and doctrinally conservative groups such as Mormons and Jehovah's Witnesses—as well as to Roman Catholics with similarly conservative beliefs about social issues like abortion (Roof and McKinney 1987).

5. On changing depictions of adolescent sexuality in movies, see Douglas 1994, Lewis 1992. On virginity-loss films specifically, see Carpenter 2002.

6. The plotline involving Donna's virginity was already pronounced in 1994 (Rexfelis).

7. Singh and Darroch 1999; Ku et al. 1998; U.S. Census Bureau 2001.

8. As in a *Penthouse Forum* (1985) letter titled, "De-Virginized—Both Ways" (i.e., through vaginal and anal sex).

9. For example, when survey researchers use the term "virgin" as shorthand for people who have never had vaginal sex or when sex educators advocate abstinence as the best protection against pregnancy and STIs, they imbue virginity loss with exceptional significance.

10. Solin 1996, 93.

11. Berger and Wenger (1973, 667) proposed to treat virginity as a social category rather than as a "residual category of . . . experience," but few researchers

have followed suit. Given my interest in virginity loss as a cultural phenomenon ("What is this thing people call virginity loss?"), as well as an experience, I have chosen to retain the conventional term. That said, many study participants did not experience the transition called virginity loss as a loss of something either positive or negative.

12. Much of this literature additionally assumes that people who have had coitus once are thereafter "sexually active" (despite research indicating that first coitus is frequently isolated) and tends to ignore activities like oral and anal sex when designating who is sexually active. For a critique and alternative approach, see Singh and Darroch 1999.

13. A handful of popular volumes on virginity loss have been published (Fleming and Fleming 1975; Bouris 1993; Crosier 1993), along with a psychoanalytic volume (Holtzman and Kulish 1997) and two memoirs (McCarthy 1997; Wolf 1997). Two early monographs were poorly documented, largely speculative, and focused almost exclusively on women (de Lys 1960; Nemecek 1958).

14. Studies addressing subjective aspects of first sex among *heterosexual* women *and* men include those by Holland, Ramazanoglu, and Thomson 1996; Rubin 1990; Sprecher, Barbee, and Schwartz 1995. Studies looking at first sex among women of *various* sexual orientations include Brumberg 1997, Thompson 1995, Tolman 1994. Wight 1994 explores sexuality among heterosexual Scottish boys.

15. Foucault (1978), among others, would argue that the scientific study arises out of, and enables, the impulse to social control.

16. Berger and Wenger 1973; Bogart et al. 2000; Kelly 2000.

17. Following Carrington's (1999) example, I use the increasingly common term "lesbigay," which includes people who identify as lesbian, gay, and bisexual, as an occasional alternative to variants of the more cumbersome expression, "gay, lesbian, and bisexual."

18. Elder 1996; Hart 1995.

19. Further information about study participants and my research methods can be found in chapter 2 and the Methodological Appendix.

20. These designations by sexual identity are based on participants' self-descriptions at the time of the interview. Presumably, anyone I interviewed could reevaluate their understanding of their sexual identity at some later juncture. No one I interviewed identified as queer without also identifying as gay, lesbian, or bisexual.

21. I chose to sample according to social class and religious background, rather than current status or practice, because people typically lose their virginity while they are dependent on their parents (or newly independent). However, my analyses take current socioeconomic status and religious beliefs and practice into account. I measured social class background by parents' occupations and educational attainment.

22. More specifically, I used a theoretical sampling strategy; see Glaser and Strauss 1967, Miles and Huberman 1994.

23. I did not have the opportunity to interview anyone raised in the Muslim or Hindu religious traditions, both of which take distinctive perspectives on gender, sexuality, and virginity. See, e.g., Mernissi 1991 and Kakar 1990, respectively.

24. On the utility of comparing "typical" groups to "exceptional" ones, see Goffman 1974. Born-again virginity has been examined in the popular press (Dobie 1995; Hayt 2002) and promoted in self-help literature (Keller 1999), but has not yet been the explicit subject of empirical research. Although about a dozen participants' sexual histories included events resembling born-again virginity, I interviewed only four self-professed born-again virgins.

25. I do not presume to explore change over time, within individual lives, in the sense that a longitudinal study can. The effects of aging/maturation and generational differences are confounded in my study. Because most Americans become sexually active during adolescence, interviewing young adults rather than teenagers further ensured that most would be nonvirgins who could reflect on virginity loss in relation to earlier and later experiences.

26. Mills 1959.

27. HIV/AIDS was widely recognized as a serious health threat to gay men in 1982–83 and to heterosexuals several years later. Basketball star Magic Johnson announced he was HIV-positive in 1991.

28. See, e.g., Bruni 1998. I explore this issue further in Carpenter 2001a.

29. Twenty-two of the final 25 people I interviewed were nonvirgins.

30. The ability to extrapolate the distribution of a practice or belief in a probability-based sample to a larger defined population is called *statistical generalizability*. Alternatively, one can generalize that the meanings and processes observed in a theoretically chosen, socially diverse nonprobability-based sample will reflect those that exist in a broader social group or groups overall. Because the vagueness of qualitative expressions like "many" and "seldom" can obscure important patterns in the data, I use a combination of such words and percentage statistics. These percentages should not be taken to imply that the distribution of phenomena in my sample can be generalized to a broader population.

31. National surveys have documented modest regional differences in Americans' approaches to sexuality, with residents of the New England, Pacific, and Mid-Atlantic states exhibiting relatively permissive attitudes, whereas people from the Southern Central and Mountain states hold comparatively conservative views (Laumann et al. 1994; Klassen, Williams, and Levitt 1989). Urbanites and suburbanites also tend to be more permissive about sex than their rural counterparts. State and local control of the public school systems also contributes to regional variation in sexual socialization (Landry, Kaeser, and Richards 1999). As the majority of people I interviewed grew up in metropolitan areas in "permis-

sive" states, my findings may not fully reflect the beliefs and experiences of the most conservative Americans. However, I deliberately sought participants with conservative stances.

32. Most of the participants who made a referral offered to initiate contact with the referee on my behalf. I stopped searching for new participants only when I found that every new person I interviewed raised the same general themes that I had heard before, a phenomenon often referred to as *saturation* (Glaser and Strauss 1967).

33. See Bernard 1994, Biernacki and Waldorf 1981. Scholars have found this to be true for a wide variety of topics typically perceived as very private (e.g., Lee and Sasser-Coen 1996). Although random sampling methods have successfully been used in survey research on sexuality (e.g., Laumann et al. 1994), such techniques are less appropriate for gathering detailed subjective accounts of the most intimate aspects of sexual life. Snowball sampling also enables the researcher to identify members of groups that are not numerically common, readily "visible," or evenly distributed throughout a population, such as lesbigay women and men. To offset the potential for bias due to the relative homogeneity of most social networks, I drew on multiple snowballs (17 in all) and interviewed no more than 5 people in a given network (most contained 2 or 3 members).

34. The interview guide is available from the author on request.

35. Research suggests that people's recollections of events perceived to be especially salient or transformative tend to be more accurate than memories of everyday events (Denzin 1989a; Berk, Abramson, and Okami 1995; Lee and Sasser-Coen 1996). Limiting the upper age of study participants to 35 also helped ensure that participants would be able to recall their virginity-loss experiences in detail. The time elapsed between virginity-loss experience and interview ranged from several months to 25 years, with an average of 9 years.

36. Three gay men described virginity as irrelevant to their lives (see chapter 2), and two heterosexual born-again Christian women interpreted virginity as an act of worship (see chapter 6).

37. More specifically, I relied on the systematic procedures referred to as grounded theory (Glaser and Strauss 1967).

38. Lakoff and Johnson 1980. Metaphors are social; that is, they are shared and communicated among individuals and social groups.

39. The concept *sexual scripts* refers to the socially learned sets of sexual desires and conduct that guide people's choices about when, where, how, why, and with whom they should be sexual (Gagnon and Simon 1973, 1987). Metaphors for virginity can also be conceptualized as frames (Goffman 1974).

40. Lorber 1993.

41. Women were twice as likely as men to have ever interpreted virginity as a gift, while men were over twice as likely to have ever seen virginity as a stigma; this gender difference was more pronounced at the time of virginity loss. Men

and women were almost equally likely to have ever viewed virginity loss as a rite of passage. Lesbians and gay men were underrepresented in the gift group and overrepresented in the stigma and process groups; bisexual women and men fell somewhere in between. See Methodological Appendix for details.

42. See Weber 1946.

43. I find it useful to conceptualize metaphorical understandings of virginity loss as cultural resources (Griswold 1987) and virginity loss itself as a cultural object—one of the meaningful social symbols that make up a cultural system (Blumer 1969). Swidler (1986, 273) defines culture as the "publicly available symbolic forms through which people experience and express meaning," including formal and informal practices, skills, habits, and styles. In other words, culture is social; it does not exist before or outside of society. Cultural resources are created, perpetuated, and altered through human action.

44. On the uses of culture, see Swidler 2001.

45. Seeking to theorize how people come to trust or distrust particular understandings of the world, sociologist Andreas Glaeser (2004, 3) differentiates between *possible* understandings—those that an individual knows to exist—and *actual* understandings, those they perceive as "true, good, reliable, and right." Possible understandings become (and remain) actual when they are validated by the people and institutions an individual accepts as authorities, are corroborated through actions or events, and when they resonate with other things a person "knows." Conversely, a person confronted with repeated evidence and authorities that counter his actual understanding will tend to reject it in favor of a new one. People vary in the degree to which they are conscious of the cultural choices they make.

46. The terms "social status" and "social identity" are not precisely synonymous. Status typically refers to social-structural aspects of group membership, whereas identity refers to social-psychological dimensions. As I am interested in both aspects of group membership, I use the terms somewhat interchangeably, generally favoring identity.

47. Budgeon 2003, 104. See also Beck and Beck-Gernsheim 1996, Bradley 1996, and Giddens 1992.

48. There are, of course, limits to the identities young people can fashion through virginity loss, not least because they cannot choose their gender or their racial/ethnic, social class, or religious background (scholars disagree as to whether sexual identity is chosen or inborn) (Budgeon 2003). That said, social identity can change over a person's lifetime. Social class and religion are most volatile, but people may also refashion their racial/ethnic identity (as when an African American "passes" as White).

49. Whatever interpretation of virginity a person favors, the life event of virginity loss offers a vehicle for achieving one aspect of adult status: sexual "maturity." See chapter 7.

NOTES TO CHAPTER I

1. On *American Pie*'s box office performance, see movies.com.

2. After a friend tells Jim that having sex feels like having one's penis immersed in a warm apple pie, he experiments with a pie baked by his mother.

3. Jim is at first offended, then proud that he was desirable enough for a girl to "use" him. Neither Michelle nor Jessica is sanctioned for taking an unorthodox perspective, but the fact that Jessica remains celibate throughout the film effectively defuses her pro-pleasure approach.

4. In my reading, whether Chris and Heather have sex on prom night is left ambiguous; by the sequel, they are clearly sexual partners. The sequels construct a relatively conservative sexual narrative for Jim and Michelle, as well—they fall in love in *American Pie 2* (2001) and get married in *American Wedding* (2003). Interestingly, mutual virginity loss solidifies Vicky's resolve to break up with Kevin before she moves away for college.

5. Seidman 1991; Irvine 1994; Rubin 1990; Weeks 1985.

6. These meanings are, of course, social creations (see Introduction). On virginity cross-culturally, see Ortner 1976; Schlegel 1991, 1995.

7. This brief history is not intended to be definitive or exhaustive; however, it does represent one of the first systematic social histories of virginity loss (as opposed to sexuality or courtship more generally). In fact, I know of no comprehensive, carefully documented histories of virginity loss in the United States or elsewhere.

8. For two superb histories of sex research, see Ericksen 1999 and Irvine 1990.

9. Smith 1994; Zabin et al. 1984.

10. These research biases have been alleviated somewhat since the 1970s as scientific studies of sexuality have increasingly begun to include youth of color and (more rarely) lesbigay youth (Ericksen 1999).

11. Aries 1985; D'Emilio and Freedman 1988; Godbeer 2002.

12. Kelly 2000; Bugge 1975; Sissa 1990. Greeks and Romans also assigned virgin women important roles in religious rituals.

13. *Oxford English Dictionary* online.

14. Bugge 1975.

15. I Corinthians I, 7:7–9 (Twentieth Century New Testament). Paul described his own sexual continence as a "gift from God." Paul's flexibility undoubtedly helped win converts from pagan populations (Brown 1988). Other theologians depicted virginity as a precious, God-given "ornament" that "armed the flesh" against incontinence (Methodius 1958, 141).

16. According to the *OED*, "virgin" originally referred to women, with references to male virgins beginning around 1300. Kelly (2000) further notes that tests of virginity status also differed by gender. The gendering of virginity stems

in part from the greater potential visibility of nonvirginity in women, due to the unique signals of pregnancy and hymeneal blood, and in part from women's historic status as property transferred from fathers to husbands at marriage (Rubin 1975; Ortner 1976). See also Bugge 1975.

17. McInerney 1999, 57.

18. *Holy Maidenhood* 1991, 228, 240. The anonymous poem was written in about 1225. Elsewhere, the poet invokes a secular form of reciprocation: the "morning-gift" of money or goods customarily "made by husband to wife the morning after the consummation of their marriage" (*Hali meidhad* 1982, 72); see also (*Holy Maidenhood* 1991, 416n48). This custom appears to be Anglo-Saxon or Nordic in origin (Foote and Wilson 1970). See also the thirteenth-century poem, "Love Ron" (Kelly and Leslie 1999).

19. Rosenberg 1973; White 1993.

20. Augustine 1980, XIII.7.

21. Kelly 2000; Payer 1993.

22. Chrysostom 1986. The claim that impure thoughts could imperil chastity/virginity resurfaced to inform Victorian ideology about women's virtue.

23. Brownmiller 1975; Dworkin 1987; Vigarello 2001.

24. As in the *Glossa Palatina*, attributed to Laurentius Hispanus (died 1248), cited by Kelly 2000, 36. See also Brundage 1987.

25. Greenberg and Bystryn 1982.

26. Kelly and Leslie 1999. Medieval ideas persisted more completely in Roman Catholic areas such as Italy and Spain.

27. Harvey 1994, 123n1.

28. Kelly 1999. See Johnson's *Song: To Celia (I)* (1616), Andrew Marvell's *To His Coy Mistress* (1650–52), and John Donne's *The Flea* (1633).

29. Act I, Scene 1, lines 141–52.

30. In Britain, Cromwell's Puritan rule represented a brief detour from the broader trend.

31. Van de Walle and Muhsam 1995.

32. Cott 1978. Middle-class opinion leaders in the mid-1700s, novelists Samuel Richardson and Daniel Defoe among them, actively denounced the sexual and other excesses of their social "betters."

33. Kelly and Leslie 1999, 21. The historical record offers little insight into the lives of peasants and the urban poor, who lacked inheritance as an incentive to preserve women's virginity, but may well have valued it for religious or other reasons.

34. Hitchcock 2002, 185. Such sexual encounters appear to have been more acceptable if the man selected partners of lower social standing than himself. Likewise, in France by the mid-1600s, mutual masturbation was popular among unwed couples intent on enjoying sexual pleasure while preserving virginity and avoiding conception (van de Walle and Muhsam 1995).

35. Although the American colonists as a group were less secular than their English contemporaries, the Puritans, notorious for their very restrictive stance toward sexuality, were only one of the religious groups to found the United States, and they held little sway outside New England (Godbeer 2002).

36. D'Emilio and Freedman 1988. This sexual system was supported by a family-centered agricultural economy, in which children were valued as workers.

37. Bundling couples were sometimes also separated by a board.

38. D'Emilio and Freedman 1988; Omolade 1983.

39. D'Emilio and Freedman 1988. Companionate marriage also grew in popularity during this period, and young people were gaining greater choice over whom they married (Rothman 1984). Some historians suggest that young people used premarital pregnancy to force marriage against parental wishes (Degler 1980).

40. Smith and Hindus 1975.

41. D'Emilio and Freedman 1988, 44.

42. Rowson 1794, 27.

43. Rowson 1794, 47.

44. Rowson 1794, 66.

45. Rowson 1794, 80. Contextual cues in the book and contemporaneous historical sources leave little doubt that *honor* and *virtue* encompass virginity, and that virginity, honor, and virtue can all be lost through vaginal sex.

46. Rowson 1794, 161.

47. Rowson 1794, 29.

48. The classic work on female passionlessness is Cott 1978. According to Rothman (1984), passionlessness rather than self-control became the prevailing ideology for women because of the earlier view that women were sexually dangerous beings who could not be trusted to control their feelings, although they could deny them. The ideology was also supported by the late-1700s scientific "discoveries" that women could conceive without orgasm and that the sexes were two incommensurate biological entities rather than inverted versions of one another, both of which paved the way for envisioning women's and men's sexual natures as natural opposites (Laqueur 1990).

49. Davidson 1986, xii. The first U.S. edition of *Charlotte Temple* was published in 1794. The novel's apparent popularity with working-class women readers suggests that the perils it portrayed resonated with less-advantaged White women as well as with their middle-class counterparts. On middle-class beliefs about working-class sexuality, see Rosenberg 1973.

50. More pragmatically, this appealing alternative to the image of women as sinful temptresses helped attract new female congregants at a time of flagging religious commitment among men (Cott 1978).

51. According to Cott 1978, the other causes predate medical support for

passionlessness. On nineteenth-century medical views on women, see Barker-Benfield 2000.

52. Rosenberg 1973. For a dissenting viewpoint, see Foucault 1978.

53. Rosenberg 1973, 139.

54. Paul Paquin, a late-1800s reformer who denounced tolerance for such practices, quoted in Rosenberg 1973, 140. See also White 1993.

55. Brandt 1987.

56. Rosenberg 1973, 141; Kinsey, Pomeroy, and Martin 1948; Lindsey and Evans 1925. Publicly admitting recourse to sex workers cast aspersions on a man's character and masculinity (White 1993). In contrast to irrevocably "fallen" women, young unmarried men who failed to control their lusts were typically thought amenable to rehabilitation, thanks to the relative invisibility of their sexual indiscretions (lacking hymeneal blood and potential pregnancy) and the fact that they were not morally elevated to begin with (Mumford 1993).

57. Rothman (1984, 54) demonstrates the narrowing of the range of acceptable sexual activities over the course of the 1800s, arguing that the new focus on premarital chastity led to the "the removal of intercourse from the range of premarital sexual behavior . . . that began with hand holding in church." Rothman calls this development the "invention of petting," but evidence from the previous century suggests that the practice of stopping at "everything but" intercourse to preserve virginity was not new. See also Hitchcock 2002, Welter 1983.

58. Nathanson 1991. When a woman lost her virginity with her husband, she irrevocably lost her innocence; if she lost her virginity outside of marriage, she also forfeited her moral integrity. Men were legally entitled to break an engagement to a woman discovered not to be a virgin.

59. Smith and Hindus 1975.

60. Greenberg 1988; Seidman 1991; Smith-Rosenberg 1975.

61. In the South in particular, the image of elite White women as paragons of asexual virtue depended on a contrast with the purported promiscuity of Black *and* of nonelite White women (Hodes 1993).

62. Parent and Wallace 1993; Gutman and Sutch 1976.

63. In addition to encouraging "natural increase," slave owners sought to improve their "stock" by such means as denying puny men access to wives. Slave marriages had no legal standing.

64. Hodes 1993.

65. Omolade 1983.

66. Jones (1985) suggests that acquiring property (which could be bequeathed) may have given Black elites additional incentive for promoting stricter sexual norms, especially regarding premarital pregnancy.

67. D'Emilio and Freedman 1988; Dill 1988. The Mexican American popu-

lation created by the U.S. annexation of northern Mexico in 1848 was rapidly outnumbered by westward-bound White settlers, but continued to expand, especially with the institution of contract-labor programs starting in the late 1800s.

68. Espiritu 2000. Between 1850 and 1934, nearly one million Chinese, Japanese, Koreans, Filipinos, and Indians immigrated to the United States, most of them men recruited for manual labor in the West. "Importing" Asian women as sex workers was officially prohibited in 1875.

69. The competing stereotype of Asian women as servile "lotus blossoms" emerged somewhat later.

70. Dreiser 1900, 90.

71. Although many critics initially denounced *Sister Carrie* as an affront to conventional morality, within a few years the novel was reissued to "wide acclaim," suggesting that middle-class America had begun to acknowledge, if not embrace, the changes taking place (Lingeman 2000, xviii).

72. These migrants were disproportionately single and widowed women (Jones 1985).

73. Nathanson 1991. These changes were facilitated by the declining need for young women's help in the home, due to shrinking family sizes and more efficient housekeeping technology. Most single White working women lived with family members.

74. Peiss 1986; Seidman 1991.

75. Bailey 1989.

76. Necking was popularly defined as sexual contact above the waist, petting as contact below the waist. Modell (1983) suggests that uncertainty about the degree of commitment implied by kissing lingered well into the 1920s.

77. In the mid-1800s, one in ten marriages was preceded by conception, compared to one in four between 1880 and 1910 (Smith and Hindus 1975). Comparable data are not available for Blacks. White youths' premarital sexual exploration was limited largely by the value on premarital virginity, especially in women, whereas working-class Blacks' was limited more by parental chaperonage (D'Emilio and Freedman 1988; Parent and Wallace 1993).

78. The crowded living conditions in which most immigrants lived often meant that children were exposed to parents' sex lives and that courting took place in public. Native-born critics discounted the possibility that these practices might result from material circumstance rather than inherent depravity.

79. White reformers established dozens of institutions for saving girls from sexual "waywardness" and in many states succeeded in raising the age of sexual consent for women from as low as 10 to 14, 16, or higher (Nathanson 1991). Anthony Comstock's crusade to curtail the circulation of "obscene" literature, such as pulp novels and story magazines, culminated in the passage of a 1873 federal law prohibiting the U.S. postal service from carrying "indecent" materials (Beisel 1997). Popularly known as the Comstock Act, this law had the inci-

dental effect of limiting access to information about birth control (Gordon 1974). Efforts to eradicate prostitution bore little fruit until the mid-1910s, when opponents' focus shifted to eradicating venereal disease (Brandt 1987; Pivar 2002). Neither the White- nor the Black-led movements achieved total success, nor did their offspring, progressivism (Seidman 1991).

80. Social purists opposed artificial birth control on the grounds that it would facilitate men's extramarital affairs and erode the authority women derived from motherhood (Gordon 1974). The increasingly powerful medical profession also opposed abortion and birth control.

81. Hodes 1993; Omolade 1983. Lynching raged from Emancipation through the early 1900s. Black women's activism in this period should be understood not as an attempt to mimic White women, although they shared purity crusaders' belief that women's innate moral superiority could be harnessed to improve men, but rather as part of a long-standing tradition of working to defend and improve life in the Black community (Jones 1985).

82. Rothman 1984; Kinsey, Pomeroy, and Martin 1948.

83. White 1993, 9. See also Mumford 1993.

84. Omolade 1983; DuBois 1899.

85. Faderman 1981.

86. Seidman 1991.

87. White 1993; Carby 1990.

88. Marks 1924, 6–7.

89. Marks 1924, 66, 58, 13.

90. Marks 1924, 11, 22, 53.

91. Marks 1924, 53.

92. Marks 1924, 165, 53.

93. Marks 1924, 155–56. See also White 1993. Hugh is "ashamed" to reveal his own standards (53). Still, his friends, far from teasing him, go to great lengths to protect his virtue.

94. Marks 1924, 249.

95. Marks 1924, 255.

96. Bailey 1989; Modell 1983.

97. The first quote comes from the University of Chicago's Paul Cressey (cited in White 1993, 87); the second is from White's (1993, 88) analysis of such researchers' work. Urban sociologies of the 1910s strongly suggest that White working-class boys and men saw sexual inexperience at marriage as highly undesirable and sexual activity as proof of masculinity.

98. This redefinition was part of a broader shift, beginning in the late nineteenth century, toward treating all manner of social "problems," including sexuality, as medical, rather than moral, matters (Nathanson 1991; Tiefer 1995; Conrad 1992).

99. D'Emilio and Freedman 1988; Gordon 1974; Nathanson 1991. The shift

from an agricultural to industrial economy meant that families "needed" fewer children to survive.

100. Seidman 1991. If African Americans perceived a crisis in the Black family, they saw it as stemming from poverty, racism, and the actions of White eugenicists (see below).

101. Hannah Stone and Abraham Stone, *A Marriage Manual,* 1939, quoted in Seidman (1991, 76). However, experts cautioned against seeing sex as an end in itself. The first converts to these theories were intellectuals and the medical community, starting around 1890.

102. Nathanson 1991.

103. Bromley and Britten 1938, 124; Butterfield 1939, 49, 89.

104. Mead 1939. See chapter 5.

105. Bromley and Britten 1938, 92.

106. Bromley and Britten 1938, 92.

107. Bromley and Britten 1938, 175.

108. Bromley and Britten 1938, 85. See also Newcomb 1937.

109. Haag 1993, 164.

110. Havelock Ellis, quoted in Haag 1993, 180–81. See also Brandt 1987.

111. Freud 1908, 197.

112. White 1993, 49; Bromley and Britten 1938, 144.

113. Bromley and Britten 1938, 60.

114. Bromley and Britten 1938.

115. Ellis 1951, 31. Ellis's compendium of American sexual folklore draws heavily on examples from the 1920s and 1930s.

116. According to Bailey (1989), dating first spread beyond its working-class origins to elite urban youth drawn to the privacy from families it offered and to the air of decadence surrounding the practice. By about 1930, dating was the norm among youth from all social strata (Modell 1983).

117. The recognition of adolescence had already been well under way when psychologist G. Stanley Hall published his landmark study, *Adolescence,* in 1904. Three-fourths of American youth were enrolled in high school in the 1920s. Deferment of marriage was recommended by adults keen on protecting "endangered" adolescents. Middle-class youth tended to perceive generation, not gender, as the central division in social life (Bailey 1989).

118. Bailey (1989) argues that the automobile, while indubitably allowing couples more privacy, accelerated rather than catalyzed ongoing changes in sexual behavior.

119. DuBois 1899.

120. Jones 1985.

121. As novelist Jessie Fauset (1928) put it, middle-class African Americans were enjoined to keep their "pearl of great price untarnished" (66). The sex-affirming lyrics of Black women blues singers notwithstanding, the bulk of empiri-

cal evidence suggests that few young Black women achieved genuine sexual lib-eration in the early twentieth century (DuCille 1993; Omolade 1983; though see Carby 1990). Black community leaders' concern was exacerbated by the proxim-ity of Black neighborhoods to vice districts. Asian Americans in West Coast cities reported similar difficulties in sheltering young community members from "vice" and racism.

122. Joyner and Laumann 2001.

123. On Blacks in the urban north, see Drake and Cayton 1945, Frazier 1932; on the rural South, see Johnson 1941.

124. Bailey 1989.

125. Lynd and Lynd 1929. Couples at such parties would pair up and neck (or more) in semiprivacy (e.g., at the host's home with lights dimmed).

126. Parent and Wallace 1993, 27.

127. *Technical virginity*, sometimes called *demi-virginity* or *half virginity*, does not appear in any dictionary I have consulted. The first uses I have found occur in the 1920s, in novels and academic papers (e.g., de Lys 1960). The latter expressions appear to have died out in the 1970s.

128. Hecht 1921, 189–90. See also Bromley and Britten 1938. Technical vir-gins who were motivated by passion or love were typically viewed in a positive light—Hugh Carver and Cynthia Day are prime examples—but those who acted out of mercenary intent could be judged harshly.

129. Rates of premarital virginity loss were higher among African American men than White men (Joyner and Laumann 2001). About one-fourth of Ameri-cans had premarital sex in 1919; between one-third and one-half did by the mid-1960s (Gebhard 1980).

130. Kinsey et al. 1953. Worried parents, physicians, and educators re-sponded by imposing curfews and parietal rules and by developing marriage manuals and college family life courses that depicted sexual fulfillment in mar-riage as dependent on premarital chastity (Bailey 1989; Moran 2000).

131. Omolade 1983, 372. See also Hine 1988.

132. On discretion, see Brumberg 1997, Rubin 1990. On contraception, see Gordon 1974. Under Margaret Sanger's leadership, birth control became widely available to *married* women by the 1930s, thus enabling them to explore the erotic side of sex.

133. Kinsey, Pomeroy, and Martin 1948; Lindsey and Evans 1925.

134. D'Emilio and Freedman 1988, 226. The shift from moral to medical un-derstandings of homosexuality was part of the broader late-1800s trend toward medicalization. The new belief that all people were inherently sexual meant that relationships between same-sex partners could no longer be presumed asexual, which rendered them increasingly unacceptable in mainstream opinion.

135. Greenberg 1988; Seidman 1991.

136. Duberman 1991; Katz 1992. These subcultures/communities had begun

to coalesce in cities like San Francisco, Boston, Chicago, and New York between 1880 and the First World War.

137. E.g., Bromley and Britten 1938, 124.

138. Bailey 1989, 153n73; Trowbridge 1952.

139. Bailey 1989; Rothman 1984.

140. Bailey 1989.

141. Such sites would eventually be immortalized in nostalgic media productions like the movie *American Graffiti* (1973) and television series *Happy Days* (aired 1974–84).

142. "Shaping the '60s . . . Foreshadowing the '70s," *Ladies Home Journal,* January 1962, quoted in Ehrenreich, Hess, and Jacobs (1986, 25). See also Moran's (2000) discussion of sex educator Mary Calderone and contemporaries.

143. Sowing wild oats might acceptably include virginity loss, provided the young man remained discreet and didn't sully a good girl's reputation in the process.

144. Such rules were seen as increasingly necessary from the late 1940s onward, as youth were deemed more likely to transgress sexual boundaries (Bailey 1989). Early marriage was especially appealing for working-class youth, whose families lived in smaller, more crowded homes and who rarely enjoyed the respite offered by residential college life (Rubin 1976).

145. Mace 1949, 101.

146. Similar patterns prevail in better-known films of the era, such as *A Summer Place* (1959), *Splendor in the Grass* (1959), and *Where the Boys Are* (1961).

147. According to the National Health and Social Life Survey (Laumann et al. 1994), 22 percent of men and 48 percent of women born between 1930 and 1944 had vaginal sex for the first time with their spouse.

148. Kinsey, Pomeroy, and Martin 1948; Kinsey et al. 1953; Nathanson and Schoen 1993; Weinberg and Williams 1980; Rubin 1976.

149. Joyner and Laumann 2001.

150. Scholars disagree as to whether the changes of this period represent a true revolution or the culmination of decades of gradual change. Compare, e.g., D'Emilio and Freedman 1988 to Seidman 1991 and Weeks 1985.

151. Ericksen 1999; Moran 2000.

152. Just under half of the women who married by age 25 had sex before marriage; rates were higher among women who married later (Kinsey et al. 1953, 287). Over 60 percent of men with at least a high school education, and 90 percent of men with less education, had sex before marriage (Kinsey, Pomeroy, and Martin 1948).

153. On problems with Kinsey's statistics, ostensibly the source of the widely cited statistic that one in ten Americans is gay, and for an alternative estimate of the proportion of lesbigay Americans, see Laumann et al. 1994.

154. D'Emilio and Freedman 1988; Katz 1992. Expanded opportunities for

lesbigay people and Cold War rhetoric linking homosexuality and communism prompted intensified oppression, including Eisenhower's 1953 executive order barring gay men and lesbians from federal employment. Gay bars began appearing in cities in the 1940s, and various "interest societies" (e.g., the Mattachine Society and Daughters of Bilitis), precursors of later activist organizations, were founded in the 1950s.

155. Raymond 1994; Herdt and Boxer 1993. Historical patterns are difficult to establish with certainty, as data on the sequencing of sexual initiation with same- and other-sex partners are rare.

156. Seidman 1991; Weeks 1985. The consumer economy, mass media, and advertising industry grew rapidly in the 1950s and 1960s. Whereas mainstream news sources generally discouraged extensive treatments of sexual topics, detailed coverage of the Kinsey Reports could be justified by their scientific status (D'Emilio and Freedman 1988).

157. Quoted in Leff and Simmons 1990, 194. Official Hollywood reaction to *Moon* strongly echoes critical reaction to *Sister Carrie*.

158. These media's early 1960s successors, like the best-selling novels *The Last Picture Show* (Larry McMurtry 1966) and *Summer of '42* (Herman Raucher 1965), likewise reflected and helped perpetuate the belief that premarital virginity was shameful in men.

159. Brown 1962, 225.

160. Brown 1962, 67.

161. The economic prosperity, earlier marriages, and pro-natalist sentiment that followed the Second World War helped bring about the baby boom (Bailey 1989; Seidman 1991).

162. Craig 2002.

163. Gagnon and Simon 1987; Joyner and Laumann 2001.

164. Muuss 1970; Modell, Furstenberg, and Herschberg 1976; Jessor and Jessor 1975.

165. Hofferth, Kahn, and Baldwin 1987; Sherwin and Corbett 1985. The Pill and the IUD became widely available to young, unmarried women in the late 1960s; the legalization of abortion in 1973 also facilitated women's sexual freedom (Gordon 1974).

166. Ehrenreich, Hess, and Jacobs 1986; Connell 1995.

167. Moffatt 1987; Reiss 1967.

168. Rubin 1990, 46. See also *Time* 1973.

169. Brumberg 1997; Thompson 1990; Tolman 1994.

170. Hofferth, Kahn, and Baldwin 1987; Joyner and Laumann 2001. A lack of data on Asian Americans prevents assessing trends over time. Analyses of trends in adolescent sexuality typically focus on attitudes about premarital sex and the ages at which youth first engage in vaginal sex (the most common definition of virginity loss but, as I have shown, not necessarily equivalent).

171. Joyner and Laumann 2001. Mahay, Laumann, and Michaels (2001) find that although the majority of men and women at every educational level favor relational sex, college-educated men and women are more likely to take a recreational stance than their less-well-educated counterparts.

172. Upchurch et al. 1998.

173. Mahay, Laumann, and Michaels 2001. A comparable analysis is not available for Asian Americans.

174. Working-class and poor teens are therefore more likely to experience unintended pregnancy (Brewster 1994; Nathanson and Schoen 1993). There is, however, some evidence that the effects of race and ethnicity outweigh those of class among Black and Latino boys, who often feel they must prove their masculinity through sexual prowess (Anderson 1995; Lauritsen 1994; Upchurch et al. 1998).

175. Herold and Goodwin 1981; Schecterman and Hutchinson 1991. Bromley and Britten (1938) observed, but did not name, a similar phenomenon among college women in the 1930s.

176. Gagnon and Simon 1987. Unmarried men receiving fellatio, presumably from prostitutes, were an exception to this rule. Kinsey and colleagues' data (1948, 1953) suggest that oral sex was fairly common among White, well-educated married couples starting in the 1930s.

177. Newcomer and Udry 1985; Thompson 1990.

178. *Dear Abby* column, January 10, 1983, quoted in Jones et al. 1984, 10.

179. Prior to the Stonewall era, "coming out" had referred to acknowledging one's homosexuality only to oneself and to other members of the lesbigay community (Cain 1993).

180. Faludi 1991; Seidman 1992; Luker 1996.

181. Dworkin 1981; MacKinnon 1989.

182. Vance 1984; Willis 1992.

183. Shalit 1999; Roiphe 1993.

184. Johnson 2002. Kamen (2000) found that many nonfeminists of the same generation shared this "both/and" position.

185. The amendment, which died in the House of Representatives, would "define marriage as strictly between a man and a woman, invalidate all state and local domestic partnership laws and nullify civil rights protections based on marital status" (American Civil Liberties Union). It was reintroduced, but did not come to a vote, in summer 2004.

186. Herdt and Boxer 1993.

187. Ku et al. 1998; Singh and Darroch 1999.

188. Holland, Ramazanoglu, and Thomson 1996; Sprecher, Barbee, and Schwartz 1995; Thompson 1995; Wight et al. 2000.

NOTES TO CHAPTER 2

1. This was the first question I asked in every interview. I have changed names and some identifying details throughout the text and tables to protect the identities of the people I interviewed.

2. I did not ask separate questions about fellatio and cunnilingus, nor did I inquire specifically about perceptions of giving versus receiving oral sex. Participants' remarks at other points in the interview indicated that some people believed that giving oral or anal sex would result in virginity loss, whereas others maintained that only a recipient could lose her or his virginity. To the best of my knowledge, only one previous study has explicitly investigated young people's own definitions of virginity loss (Berger and Wenger 1973). On the definitional ambiguity of "sex," see Sanders and Reinisch 1999, Bogart et al. 2000.

3. Five of the 12 heterosexuals who adopted a lesbigay-inclusive definition of virginity loss said they did so because of discussions with lesbigay friends or because of professional training.

4. Rich 1980. This pattern also reflects the widespread tendency, described by anthropologist Gayle Rubin (1984), for social groups to place sexual activities in a moral hierarchy, with vaginal sex occupying the place of honor.

5. A number of radical lesbian feminists have taken a similar stance, claiming that virginity among women who have had sex only with other women is potentially transgressive (Dworkin 1987; Jo 1993; Kitzinger and Wilkinson 1994).

6. Raymond 1994. These men were born in 1967 and 1969, and therefore were teenagers in the early 1980s. None of the younger gay men or any of the lesbians, concurred that virginity was inherently irrelevant to lesbigay sexuality.

7. Given the prevalence of anti-gay sentiment in the United States overall, heterosexual participants' stance on same-sex virginity loss is striking; it may be due in part to the relatively high level of education among respondents overall and their metropolitan mid-Atlantic location (education, metropolitan residence, and north/mid-Atlantic location being positively associated with tolerance for sexual diversity) (Laumann et al. 1994). Heterosexuals born between 1973 and 1980 were much more likely than their older counterparts to believe that same-sex virginity loss was possible for both women and men (86 percent and 56 percent, respectively).

8. A few people mentioned acquaintances who felt otherwise; and several women who worked in health-care professions recalled female patients from South Asia and Africa who feared that a pelvic exam would compromise their virginity.

9. Quoted in Bailey 1989, 80.

10. Twenty-nine percent of those who hadn't engaged in oral sex before vaginal sex saw oral sex as resulting in virginity loss, compared with 13 percent of those who had experienced oral sex before coitus.

11. Fourteen of the 36 nonvirgin heterosexuals had engaged in oral or anal sex on repeated occasions with at least one partner prior to their virginity-loss partner; another seven had manual sex regularly with pre-virginity-loss partners. A few referred to themselves as technical virgins. For lesbigay participants, kissing and bodily and genital touching were the primary forms of foreplay.

12. Ali and Scelfo 2002; Jarrell 2000. Despite a dearth of historic data on fellatio and cunnilingus among U.S. adolescents, popular commentators have speculated that oral sex is becoming increasingly common among youth, either because they have adopted Clinton's definition of oral sex as "not sex" (and thus may engage in it while remaining virgins) or because media coverage of the impeachment introduced teens to the practice (making them interested in trying it). It may also be that, since Clinton-Lewinsky, adults have a greater propensity to perceive oral sex—among teens or anyone—as real sex, and thus have become concerned about it. The Clinton controversy has had the welcome effect of encouraging more social scientists to specify which physical acts they're referring to when they talk about "sex" or "virginity loss" (e.g., Bearman and Brückner 2001).

13. The one virgin gay man expected to lose his virginity through anal sex with another man, the one virgin lesbian through oral sex with another woman, and the one virgin bisexual woman through vaginal sex with a man. This gender difference appears to result from the tendency of lesbian and bisexual women to come out at later ages than their male counterparts (Savin-Williams 2003).

14. In 1995, for instance, the average age at first vaginal sex for teens in Los Angeles County was 16.6 for White boys and girls, 15.0 for Black boys, 16.3 for Black girls, 16.5 for Latinos, 17.3 for Latinas, and over 18 for Asian Americans (Upchurch et al. 1998).

15. Herdt and Boxer 1993.

16. Yet, surprisingly, the one man and one woman who had been raped by acquaintances when they were virgins did not apply their own definitions to themselves; they both described themselves as having lost their virginity when they were raped.

17. Brownmiller 1975; McCaughey 1997.

18. Darling, Davidson, and Passarello 1992; Holland, Ramazanoglu, and Thomson 1996; Rubin 1990; Sprecher, Barbee, and Schwartz 1995.

19. Sanders and Reinisch 1999.

NOTES TO CHAPTER 3

1. Bream 1998.

2. March 1999 interview, quoted in *Houston Chronicle* 2000.

3. Smoron 1999; Strauss 1991.

4. *Pittsburgh Post-Gazette* 2000.

5. Renfrew 2000.

6. Knight 2000.

7. The criteria for determining the worth of any particular gift appear to be fairly universal (Belk and Coon 1993). Gifts are more valuable if they are unique (an original painting), carry symbolic value (a diamond "is forever"), comprise the giver's time or activities (home-baked cookies), or can be seen as an extension of the giver's self (a kidney). Also valuable are gifts that involve the sacrifice of the giver's pleasure or goals in favor of the partner's. Virginity's uniqueness may make it an ideal sacrificial gift.

8. Reported in the British magazine, *Celebrate,* quoted in *Houston Chronicle* 2000.

9. Reported in the *San Francisco Chronicle,* quoted in *Houston Chronicle* 2000.

10. Singh and Darroch 1999.

11. Gold 2001.

12. Joyce 2002; Helligar 2002.

13. Oldenburg 2002.

14. Tauber, Gold, and Leger 2002, 50.

15. Haskell 2003. The juicier bits of the interview were picked up by the Associated Press.

16. This chapter's analysis draws primarily on the work of Mauss 1925, Schwartz 1967, and Gouldner 1960. See also Blau 1964 and Levi-Strauss 1969. In his classic treatise on gift exchange, Mauss marshaled evidence from Western and non-Western cultures to argue that gift giving possesses a similar structure and function wherever it occurs, challenging earlier scholars' assumption that gifts in "primitive" societies represented a form of commerce, as distinct from the spontaneous and ulterior-motive-free gifts in their own "civilized" cultures. For critiques of Mauss, see Parry 1986.

17. Exchanging gifts of similar value is seen as ideal. A person who responds to the present of a ruby bracelet with a paperback novel, for instance, will have failed to "repay" the initial gift. "Overpaying" with an excessively large gift would be no more appropriate, as it would place the recipient's partner too deeply in his debt.

18. Alternatively, exchanging a series of gifts, each slightly more valuable than the last, tends to increase interpersonal indebtedness. Reciprocating a gift with an identical item is frowned upon, because doing so effectively cancels the obligation to reciprocate, defeating the development of social ties that gift exchange is meant to foster (Schwartz 1967).

19. Mauss 1925, 10–11.

20. In societies more homogeneous than the contemporary United States and in which there is a stronger consensus on sexual standards, it may be easier to bring successful sanctions against partners who fail to reciprocate (Lindisfarne

1994; Rubin 1976). In the homogeneous societies Mauss analyzed, the structure of gift giving tended to empower the giver via the recipient's debt to him or her.

21. Like Spears, Shields as an adolescent simultaneously embodied youthful innocence and adult sexuality. She rose to fame playing a child prostitute who sold her virginity in Louis Malle's 1978 film *Pretty Baby,* and spent the early 1980s as sultry spokesgirl for Calvin Klein jeans, proclaiming "Nothing comes between me and my Calvins" (Maurstad 1996). Yet Shields also likened her virginity to a gift intended for her future husband. "Being a virgin is nothing to be ashamed of. It's sacred," she told *Redbook* magazine (McCaughey 1991). As a young adult, she encouraged other women to follow her example and, even at the ripe old age of 30, shied away from publicly admitting that she and tennis champion Andre Agassi were lovers (*South China Morning Post* 1995).

22. Until very recently, laws accordingly treated rape as a property crime against a father/husband, rather than as a sexual crime against the woman herself. On women's status as the property of fathers and husbands, see Rubin 1975, Ortner 1976. On rape and virginity historically, see Brownmiller 1975, Dworkin 1987.

23. The gift metaphor dovetails with traditional beliefs about gender in other areas of social life, such as the notions that women are natural nurturers, inherently different from men, and ought to place family before other concerns.

24. Two-fifths (14) of the women I interviewed saw virginity as a gift at the time of their own virginity loss, as did one-fifth (5) of the men, two of whom were virgins at the time of the interview. Three-fifths (20) of women and one-third (10) of men had ever likened virginity to a gift. Women's greater tendency to interpret virginity as a gift is consistent with the tendency for women but not men to interpret sexual acts of all kinds as gifts (Gilfoyle, Wilson, and Brown 1993).

25. Kelly and her friends particularly identified with Katherine Danziger, the heroine of Judy Blume's popular teen novel, *Forever* (1975). Nearly one-fourth of the women I interviewed, across all interpretive groups, mentioned *Forever* as a source of information about virginity loss. Continually in print since 1975, *Forever* tells the story of high school senior Katherine's decision to lose her virginity, which she perceives as a gift, with her beloved boyfriend, Michael. Although she eventually decides to end the relationship, Katherine has no regrets. Less pleasant fates befall female characters who approach sex casually, however.

26. Only three people in the study had actively tried to remain virgins until marriage. Two saw virginity as a gift, while the third viewed it as an act of worship (see chapter 6). One of the three lost her virginity with a man she expected to marry (but did not); the other two were virgins when I interviewed them. This relative disinterest in confining virginity loss to marriage reflects broader social trends, including steadily increasing ages at first marriage (which make it harder

to wait) and growing approval of all forms of nonmarital sex, and stands in dramatic contrast to the beliefs espoused by the White working-class teen women Thompson (1984) interviewed in the early 1980s, as well as the typical stance among women who came of age before the sexual revolution (Bell and Coughey 1980; Gagnon and Simon 1987; Rubin 1990).

27. Kevin Cleary, a 22-year-old, heterosexual White college senior, had, subsequent to losing his own virginity (which he'd seen as a stigma), started dating a devout Roman Catholic who convinced him that sex should be reserved for couples who were betrothed or (ideally) spouses.

28. Kelly had lived with her mother and stepfather, who introduced the family to the Lutheran church. As an adult, Kelly considered herself religious even though she went to church only on holidays.

29. Belk and Coon 1993. In contrast with Kelly, some people, such as Danielle Rice, described virginity as a lost or transferred part of the self: "something private a woman gives up."

30. On the extended self, see especially Belk and Coon 1993; see also Fox and Swazey 1978 on the literally shared self involved in organ transplants.

31. Schwartz 1967.

32. Haskell 2003.

33. Of the nonvirgins in this group, only three had not been in love with their virginity-loss partners; two of the exceptions had liked their partners very much, one had been raped by a friend.

34. Everyone in this group told their virginity-loss partner that they were a virgin. The majority recalled discussing their virginity openly with friends, and none sought deliberately to conceal it.

35. Six of the 17 nonvirgins in this group reported close calls, as did one of two virgins.

36. Ten of 17 reported mutual virginity loss.

37. Fine 1988; Horowitz 1983; Lees 1986; Thompson 1990.

38. These figures exclude the highest and lowest outlier in each group.

39. Only one bisexual man, one lesbian, and one bisexual woman had seen virginity as a gift at the time of their virginity loss. A virgin gay man also viewed virginity as a gift. One gay man, two lesbians, and two bisexual women had held but rejected the gift perspective prior to virginity loss.

40. The stories of the lesbigay women and men who *did* favor the gift metaphor closely resembled those of their heterosexual counterparts.

41. Like many people, he means vaginal penetration, but sees this as so obvious that he doesn't feel the need to specify further.

42. Study participants of every interpretive stripe noted similar patterns, as have scholars (e.g., Thompson 1984).

43. When I asked what he meant by horror stories, Bryan cited his worst-case scenario: "party situations" in which "virgins . . . hoo[k] up with people

that they didn't even want to have sex with . . . and it's terrible because . . . it's just not special."

44. Faderman 1993; Levine 1995.

45. Ehrenreich, Hess, and Jacobs 1986; Rubin 1990. Women of this generation are responsible for launching third-wave feminism (Kamen 2000).

46. On "new" masculinities, see Connell 1995, Kimmel 1995.

47. Recent studies show corresponding increases in the average age at which boys first have vaginal sex and in the proportion of boys who disapprove of premarital sex (Ku et al. 1998; Sonenstein et al. 1998).

48. Thornton and Camburn 1989; Brewster et al. 1998; Meier 2003.

49. Sprecher, Barbee, and Schwartz (1995) compared young people who were 17 and older when they first had vaginal sex to those who were 16 and younger.

50. Kinsman et al. 1998; Billy and Udry 1985b.

51. Thompson 1990.

52. Most of the people who saw virginity as a gift and were generally satisfied with the way they lost theirs, like Karen and Kelly, were willing, even eager, to share the news with their close friends.

53. Laumann et al. 1994.

54. Landry, Kaeser, and Richards 1999.

55. Of the remaining four, two spoke of maintaining virginity as an act of worship and two had left the church as teenagers, around which time they'd begun to see virginity as a stigma. Two of the ten had become conservative Protestants as adults.

56. Belk and Coon 1993. This interpretation makes sense either assuming that Scott himself saw virginity as a gift or (more likely) that he believed that Julie did; or if he assumed (as many people do) that women always bleed when they lose their virginity, and, when he didn't see physical signs, he assumed the worst.

57. A person who gives an initial gift takes a particular risk, for she and her chosen recipient have set no precedent of ongoing exchange (Mauss 1925).

58. This practice can be interpreted either as a type of direct reciprocation or as a form of indirect reciprocation in which each person gives to a member of her social group, expecting to receive from a different member (Mauss 1925).

59. Compared with those who believe, like Kelly Lewis, that the part is merely shared. See note 30 above.

60. The other three women's stories closely resemble Julie's. It was not always clear from the interviews whether these young men drew on specific knowledge about their girlfriends' beliefs or on the common assumption that women view virginity as a gift.

61. On gender and sexual agency during adolescence and/or at sexual initia-

tion, see Holland, Ramazanoglu, and Thomson 1996, Laumann et al. 1994, Thompson 1995, Tolman 1994, Wight et al. 2000.

62. This was true across interpretive stances.

63. Alternatively, they may have been reluctant to challenge beliefs they'd held from very early ages, simply preferred taking a traditionally feminine stance, or told me what they thought I wanted to hear from women.

64. One of these three, Charlotte Brandt, wasn't disappointed with her virginity-loss experience, but rather found herself, immediately afterwards, in a context where the kinds of relationships she wanted were impossible (a college campus where casual sex was the norm). She felt that calling herself a born-again virgin made her abstinence easier to explain.

65. Eleven out of 19 gifters (including virgins) maintained that virginity was renewable, compared with 7 of 19 processers and 5 of 19 stigmatized (all of whom had adopted the process frame by the time of our interview). I discuss the fourth born-again virgin, who viewed virginity as an act of worship, in chapter 6.

66. On Asians' and Asian Americans' tendency toward reticence around sexuality, see Espiritu 2000, Takagi 1996.

67. Bryan described the male-female divide in his high school as less absolute, perhaps because of his involvement with the virginity-friendly coed AIDS-awareness group.

68. Referring to the award-winning 1968 film *The Graduate,* in which 21-year-old Benjamin Braddock (Dustin Hoffman) has an affair and loses his virginity with 40-something Mrs. Robinson (Anne Bancroft).

69. See, e.g., Martin 1998, Komter 1989, Blumstein and Schwartz 1983.

70. Aneshensel, Fielder, and Becerra 1989; Thompson 1995.

71. Zerubavel (1996) discusses the tendency to dichotomize and the perceived differences between having sex zero and one times, versus one and two times.

72. Two-thirds of gifters who lost their virginity under nonideal circumstances found secondary virginity plausible, compared with less than two-fifths of gifters whose experiences were nearly ideal. People whose first experiences were "perfect" simply might not have seen second chances as helpful, and may even have seen them as threatening their own perspectives on virginity.

73. Chan 1994; Cochran, Mays, and Leung 1991; Meston, Trapnell, and Gorzalka 1996; Upchurch et al. 1998.

74. Such conservatism and reticence should not be confused with the stereotype of asexuality often misattributed to Asian Americans (Espiritu 2000).

75. Steele 1999; Sutton et al. 2002.

76. This is not to suggest that Hispanic cultures are unitary; however, empirical research indicates that certain beliefs and practices transcend intragroup diversity (Espin 1984; Raffaelli and Ontai 2001).

77. On African American women interpreting virginity in ways consistent with the gift metaphor, see Anderson 1995, Sterk-Elifson 1994, White 1999, Mahay, Laumann, and Michaels 2001. Scholars have traced Black women's relatively conservative sexual beliefs in part to their participation in conservative Protestant churches (at high rates nationwide), and in part to Black families' efforts to socialize their daughters to adopt sexual standards that counteract popular stereotypes denigrating them as promiscuous. Wyatt (1997) points out that Black women's beliefs and behavior around early sexuality have been obscured by researchers' tendency to neglect middle-class and affluent Blacks.

78. The links between social identity and approaches to virginity may remain stronger in the South and western Midwest, where gender norms are more traditional, Christian beliefs more conservative and pervasive, and public school systems less likely to provide comprehensive sex education (Landry, Kaeser, and Richards 1999; Laumann et al. 1994; Rice and Coates 1995).

79. National studies tracking changing ages at first vaginal sex and attitudes about premarital sex also indicate such a trend (Ku et al. 1998; Sonenstein et al. 1998), as do a handful of studies exploring subjective aspects of adolescent sexuality (Risman and Schwartz 2002; Sprecher and Regan 1996).

80. The close parent-child relationships reported by many members of this group may have disposed them toward adopting their parents' ideals. Previous studies have shown that adolescents' beliefs about sexuality tend to resemble those of their parents, with relatively conservative parents raising relatively conservative children, and religious youth subscribing to more conservative sexual beliefs and behaviors than their more secular peers (Thornton and Camburn 1989; Meier 2003).

81. On peer influence over sexual beliefs and behavior, which tends to increase over the course of adolescence as parental influence declines, see Jessor and Jessor 1975; DeLamater 1987; Herold and Goodwin 1981. Billy and Udry (1985a, 1985b) found somewhat different peer-influence patterns by race and gender. Teens' sexual beliefs and behavior typically resemble those of their closest friends, in part because of socialization and in part because teens acquire friends who share their sexual status.

82. The women and men I interviewed did, however, feel free to reject the traditional Christian injunction to reserve sex/virginity loss for marriage; this may reflect a (perhaps uniquely American) "this religion but done my way" approach toward religious doctrine.

83. See also Omolade 1983, Wyatt 1997. Tolman (1996) found a similar pattern among urban Latinas, who are also popularly viewed as promiscuous.

1. All quotes in this section from E-Bay Sucks (n.d.); Wylie 1999; Reiter 1999; *New York Post* 1999.

2. Another version of the story circulated in which Cornworth's virginity drew only embarrassingly low bids.

3. Wylie 1999.

4. The possibility of the commercial exploitation of virginity prompted much outcry from moral conservatives in the case of another virginity-related Internet hoax, in July 1998, when two alleged 18-year-olds, Mike and Diane, announced their plan to lose their mutual virginity live on the Web on August 4, 1998.

5. Goffman 1963, 3. The stigmatizing process unfolds in the same manner whether the deviant attribute is actually perceived or merely inferred. Social discrediting hinges on the distinction between actual and virtual social identity; a person is discredited when their actual identity (who they really are) is discrepant from their virtual identity (who they appear to be). We generally assume that the people we meet are what they appear to be, lacking concrete reasons to think otherwise (Goffman 1959).

6. Such labeling often entails negative stereotyping (Heatherton et al. 2000). The stereotypes associated with a stigma are often interpreted as evidence of the stigma. For instance, virgin men are often derogated as unpopular, unattractive, and effeminate; those traits, conversely, may be viewed as indicating a man's virginity.

7. Goffman 1963.

8. Goffman (1963) distinguishes between *passing* (deliberate concealment) and *covering* (using subtle strategies to minimize a stigma).

9. One common claim is that virgin women's gait differs from that of nonvirgins. On the folklore of detecting virginity, and the fallibility of tests of virginity (including physiological tests), see Kelly 2000, Weis 1985.

10. See especially Jones et al. 1984.

11. For example, in the United States, HIV/AIDS has been highly stigmatizing in part because many of the first sufferers came from relatively powerless, already-stigmatized social groups—gay men and injection-drug users (Brandt 1987; Sontag 1989).

12. One-fifth of the women (7) and about three-fifths of the men (16) had thought of virginity as a stigma at some point in their lives. Four women and 15 men saw virginity as a stigma at the time of their own virginity loss.

13. By using this term, I mean only that these men and women saw themselves as stigmatized at the time they lost their virginity, not that they were inherently stigmatized or that others agreed with their self-assessments. Stigma is, as noted above, socially constructed and highly contextual.

14. The classic sociological treatise on stigma is Erving Goffman's (1963)

Stigma: Notes on the Management of Spoiled Identity. This chapter also relies on the work of Jones et al. 1984, Link and Phelan 2001, and Heatherton et al. 2000.

15. Of the 19 people in this group, 9 lost their virginity with a boyfriend or girlfriend, 3 with a close friend, 3 with an acquaintance, and 4 with a virtual stranger.

16. Most of these men and women were relatively young (16 or under) at virginity loss.

17. On people's reluctance to expose others and tendency to give them the benefit of the doubt, see Goffman 1963, Jones et al. 1984.

18. On the stigma of homosexuality, see Plummer 1979. Young adults in one recent study spoke of "first sex" in ways that indicated they saw it as a means of demonstrating their heterosexuality; this pattern was more pronounced among the men than the women, perhaps because masculinity has historically been linked more closely to sexual performance than has femininity (Holland, Ramazanoglu, and Thomson 1996). Gay and bisexual boys tend to describe sexual encounters with girls as something they did to "test" their sexual identity, whereas lesbian and bisexual girls characterize sex with boys as something they'd "expected" (Herdt and Boxer 1993; Savin-Williams 2003; though see Raymond 1994).

19. This was true regardless of the sex of the partner with whom they lost their virginity. That Kendall did not *consciously* experience his virginity and homosexuality as a dual stigma may be due to his relative youth and early stage in coming out when he lost his virginity. See Goffman 1963 on the co-presence of stigmas.

20. Four of the 6 gay men who saw virginity as relevant to their lives (i.e., to same-sex sexuality) interpreted it as a stigma at the time of virginity loss, as did one of two bisexual men.

21. Two-thirds of the stigma group expected *intense* physical pleasure from virginity loss.

22. Anderson 1995.

23. Bowser 1994.

24. Mahay, Laumann, and Michaels 2001; Upchurch et al. 1998.

25. Put differently, these young men incorporated what Robert Staples (1995) called the myth of Black sexual superiority, originally a racist stereotype imposed on Black men, into their self-identity.

26. White 1999; Anderson 1995; Sterk-Elifson 1994; Wyatt 1997.

27. My research supports studies finding greater gender disparity among Blacks than Whites (e.g., Wilson 1986; Upchurch et al. 1998). Mahay, Laumann, and Michaels (2001) found greater gender disparities in beliefs and smaller differences in behavior among African Americans than European Americans.

Bowser (1994) argues that the sexual double standard is less pronounced among Blacks than Whites.

28. On interracial dating and sexual relationships, see Ford, Sohn, and Lepkowski 2003.

29. Wyatt (1997) traces this mistrust to attitudes that developed during slavery and Reconstruction, when Black women could not control their sexuality and Black men could not protect their wives and daughters as they believed they ought to do. See also Collins 2004, Staples 1995.

30. My research supports previous studies suggesting that perceptions of peers' behavior are more influential than peers' actual behavior and that close friends' beliefs and behaviors have a greater impact than those of acquaintances (Billy and Udry 1985b; Kinsman et al. 1998).

31. Heavy petters in the stigma group typically had encounters with several (often casual) partners, while remaining virgins.

32. If Pam had subscribed to the "feminine" view of virginity as a gift, her excitement might have stemmed from a sense that receiving Marty's virginity would prove she was special to him. However, her interest in having sex in a weeks-old relationship suggests she was inclined to view virginity as a stigma or process. By a similar token, HIV-negative individuals may sympathize with people who have contracted HIV from blood transfusions because it is easy to think, "That could have been me." Jones et al. (1984) note that ambivalent reactions to stigmatized people are much theorized but not widely tested empirically.

33. Goffman 1963; Jones et al. 1984. Although one might imagine that people who drew on the stigma frame would prefer experienced partners for their ostensibly greater willingness to have sex, no one I interviewed suggested as much.

34. Bromley and Britten (1938) note similar patterns.

35. Alternatively, individuals may seek to overcome their stigma by mastering skills seen as off limits to people with that stigma—for instance, a virgin might seek attractive romantic partners—or by putting an unconventional spin on their identity, such as extolling "virgin chic." In my study, the first practice was extremely rare among the stigmatized and the second nonexistent; however, gifters and processers used these strategies when confronted by people who saw them as stigmatized.

36. Goffman (1959, 1963) argues that strangers are especially likely to protect one another from losing face in awkward social situations.

37. One of the hallmarks of stigmas is their capacity for disrupting social interactions (Jones et al. 1984). Despite posing few pitfalls for ordinary interactions, virginity may well disrupt those in which sexuality plays a central role, such as romantic relationships and friendships that rely on sexual banter for amusement. Although Bill's stigma disrupted his interaction with Diane, she did-

n't attribute the disruption to his stigma, even though his awkwardness gave her reason to question his appearance as a normal, i.e., *nonvirgin,* adult man. She may have been giving him the benefit of the doubt (Goffman 1959).

38. See Goffman (1963) on the tendency of stigmas to leave lasting marks after their removal, and on the tendency of people who have overcome a stigma to conceal their former stigmatized status. People who are seen as not responsible for their stigma (like virgins, who are born that way) typically receive more favorable treatment than people who are thought to have caused, or perpetuated, theirs (Jones et al. 1984). Since virginity is universal, the extent of a person's shame at having his *former* virginity discovered seems to depend on whether he lost his virginity in stigmatizing conditions.

39. The fact that he'd lost one motivation for pursuing sex—getting rid of virginity—made it easier for him to delay. Bill might have been less sensitive to Diane's reaction had he not felt so intensely stigmatized in the first place.

40. In this, they resemble the women who retained their vision of virginity as a gift even after disempowering experiences.

41. Holland et al. (1996), for instance, found that making fun of male performance was one of the few ways young British women felt able to assert themselves during virginity loss.

42. The third is Scott Lindstrom, a 25-year-old, heterosexual White man from a working-class family. When he lost his virginity at age 19, his girlfriend angrily accused him of sexual ineptitude. In contrast, Don Coulter (32, heterosexual, White, working-class background) said his girlfriend responded sympathetically to his clumsy performance and was pleased by his virginity. None of the men who concealed their virginity from male partners reported discovery or ridicule.

43. When I asked if there was an ideal age for virginity loss, people who favored the stigma frame named lower ages than any other group, with more than two-thirds approving of virginity loss at 15 or younger (compared with about one-third of gifters and processers). Several gifters and processers believed that they would have seen their virginity as stigmatizing if they hadn't lost it when they did.

44. Emma explained that, at the time, Jonathan had identified himself as bisexual; he came out as gay in college.

45. This ability is one of stigmatized people's few sources of power (Jones et al. 1984).

46. Goffman 1963; Jones et al. 1984.

47. Goffman 1963. No one reported being sanctioned for hiding virginity from friends, but doing so directly was relatively rare, unless all friends were equally eager to deny virginity and moderated their inquisitiveness accordingly.

48. One of the two viewed virginity as a stigma, the other saw it as a rite of passage.

49. At the time of virginity loss, or ever. "Younger" women were born between 1973 and 1980, "older" between 1962 and 1972.

50. These stereotypes apply to Black women and urban Latinas with particular virulence (Tolman 1996; Wyatt 1997); however, Asian American women also contend with the sexualized "Dragon Lady" stereotype (Espiritu 2000). Furthermore, White and Asian American women are less likely than African American women and Latinas to follow religious traditions that promote the idea that virginity is a gift.

51. On stigma and rape, see Sheffield 1997.

52. Rough sex may help some rape victims work through the trauma they experienced (Herman 1997). Ed described recognizing his sexual attraction to men and acting on it as two steps in the same extended learning process. (See also chapter 5.) Having sex with another man, Ed said, "didn't change how I thought of things . . . [b]ecause the change happened when I realized, several months before, that I was attracted to some men. And it was dealing with that attraction that changed things. Actually doing something about it just seemed . . . a natural progression after the attraction."

53. By a similar token, I interviewed several people who had retrospectively added oral sex to the activities they believed could result in virginity loss but who declined to apply those definitions to their own experiences with oral sex before vaginal sex (Carpenter 1999).

54. None of the Latinos, Latinas, or Asian Americans I interviewed had seen their virginity as a stigma.

55. Rubin 1990; Sprecher and Regan 1996; Thompson 1995.

56. The increasing visibility of lesbigay life has not only made it more imperative for lesbigay people to *openly* demonstrate their sexual identity, but also has reduced the degree to which heterosexuality is taken for granted, such that heterosexuals are increasingly required to "prove" their sexual identity.

NOTES TO CHAPTER 5

1. Malinowski 1929; Mead 1939. Given the relative permissiveness of the sexual cultures these books described, it is likely that many readers' interest was of a rather prurient nature. French anthropologist Arnold Van Gennep, who was first to recognize the structural similarities between the rituals celebrating such transitions, loathed the term "puberty rites" and was adamant that scholars should distinguish between rites of physiological puberty and social puberty. Mead and Malinowski were major figures in Anglo-American anthropology's campaign to influence the public sphere in the wake of World War I (MacClancy 1996).

2. This discussion relies primarily on the works of Glaser and Strauss 1971, Turner 1969, and van Gennep 1908. Van Gennep coined the term *rite of passage*

and demonstrated that, whatever the specific statuses involved (e.g., virginity to nonvirginity, single to married), rites of passage shared a three-step process: separation from the initial status (virgin, single person); the transition, often surrounded by a period of liminality (sexual exploration and virginity loss, betrothal and wedding); and incorporation into the new status (nonvirgin, spouse). In some passages, the transitional period is elaborate enough to constitute an independent state—as adolescence does in the passage from childhood to adulthood in the contemporary West. The liminal phase of a passage, in which a person hovers "betwixt and between" established social statuses, is typically seen as a time of danger both for the person making the passage and for the society of which she is a part (Douglas 1966).

3. On the passage from childhood to adulthood in non-Western contexts, see Muuss 1970, Schlegel 1995.

4. For example, Neil Simon's 1986 play, *Biloxi Blues*.

5. Products of their time, early anthropologists tended to think of virginity primarily as an attribute of women and to frame becoming sexually active as critical to achieving manhood (whereas they framed motherhood as crucial to womanhood). As van Gennep (1908) wrote, "A woman's first coitus has a ritual character which gives rise to a whole series of rites pertaining to the loss of virginity" (176). On virginity loss as a rite of achieving manhood, see Holland, Ramazanoglu, and Thomson 1996.

6. In her 1970 book, *Culture and Commitment: A Study of the Generation Gap,* and in a regular column for *Redbook* magazine from 1963 to 1979, Mead harnessed anthropological research to reassure parents worried about the psychological health and sexual development of their offspring (Mitchell 1996). At the time, *Redbook*'s audience included both genders.

7. Three-fourths of the men and women who drew on this metaphor spoke of it primarily as a learning process, while one-fourth dwelled on its role in conferring adulthood.

8. Some sociologists prefer the term "status passage," to emphasize the social statuses involved in such transitions (e.g., Glaser and Strauss 1971). "Process" was the term used most often by study participants.

9. Turner 1969, 103.

10. In general, an initiate's control over a rite of passage can be limited by her relative ignorance about the status she hopes to assume.

11. Some passages, like marriage, are accomplished through formal institutions and agents (e.g., clergy and state officials), whereas others are achieved through informal channels (Glaser and Strauss 1971).

12. Two-fifths of the women I interviewed and one-fifth of the men favored the process metaphor when they lost their virginity; however, men and women were almost equally likely *ever* to employ it (61 percent and 52 percent, respectively).

13. On Americans' tendency to deem gender relevant to virtually every aspect of social life and the pervasiveness of gender as a social category, see Lorber 1993, West and Zimmerman 1987.

14. Glaser and Strauss (1971) advocate analyzing status passages in terms of variation in desirability, irrevocability, and inevitability, all of which affect the way people approach a passage. Insofar as contemporary Western societies treat sexual activity as an essential ingredient of human happiness (Foucault 1978; Weeks 1985) and as few Americans pursue lifelong celibacy (Donnelly et al. 2001; Laumann et al. 1994), we would expect virginity loss to be perceived as desirable and inevitable.

15. Rich 1980.

16. Savin-Williams 2003.

17. One was Tessa Hauser, a 32-year-old White lesbian, who lost her virginity with her first girlfriend, Becka. Tessa (who had dated men before) concealed her virginity from Becka, who'd been openly gay for years, until after they had sex because she feared Becka would be reluctant to have sex with a woman who'd never had sex with a woman. The other was Tricia Watson, a 20-year-old White heterosexual student, whose curiosity about sex inspired her to lose her virginity with a stranger whom she never expected to see again, and with whom (ironically) she preferred not to share something so personal as her sexual history.

18. Four years later, when I interviewed Meghan, she said both of her parents had indicated that they knew she was having sex, but they avoided acknowledging it explicitly.

19. Van Gennep 1908, 175. Van Gennep called first-time rites of passage "founding ceremonies."

20. Ten White women (of 26), 2 Asian American women (of 2), one African American woman (of 3), and one Latina (of 2) interpreted virginity as a process at the time of virginity loss. (These figures include virgins.)

21. Tolman 1996; Wyatt 1997.

22. On these sexual stereotypes, see Espiritu (2000). The desire to reject both stereotypes is one possible reason that the two Asian American women I interviewed approached their own virginity loss as a rite of passage; their self-identification as bisexual may also have played a role. The reader should bear in mind that I interviewed too few Asian women to reach definitive conclusions about how their interpretations and experiences might differ from women from other backgrounds.

23. Tom's sexual career exemplifies Glaeser's (2004) account of the process of adopting a new understanding of a situation after one's previous understanding has been invalidated (see Introduction).

24. It is interesting that Tom didn't simply apply the gift metaphor to gay marriage, a topic already on gay activist agendas in the early 1990s; rather, he

seems to have accepted the Church's (and state's) understanding of marriage as exclusive to heterosexuals.

25. Glaser and Strauss 1971.

26. Herdt and Boxer 1993.

27. Despite coming out to himself early in college, "I never said that I was gay to anyone out loud until I was 22."

28. Raymond 1994; Savin-Williams 2003. Even fewer teens and young adults openly identified as gay in the early and mid-1990s, when the participants in question lost their virginity.

29. Specifically, 71 percent of lesbians, 11 percent of gay men, and 50 percent of bisexuals saw virginity as a process *at the time* of virginity loss, compared with 33 percent of heterosexual women and men (these figures include virgins). In addition to Tom, 3 of the 4 lesbians who saw their own virginity loss as a process explicitly mentioned the intertwining of the coming out and virginity-loss processes, as did one of the 3 bisexual women (a virgin). Although 2 of the 4 lesbians and 2 of the 3 bisexual women in the passage group came out *after* losing their virginity, it appears that their understandings were influenced by sexual identity, insofar as they were, more or less consciously, already in the process of recognizing and dealing with their desires for same-sex partners.

30. Concurrent passages may complicate or facilitate one another; see Glaser and Strauss 1971.

31. Comedian Ellen DeGeneres came out personally and as a television character, to great fanfare, on her eponymous sitcom in 1996. Lesbigay youth groups across the U.S. sponsored "Come out with Ellen" parties and the like (Walters 2001).

32. Phelan 1989; Stein and Plummer 1994.

33. Herdt and Boxer 1993; Savin-Williams 2003.

34. Even if they had thought about STIs, Abby reasoned retrospectively, the risk of contracting one through woman-woman sex was very low. Lesbians' decisions about safer sex represent one of the few issues where sexual identity clearly outweighed interpretive stances in influencing sexual behavior.

35. Glaser and Strauss (1971) recommend analyzing status passages in terms of variations in duration, rate, significance, desirability, irrevocability, and inevitability. About half of the processers, including Jennifer and Abby Rosen, viewed virginity loss as a long and gradual passage. Two-thirds explicitly said that they had expected to feel transformed by virginity loss; several others hadn't expected to feel transformed, but did.

36. Interestingly, the only female character to survive in *Halloween* (and many other horror films) is a virgin, a fact made much of in the 1997 satire/homage *Scream,* and analyzed by film scholar Carol Clover (1992).

37. The content of sex education programs in U.S. public schools varies tremendously by region and school district, in part because school curricula are

locally controlled (Landry, Kaeser, and Richards 1999). In 2001, Virginia was an abstinence-plus state (NARAL 2001). See also chapter 6.

38. Twelve of the 17 in this group lost their virginity within a year (in either direction) of high school graduation.

39. Although Jennifer had known it was possible to get HIV from heterosexual sex (it was 1990), preventing pregnancy had been her primary concern.

40. Glaser and Strauss 1971. Andy's supportive, encouraging response to Jennifer's distress also seems to exemplify this tendency.

41. Weis 1985; Sprecher, Barbee, and Schwartz 1995.

42. Sharon Thompson (1990, 1995) found that adolescent girls who discussed sex openly with their mothers—as Jennifer did—were disproportionately likely to be "pleasure narrators." Jennifer's story supports Thompson's contention with regard to emotional pleasure if not physical enjoyment.

43. Turner 1969.

44. Espin 1984; Hovell et al. 1994; Raffaelli and Ontai 2001.

45. Aneshensel, Fielder, and Becerra 1989; Upchurch et al. 1998.

46. Repeating an activity that engendered a transition, in order to make it harder to undo or back away from (i.e., to "stick" it), is especially common in the case of desirable but tenuous passages (Glaser and Strauss 1971).

47. One-fifth of working-class men and women I interviewed drew on the process frame at the time of their virginity loss, compared with over one-third of their middle-class counterparts.

NOTES TO CHAPTER 6

1. Mast 2001, 16.

2. Advertisement copy (Respect, Inc. 2004).

3. SR defines sex as "the physical and personal act of male and female genital union, sexual intercourse" (Mast 2001, 6). See also Teen-Aid's high school text, *Sexuality, Commitment, and Family,* and the Human Sexuality: Values and Choices curriculum, especially Teen Talk. For a review of curricula, see U.S. House of Representatives 2004.

4. Mast 2001, 6, 12. This rhetoric resonates richly with that of 1890s-era social purity campaigns (see chapter 2).

5. Mast 2001, 80.

6. Dailard 2001; Landry, Kaeser, and Richards 1999.

7. Definitions adapted from Landry, Kaeser, and Richards 1999. A 2004 study commissioned by California representative Henry Waxman found that 11 of the 13 curricula used most often by SPRANS grantees "contain false, misleading, or distorted information about reproductive health" (U.S. House of Representatives 2004, i). *Sex Respect* often cites scientific research in misleading ways (Moran 2000; Trudell and Whatley 1991). For example, despite acknowledging

that there is only one substantiated case of HIV transmission through saliva, the SR student workbook recommends avoiding tongue kissing entirely as a precaution (Mast 2001, 63). The research cited actually advises against tongue kissing *people known to have HIV.*

8. Landry, Kaeser, and Richards 1999.

9. Although only 69 percent of school districts have formal policies requiring some form of sex education, 86 percent of students live in districts that require sex education (Landry, Kaeser, and Richards 1999).

10. Kaplan and Springen 1991; Mast 2001.

11. Landry, Kaeser, and Richards 1999. See also Advocates for Youth and SIECUS 2001.

12. Darroch, Landry, and Singh 2000.

13. Funding restrictions, local officials' desire to avoid controversy, and discomfort and lack of training on the part of teachers have all contributed to self-censorship (Irvine 2002).

14. KFF 2000.

15. Dailard 2001; Landry, Kaeser, and Richards 1999.

16. Advocates for Youth and SIECUS 2001; Irvine 2002; Moran 2000; Walters 2001. Although moral conservatives historically opposed any sex education in public schools, arguing that such decisions should be left to families, their emergence as a major political force in the late 1970s combined with widespread recognition, in the mid-1980s, that the HIV/AIDS epidemic required a sex education-type response, to produce their current stance.

17. Title V was passed by Congress as a provision of the 1996 Temporary Assistance to Needy Families Act (TANF). Although TANF has expired, Congress reauthorized the welfare system and Title V.

18. California has been a consistent hold-out from Title V funding (Advocates for Youth and SIECUS 2001); in 2004, Arizona and Pennsylvania followed suit.

19. Section 510(b) of Title V of the Social Security Act: L. 104–193. More specifically, "Title V and AFLA require that programs not be inconsistent with any of the eight points, SPRANS-CBAE requires that all programs funded be responsive to each of the eight points" (SIECUS Legislative Action Center).

20. SIECUS 1996, 7. SIECUS's Guidelines for Comprehensive Sexuality Education are, properly speaking, not a sex education curriculum but a highly detailed guide to developing one.

21. Advocates for Youth and SIECUS 2001; Dailard 2001.

22. Moran (2000) and Trudell and Whatley (1991) contend that popular public school abstinence-only curricula are implicitly imbued with Christian morality. Note also the phrase "gifts from up above" in this chapter's opening quote.

23. True Love Waits (TLW). The page goes on to describe the dangers of

STIs, including HIV/AIDS, and such apparently inescapable emotional/psychological consequences as: "Those who participate in premarital sex experience emotional damage that may lead to an increased chance of mental depression and emotional despair" and "There is no way that premarital sex of any kind could be a plus for your future marriage. It only causes suspicion, mistrust, and regret."

24. By 2002, the TLW pledge had been reworded, with "a commitment to . . . my friends" replacing "to . . . those I date," "sexually abstinent" replacing "sexually pure," and "biblical marriage relationship" replacing "covenant. . . ." TLW materials are promoted primarily at churches; however, "pledge clubs" can be found in some public schools (Bearman and Brückner 2001). Like Sex Respect, TLW promotes secondary virginity for unmarried people who have already had sex.

25. Crim.

26. True Love Waits.

27. Conservative Protestant denominations rank among the fastest-growing religious groups in America and, despite representing a minority of the American populace, they have become politically very powerful (American Religion Data Archive; Woodberry and Smith 1998).

28. In fact, for a conservative Christian, Carrie struck me as remarkably open-minded, sex positive, and gay friendly. For instance, she explained her belief that it was possible to lose one's virginity with a same-sex partner by saying, "I wouldn't want to just categorize [virginity loss] to one kind of physical act . . . because that takes away so much of the beauty and significance of what sex is."

29. See chapter 3. Both Carrie and Kate told me they knew men who shared their beliefs; however, I was unable to locate any who were willing to take part in the study. Additional factors distinguishing people who see virginity as an act of worship from those who see it as a gift include the former group's absolute insistence on retaining virginity until marriage, their understanding of God as the rightful decision maker in the realm of personal relationships, and their very restrictive stance on sexual intimacy, including kissing, before betrothal or marriage.

30. According to my and other studies (Sprecher and Regan 1996; Bearman and Brückner 2001).

31. Gallagher and Smith 1999; Stacey 1991.

32. Of the 6 currently practicing conservative Protestants, 4 had been raised in such denominations; another 4 study participants had withdrawn from their churches/denominations as adults. Thus, I interviewed a total of 10 former or currently practicing conservative Protestants.

33. My sampling methods prohibit making generalizations about the prevalence of particular beliefs; more study is needed.

34. Woodberry and Smith 1998; Irvine 2002.

35. Widmer, Treas, and Newcomb 1998; Dailard 2001; Harding and Jencks 2003.

36. The relative popularity of the gift metaphor among conservative/devout Christians is consistent with conservative denominations' promotion of traditional gender and sexual ideologies, and the gift metaphor's Christian roots.

37. Thornton and Camburn 1989; Paradise et al. 2001; Petersen and Donnenwerth 1997; Brewster et al. 1998; Meier 2003.

38. Kirby 2001, 2002. The Effective Research and Programs Task Force of the National Campaign to Prevent Teen Pregnancy considered program evaluations to be scientifically sound if they used an experimental or quasi-experimental design, waited a minimum of 6 months after the program to collect follow-up data, had a sample size of at least 100 youth, and measured effects on behavior rather than attitudes or intentions.

39. Kirby 2001; U.S. House of Representatives 2004; Advocates for Youth and SIECUS 2001. One independent review (i.e., conducted by a party other than the curriculum's producer or a partisan think-tank) found that, of 10 programs evaluated as successful by the conservative Heritage Foundation, only one (*Not Me, Not Now*) was associated with delayed sex and lower pregnancy rates; yet, the study design couldn't rule out alternative explanations (Kirby 2002).

40. In 2001, 62.3 percent of U.S. twelfth-grade girls and 60.7 percent of boys reported having had vaginal sex (Grunbaum et al. 2003). About 80 percent of young adults (18 to 24) report having had vaginal sex (KFF 2003). For data on condom effectiveness, see World Health Organization 2000.

41. CDC 1997. The report also notes that "studies of hundreds of couples show that consistent condom use is possible when people have the skills and motivations to do so."

42. Grunseit and Kippax 1993; Kirby 1997, 2002; Jemmott, Jemmott, and Fong 1998. Evaluations often group comprehensive and abstinence-plus programs together because both provide accurate information about contraception.

43. Advocates for Youth and SIECUS 2001; Office of National AIDS Policy 2000. In 2003, allegedly under pressure from "higher-ups in the Bush administration," the CDC discontinued Programs That Work and removed from its Web site all information about the proven-to-be-effective comprehensive sex education programs (Union of Concerned Scientists 2004).

44. Alford 2003; Singh and Darroch 2000. Ages at first sex are slightly higher among Europeans.

45. David et al. 1990; Singh and Darroch 2000; Planned Parenthood Federation of America 1999. European teens also use more effective methods of contraception than their U.S. counterparts.

46. Jones et al. 1985.

47. On media, see Carpenter 1998, 2001b, Jones et al. 1985. On adults' atti-

tudes, see Schalet 1998; Harding and Jencks 2003; Widmer, Treas, and New-comb 1998.

48. Carpenter 2001b; David et al. 1990; Widmer, Treas, and Newcomb 1998; Schalet 1998; Schmidt et al. 1994.

49. Patterns of religiosity account in part for these cross-national differences in outlook and public policy (Furstenberg 1998; Westoff 1988).

50. As per provision E of the Title V definition of abstinence education. Note that the term used by the definition's authors—"likely"—is open to a wide range of interpretations.

51. Advocates for Youth and SIECUS 2001, 15.

NOTES TO CHAPTER 7

1. World Health Organization 2002. David Satcher's definition is quite similar (U.S. Surgeon General 2001).

2. One of the two was Carrie Matthews, profiled in chapter 6; the other was Chris Albrecht, a heterosexual Southern Baptist man who saw virginity as a gift (see chapter 3).

3. Study by Peter Bearman and Hannah Brückner, discussed in Altman 2004. In this nationally representative survey, nearly 90 percent of teenagers who pledged virginity until marriage (as part of True Love Waits or similar campaigns) did have sex before marriage. Forty percent of sexually active pledgers used condoms in the last year, compared with 60 percent of nonpledgers. The study did not assess interpretive frames for virginity loss; however, the pledge is consistent with the act-of-worship and gift frames.

4. Horowitz 1983; Lees 1986; Thompson 1995.

5. Such feelings might, of course, be mitigated by the belief that God forgives mistakes. The only study to address this possibility suggests, based on longitudinal survey data, that teens who break their pledges to remain virgins until marriage experience similar changes in self-esteem as nonpledgers who have sex (Bearman and Brückner 2001).

6. For a similar argument, see Furstenberg 1998.

7. On pledger/nonpledger marriage rates, see Altman 2004; on age at marriage and divorce rates, see Bramlett and Mosher 2001. Abstinence-only advocates have recently begun explicitly to address this critique, albeit not very satisfactorily; see, e.g., http://www.sexrespect.com/FundInfo.html.

8. Irvine 2002; Landry, Kaeser, and Richards 1999; Moran 2000.

9. Dailard 2001, 12.

10. Union of Concerned Scientists 2004.

11. Navarro 2004.

12. Should moral conservatives succeed in their efforts to rescind abortion rights and limit unmarried youths' access to contraception, young Americans (es-

pecially women) may once again find themselves valuing virginity out of fear of unintended pregnancy and/or contracting STIs.

13. Irvine 2002.

14. Jehl 1994.

15. Dailard 2001.

16. Laumann et al. 1994; Widmer, Treas, and Newcomb 1998.

17. Hackstaff 1999.

18. National Coalition Against Censorship 2001; Simson and Sussman 2000.

19. Irvine 2002.

20. U.S. House of Representatives 2004, i. The study focused on SPRANS-CBAE grantees. I suspect that this critique will result in greater medical accuracy in abstinence-only curricula rather than a shift to comprehensive programs.

21. For example, in Wisconsin (Kaplan and Springen 1991, 69).

22. Advocates for Youth and SIECUS 2001.

23. Carpenter 1998; Sutton et al. 2002. They have also been the targets of moral conservative-sponsored consumer advertising boycotts intended to force the removal of such content (Larsen 1990).

24. KFF n.d. For example, the "Entertainment Media Partnership" among the Kaiser Family Foundation, Viacom, and public health initiative, KNOW HIV/AIDS.

25. Stern 2002; Wray and Steele 2002.

26. In other words, virginity loss is significant because of the ways young people use virginity loss, in what they ask it, as a cultural object, to help them do. Conversely, social identities also guide and constrain people's choice of metaphors. See Introduction.

27. Mortimer and Larson 2002; Furstenberg et al. 2004.

28. Elder 1987. For a similar argument, albeit one influenced by functionalism, see Muuss 1970.

29. For similar arguments, see Kamen 2000, Risman and Schwartz 2002.

NOTES TO METHODOLOGICAL APPENDIX

1. Denzin 1989a; Riessman 1993.

2. Denzin 1989b; Mies 1983; Reinharz 1983.

Bibliography

Works and organizations frequently cited have been identified by the following abbreviations:

AJS   *American Journal of Sociology*
ASR   *American Sociological Review*
ASB   *Archives of Sexual Behavior*
CDC   Centers for Disease Control and Prevention
FPP   *Family Planning Perspectives*
JAMA   *Journal of the American Medical Association*
JMF   *Journal of Marriage and the Family*
JSR   *Journal of Sex Research*
KFF   Henry J. Kaiser Family Foundation
SIECUS   Sexuality Information and Education Council
         of the United States

Advocates for Youth and SIECUS. 2001. *Toward a sexually healthy America: Roadblocks imposed by the federal government's abstinence-only-until-marriage education program.* New York: Advocates for Youth and SIECUS.

Alford, Sue. 2003. *The facts: Adolescents at risk for sexually transmitted infections.* Advocates for Youth. http://www.advocatesforyouth.org/publications/factsheet/fssti.htm.

Ali, Lorraine, and Julie Scelfo. 2002. Choosing virginity. *Newsweek,* December 9.

Altman, Lawrence K. 2004. Study finds that teenage virginity pledges are rarely kept. *New York Times,* March 10.

American Civil Liberties Union. ACLU denounces proposed anti-gay constitutional amendment that would deny millions of American families their fundamental rights. Press release, May 15, 2000. http://www.aclu.org/Lesbian-GayRights/LesbianGayRights.cfm?ID=10349&c=101.

American Religion Data Archive. http://www.thearda.com/.

Anderson, Elijah. 1995. Sex codes and family life among poor inner-city youths.

In *African-American youth: Their social and economic status in the United States,* edited by R. L. Taylor, 179–200. Westport, CT: Praeger.

Aneshensel, Carol S., Eve P. Fielder, and Rosina M. Becerra. 1989. Fertility and fertility-related behavior among Mexican-American and non-Hispanic white female adolescents. *Journal of Health and Social Behavior* 30:56–76.

Aries, Philippe. 1985. St. Paul and the flesh. In *Western sexuality: Practice and precept in past and present times,* edited by P. Aries and A. Bejin, 36–39. Oxford: Blackwell.

Augustine. 1980. *The confessions.* Translated by J. Gibb and W. Montgomery. New York: Garland.

Bailey, Beth L. 1989. *From front porch to back seat: Courtship in twentieth-century America.* Baltimore: Johns Hopkins University Press.

Barker-Benfield, G. J. 2000. *The horrors of the half-known life: Male attitudes toward women and sexuality in nineteenth-century America.* New York: Routledge. (Orig. pub. 1974.)

Bearman, Peter S., and Hannah Brückner. 2001. Promising the future: Virginity pledges and first intercourse. *AJS* 106:859–912.

Beck, Ulrich, and Elisabeth Beck-Gernsheim. 1996. Individualisation and "precarious freedoms." In *Detraditionalisation: Critical reflections on authority and identity,* edited by P. Heelas, S. Lash, and P. Morris. Oxford: Blackwell.

Beisel, Nicola. 1997. *Imperiled innocents: Anthony Comstock and family reproduction in Victorian America.* Princeton, NJ: Princeton University Press.

Belk, Russell W., and Gregory S. Coon. 1993. Gift giving as agapic love: An alternative to the exchange paradigm based on dating experiences. *Journal of Consumer Research* 20:393–417.

Bell, Robert R., and Kathleen Coughey. 1980. Premarital sexual experience among college females, 1958, 1968, and 1978. *Family Relations* 29:353–357.

Berger, David G., and Morton G. Wenger. 1973. The ideology of virginity. *JMF* 35:666–676.

Berk, Richard, Paul R. Abramson, and Paul Okami. 1995. Sexual activities as told in surveys. In *Sexual nature/sexual culture,* edited by P. R. Abramson and S. D. Pinkerton. Chicago: University of Chicago Press.

Bernard, H. R. 1994. *Research methods in cultural anthropology.* Thousand Oaks, CA: Sage.

Biernacki, Patrick, and Dan Waldorf. 1981. Snowball sampling: Problems and techniques of chain referral sampling. *Sociological Methods and Research* 10:141–163.

Billy, John O. G., and J. Richard Udry. 1985a. Influence of male and female best friends on adolescent sexual behavior. *Adolescence* 20:21–32.

———. 1985b. Patterns of adolescent friendship and effects on sexual behavior. *Social Psychology Quarterly* 48:27–41.

Blau, Peter M. 1964. *Exchange and power in social life.* New York: Wiley.

Blume, Judy. 1975. *Forever.* New York: Pocket Books.

Blumer, Herbert. 1969. *Symbolic interactionism: Perspective and method.* Berkeley: University of California Press.

Blumstein, Philip, and Pepper Schwartz. 1983. *American couples: Money, work, and sex.* New York: William Morrow.

Bogart, Laura M., Heather Cecil, David A. Wagstaff, Steven D. Pinkerton, and Paul R. Abramson. 2000. Is it "sex"? College students' interpretations of sexual behavior terminology. *JSR* 37:108–116.

Bouris, Karen. 1993. *The first time: What parents and teenage girls should know about "losing your virginity."* Berkeley, CA: Conari.

Bowser, Benjamin P. 1994. African-American male sexuality through the early life course. In *Sexuality across the life course,* edited by A. S. Rossi, 127–150. Chicago: University of Chicago Press.

Bradley, Harriet. 1996. *Fractured identities: Changing patterns of inequality.* Cambridge, UK: Polity.

Bramlett, Matthew D., and William D. Mosher. 2001. *First marriage dissolution, divorce, and remarriage: United States.* Advance Data Report 323. Atlanta, GA: CDC.

Brandt, Allan M. 1987. *No magic bullet: A social history of venereal disease in the United States since 1880.* 2nd ed. Oxford: Oxford University Press.

Bream, Jon. 1998. Girl power: Success has come swiftly for Britney Spears. *Star Tribune* (Minneapolis), December 25.

Brewster, Karin L. 1994. Race differences in sexual activity among adolescent women: The role of neighborhood characteristics. *ASR* 59:408–424.

Brewster, Karin L., Elizabeth C. Cooksey, David K. Guilkey, and Ronald R. Rindfuss. 1998. The changing impact of religion on the sexual and contraceptive behavior of adolescent women in the United States. *JMF* 60:493–504.

Bromley, Dorothy D., and Florence H. Britten. 1938. *Youth and sex: A study of 1300 college students.* 3rd ed. New York: Harper and Brothers.

Brown, Helen Gurley. 1962. *Sex and the single girl.* New York: B. Geis/Random House.

Brown, Peter. 1988. *The body and society: Men, women and sexual renunciation in early Christianity.* New York: Columbia University Press.

Brownmiller, Susan. 1975. *Against our will: Men, women, and rape.* New York: Simon and Schuster.

Brumberg, Joan Jacobs. 1997. *The body project.* New York: Random House.

Brundage, James. 1987. *Law, sex, and Christian society in medieval Europe.* Chicago: University of Chicago Press.

Bruni, Frank. 1998. For Starr Probe, the Devil's in the Definition. *New York Times,* August 16.

Budgeon, Shelley. 2003. *Choosing a self: Young women and the individualization of identity.* Westport, CT: Praeger.

Bugge, John M. 1975. *Virginitas: An essay in the history of a medieval ideal.* The Hague: Martinus Nijhoff.

Butterfield, Oliver. 1939. *Love problems of adolescence.* New York: Emerson.

Cain, Roy. 1993. Disclosure and secrecy among gay men in the United States and Canada: A shift in views. In *American sexual politics,* edited by J. C. Fout and M. S. Tantillo, 289–309. Chicago: University of Chicago Press.

Carby, Hazel. 1990. "It just be's that way sometime": The sexual politics of black women's blues. In *Unequal sisters: A multicultural reader in U.S. women's history,* edited by E. C. DuBois and V. L. Ruiz, 238–249. New York: Routledge.

Carpenter, Laura M. 1998. From girls into women: Scripts for sexuality and romance in *Seventeen* magazine, 1974–1994. *JSR* 35:158–168.

———. 1999. Virgin territories: The social construction of virginity loss in the contemporary United States. Ph.D. dissertation, Department of Sociology, University of Pennsylvania.

———. 2001a. The ambiguity of "having sex": The subjective experience of virginity loss in the United States. *JSR* 38:127–139.

———. 2001b. The first time/das erstes Mal: Approaches to sexuality in U.S. and German teen magazines. *Youth and Society* 32 (3):31–61.

———. 2002. Gendering virginity loss in popular film. Paper presented at the annual meeting of the National Women's Studies Association, Las Vegas, NV.

Carrington, Christopher. 1999. *No place like home: Relationships and family life among lesbians and gay men.* Chicago: University of Chicago Press.

CDC. 1997. *Questions and answers about male latex condoms to prevent sexual transmission of HIV.* Atlanta: CDC.

Chan, Connie S. 1994. Asian-American adolescents: Issues in the expression of sexuality. In *Sexual cultures and the construction of adolescent identities,* edited by J. M. Irvine, 88–99. Philadelphia: Temple University Press.

Chrysostom, St. John. 1986. *On marriage and family life.* Translated by Catharine P. Roth and David Anderson. Crestwood, NY: St. Vladimir's Seminary Press.

Clover, Carol J. 1992. *Men, women, and chain saws: Gender in the modern horror film.* Princeton, NJ: Princeton University Press.

Cochran, Susan D., Vickie M. Mays, and Laurie Leung. 1991. Sexual practices of heterosexual Asian-American young adults: Implications for risk of HIV infection. *ASB* 20:381–391.

Collins, Patricia Hill. 2004. *Black sexual politics: African Americans, gender, and the new racism.* New York: Routledge.

Connell, R. W. 1995. *Masculinities.* Berkeley: University of California Press.

Conrad, Peter. 1992. Medicalization and social control. *Annual Review of Sociology* 18:209–232.

Cott, Nancy F. 1978. Passionlessness: An interpretation of Victorian sexual ideology, 1790–1850. *Signs* 4:219–236.

Craig, Maxine Leeds. 2002. *Ain't I a beauty queen? Black women, beauty, and the politics of race.* Oxford: Oxford University Press.

Crim, David. "Special Date," Parents/tips. True Love Waits/Lifeway Christian Resources. Accessed August 4, 2004. http://www.lifeway.com/tlw/par_tips .asp.

Crosier, Louis M., ed. 1993. *Losing it: The virginity myth.* Washington, DC: Avocus.

Dailard, Cynthia. 2001. Sex education: Politicians, parents, teachers, and teens. *Guttmacher Report on Public Policy* 4 (1):9–12.

Darling, Carol Anderson, J. Kenneth Davidson, Sr., and Lauren C. Passarello. 1992. The mystique of first intercourse among college youth: The role of partners, contraceptive practices, and psychological reactions. *Journal of Youth and Adolescence* 21:97–117.

Darroch, Jacqueline, David Landry, and Susheela Singh. 2000. Changing emphases in sexuality education in U.S. public secondary schools, 1988–1999. *FPP* 32:204–211.

David, Henry P., Janine M. Morgall, Mogens Osler, Niels K. Rasmussen, and Birgitte Jensen. 1990. United States and Denmark: Different approaches to health care and family planning. *Studies in Family Planning* 21:1–19.

Davidson, Cathy N. 1986. Introduction to *Charlotte Temple* by Susanna Rowson. Oxford: Oxford University Press.

Degler, Carl N. 1980. *At odds: Women and the family in America from the revolution to the present.* New York: Oxford University Press.

DeLamater, John. 1987. A sociological approach. In *Theories of human sexuality,* edited by J. Geer and W. O'Donahue, 237–255. New York: Plenum.

de Lys, Claudia. 1960. *To be or not to be a virgin.* New York: Robert Speller and Sons.

D'Emilio, John, and Estelle B. Freedman. 1988. *Intimate matters: A history of sexuality in America.* New York: Harper and Row.

Denzin, Norman K. 1989a. *Interpretive biography.* Newbury Park, CA: Sage.

———. 1989b. *The research act: A theoretical introduction to sociological methods.* Englewood Cliffs, NJ: Prentice Hall.

Dill, Bonnie Thornton. 1988. Our mothers' grief: Racial-ethnic women and the maintenance of families. *Journal of Family History* 13:415–431.

Dobie, Kathy. 1995. Hellbent on redemption. *Mother Jones,* January/February.

Donnelly, Denise, Elisabeth Burgess, Sally Anderson, Regina Davis, and Joy Dillard. 2001. Involuntary celibacy: A life course analysis. *JSR* 38:159–169.

Douglas, Mary. 1966. *Purity and danger.* London: Routledge.

Douglas, Susan J. 1994. *Where the girls are: Growing up female with the mass media.* New York: Times Books/Random House.

Drake, St. Clair, and Horace Cayton. 1945. *Black metropolis.* New York: Harcourt, Brace.

Dreiser, Theodore. 1900. *Sister Carrie.* Reprint, New York: Penguin Putnam, 2000.

Duberman, Martin B. 1991. *About time: Exploring the gay past.* Rev. ed. New York: Meridian.

DuBois, W. E. B. 1899. *The Philadelphia negro.* Reprint, Philadelphia: University of Pennsylvania, 1995.

DuCille, Ann. 1993. Blues notes on black sexuality: Sex and the texts of Jessie Fauset and Nella Larsen. In *American sexual politics,* edited by J. C. Fout and M. S. Tantillo, 193–219. Chicago: University of Chicago Press.

Dworkin, Andrea. 1981. *Pornography: Men possessing women.* New York: Perigee Books.

———. 1987. *Intercourse.* New York: Free Press.

E-Bay Sucks. Francis Cornworth: Young man's virginity. Please look. Accessed February 22, 2002. www.wtfman.com/mcd/dick2.htm.

Ehrenreich, Barbara, Elizabeth Hess, and Gloria Jacobs. 1986. *Re-making love: The feminization of sex.* New York: Doubleday.

Elder, Glen H., Jr. 1987. Adolescence in historical perspective. In *Handbook of adolescent psychology,* edited by A. Adelson, 3–46. New York: Wiley.

Elder, Lindsey. 1996. *Early embraces.* Los Angeles: Alyson.

Ellis, Albert. 1951. *The folklore of sex.* New York: Charles Boni.

Ericksen, Julia A. 1999. *Kiss and tell: Surveying sex in the twentieth century.* Cambridge, MA: Harvard University Press.

Espin, Oliva M. 1984. Cultural and historical influences on sexuality in Hispanic/Latin women: Implications for psychotherapy. In *Pleasure and danger: Exploring female sexuality,* edited by C. Vance, 149–164. London: Routledge.

Espiritu, Yen Le. 2000. *Asian American women and men.* Thousand Oaks, CA: Sage.

Faderman, Lillian. 1981. *Surpassing the love of men: Romantic friendship and love between women from the Renaissance to the present.* New York: William Morrow.

———. 1993. The return of butch and femme: A phenomenon in lesbian sexuality of the 1980s and 1990s. In *American sexual politics,* edited by J. C. Fout and M. S. Tantillo, 333–351. Chicago: University of Chicago Press.

Faludi, Susan. 1991. *Backlash: The undeclared war against American women.* New York: Crown.

Fauset, Jessie Redmon. 1928. *Plum bun: A novel without a moral.* Reprint, London: Pandora, 1985.

Fine, Michelle. 1988. Sexuality, schooling and adolescent females: The missing discourse of desire. *Harvard Educational Review* 58:29–53.

Fleming, Karl, and Anne Taylor Fleming. 1975. *The first time.* New York: Simon and Schuster.

Foote, Peter G., and David M. Wilson. 1970. *The Viking achievement: A survey of the society and culture of early medieval Scandinavia.* New York: Praeger.

Ford, Kathleen, Woosung Sohn, and James M. Lepkowski. 2003. Ethnicity or race, area characteristics, and sexual partner choice among American adolescents. *JSR* 40:211–218.

Foucault, Michel. 1978. *The history of sexuality.* Vol. 1. New York: Vintage.

Fox, Renee C., and Judith P. Swazey. 1978. *The courage to fail: A social view of organ transplants and dialysis.* Chicago: University of Chicago Press.

Frazier, E. Franklin. 1932. *The Negro family in Chicago.* Chicago: University of Chicago Press.

Freud, Sigmund. 1908. "Civilized" sexual morality. In *The standard edition of the complete psychological works of Sigmund Freud,* 177–204. Reprint, London: Hogarth, 1953.

Furstenberg, Frank F., Jr. 1998. When will teenage childbearing become a problem? The implications of Western experience for developing countries. *Studies in Family Planning* 29:246–253.

Furstenberg, Frank F., Jr., Sheela Kennedy, Vonnie C. McLoyd, Ruben G. Rumbaut, and Richard A. Settersten, Jr. 2004. Growing up is harder to do. *Contexts* 3 (3):33–41.

Gagnon, John H., and William Simon. 1973. *Sexual conduct: The social sources of human sexuality.* Chicago: Aldine.

———. 1987. The sexual scripting of oral genital contacts. *ASB* 16:1–25.

Gallagher, Sally K., and Christian Smith. 1999. Symbolic traditionalism and pragmatic egalitarianism: Contemporary evangelicals, families, and gender. *Gender and Society* 13:211–233.

Gebhard, Paul. 1980. Sexuality in the post-Kinsey era. In *Changing patterns of sexual behavior,* edited by W. C. Arnytage, R. Chester, and J. Reel, 47–48. New York: Academic Press.

Giddens, Anthony. 1992. *The transformation of intimacy.* Stanford, CA: Stanford University Press.

Gilfoyle, Jackie, Jonathan Wilson, and Brown. 1993. Sex, organs, and audiotape: A discourse analytic approach to talking about heterosexual sex and relationships. In *Heterosexuality,* edited by C. Kitzinger and S. Wilkinson, 209–230. London: Sage.

Glaeser, Andreas. 2004. Steps to a sociology of understanding. Paper presented at the annual meeting of the American Sociological Association, San Francisco.

Glaser, Barney G., and Anselm L. Strauss. 1967. *The discovery of grounded theory: Strategies for qualitative research*. Chicago: Aldine.

———. 1971. *Status passage*. Chicago: Aldine-Atherton.

Godbeer, Richard. 2002. *Sexual revolution in early America*. Baltimore: Johns Hopkins University Press.

Goffman, Erving. 1959. *The presentation of self in everyday life*. New York: Anchor-Doubleday.

———. 1963. *Stigma: Notes on the management of spoiled identity*. New York: Simon and Schuster.

———. 1974. *Frame analysis: An essay on the organization of experience*. Cambridge, MA: Harvard University Press.

Gold, Todd. 2001. Britney can't wait. *US Weekly*, June 4.

Gordon, Linda. 1974. *Woman's body, woman's right: Birth control in America*. New York: Penguin.

Gouldner, Alvin W. 1960. The norm of reciprocity: A preliminary statement. *ASR* 25:161–178.

Greenberg, David F. 1988. *The construction of homosexuality*. Chicago: University of Chicago Press.

Greenberg, David F., and Marcia H. Bystryn. 1982. Christian intolerance of homosexuality. *AJS* 88:515–548.

Griswold, Wendy. 1987. A methodological framework for the sociology of culture. *Sociological Methodology* 14:1–35.

Grunbaum, Jo Anne, Laura Kann, Steve Kinchen, James Ross, Joseph Hawkins, Richard Lowry, William A. Harris, Tim McManus, David Chyen, and Janet Collins. 2003. Youth Risk Behavior Surveillance—United States. *Morbidity and Mortality Weekly Report* 53 (SS02):1–96.

Grunseit, A., and S. Kippax. 1993. *Effects of sex education on young people's sexual behavior*. Geneva: World Health Organization.

Gutman, Herbert, and Richard Sutch. 1976. Victorians all? The sexual mores and conduct of slaves and their masters. In *Reckoning with slavery: A critical study in the quantitative history of American Negro slavery*, edited by P. A. David, H. G. Gutman, R. Sutch, P. Temin, and G. Wright, 134–162. New York: Oxford University Press.

Haag, Pamela S. 1993. In search of "the real thing": Ideologies of love, modern romance, and women's sexual subjectivity in the United States, 1920–40. In *American sexual politics*, edited by J. C. Fout and M. S. Tantillo, 161–191. Chicago: University of Chicago Press.

Hackstaff, Karla B. 1999. *Marriage in a culture of divorce*. Philadelphia: Temple University Press.

Hali meidhad. 1982. Translated and edited by B. Millett. London: Oxford University Press/Early English Text Society.

Hall, G. Stanley. 1905. *Adolescence.* New York: Appleton.

Harding, David J., and Christopher Jencks. 2003. Changing attitudes toward premarital sex: Cohort, period, and aging effects. *Public Opinion Quarterly* 67:211–226.

Hart, Jack. 1995. *My first time.* Los Angeles: Alyson.

Harvey, A. D. 1994. Virginity and honour in *Measure for Measure* and Davenant's *The Law Against Lovers. English Studies* 75:123–132.

Haskell, Robert. 2003. Burning Spears. W. August. http://www.style.com/w/feat_story/070903/full_page.html.

Hayt, Elizabeth. 2002. It's never too late to be a virgin. *New York Times,* August 4.

Heatherton, Todd F., Robert E. Kleck, Michelle R. Hebl, and Jay G. Hull, eds. 2000. *The social psychology of stigma.* New York: Guilford.

Hecht, Ben. 1921. *Erik Dorn.* New York: Putnam.

Helligar, Jeremy. 2002. Britney on the brink. *US Weekly,* September 2.

Herdt, Gilbert, and Andrew Boxer. 1993. *Children of Horizons: How gay and lesbian teens are leading a new way out of the closet.* 2nd ed. Boston: Beacon Press.

Herman, Judith L. 1997. *Trauma and recovery.* Rev. ed. New York: Basic Books.

Herold, Edward S., and Marilyn Shirley Goodwin. 1981. Adamant virgins, potential nonvirgins, and nonvirgins. *JSR* 17:97–113.

Hine, Darlene Clark. 1988. Rape and the inner lives of black women in the Middle West: Preliminary thoughts on the culture of dissemblance. *Signs* 14:912–920.

Hitchcock, Tim. 2002. Redefining sex in eighteenth-century England. In *Sexualities in history,* edited by K. M. Phillips and B. Reay. New York: Routledge.

Hodes, Martha. 1993. The sexualization of reconstruction politics: White women and black men in the South after the Civil War. In *American sexual politics,* edited by J. C. Fout and M. S. Tantillo, 59–74. Chicago: University of Chicago Press.

Hofferth, Sandra L., Joan R. Kahn, and Wendy Baldwin. 1987. Premarital sexual activity among U.S. teenage women over the past three decades. *FPP* 19:46–53.

Holland, Janet, Caroline Ramazanoglu, and Rachel Thomson. 1996. In the same boat? The gendered (in)experience of first heterosex. In *Theorising heterosexuality,* edited by D. Richardson, 143–160. Bristol, PA: Open University Press.

Holtzman, Deanna, and Nancy Kulish. 1997. *Nevermore: The hymen and the loss of virginity.* Northvale, NJ: Jason Aronson.

Holy Maidenhood. 1991. In *Anchoritic spirituality: Ancrene Wisse and associated works,* edited by A. Savage and N. Watson. New York: Paulist Press.

Horowitz, Ruth. 1983. *Honor and the American dream: Culture and identity in a Chicano community.* New Brunswick, NJ: Rutgers University Press.

Houston Chronicle. 2000. Church praises Britney for being virgin. December 18.

Hovell, Mel, Carol Sipan, Elaine Blumberg, Cathie Atkins, C. Richard Hofstetter, and Susan Kreitner. 1994. Family influences on Latino and Anglo adolescents' sexual behavior. *JMF* 56:973–986.

Ingrassia, Michelle. 1994. Virgin cool. *Newsweek,* October 17.

Irvine, Janice M. 1990. *Disorders of desire: Sex and gender in modern American sexology.* Philadelphia: Temple University Press.

———. 1994. Cultural differences and adolescent sexualities. In *Sexual cultures and the construction of adolescent identities,* edited by J. M. Irvine, 3–28. Philadelphia: Temple University Press.

———. 2002. *Talk about sex: The battles over sex education in the United States.* Berkeley: University of California Press.

Jarrell, Anne. 2000. The face of teenage sex grows younger. *New York Times,* April 2.

Jehl, Douglas. 1994. Surgeon General forced to resign by white house. *New York Times,* December 10.

Jemmott, J. B., L. S. Jemmott, and G. T. Fong. 1998. Abstinence and safer sex HIV risk-reduction interventions for African American adolescents: A randomized controlled trial. *JAMA* 279:1529–1536.

Jessor, Shirley L., and Richard Jessor. 1975. Transition from virginity to non-virginity among youth: A social-psychological study over time. *Developmental Psychology* 11:473–484.

Jo, B. 1993. "Virgin" means never having been heterosexual—Virgins do exist. *off our backs.* January.

Johnson, Charles S. 1941. *Growing up in the Black Belt: Negro youth in the rural south.* Washington, DC: American Council on Education.

Johnson, Merri Lisa. 2002. Fuck you and your untouchable face: Third wave feminism and the problem of romance. In *Jane sexes it up: True confessions of feminist desire,* edited by M. L. Johnson, 13–50. New York: Four Walls Eight Windows.

Jones, Edward E., Amerigo Farina, Albert H. Hastorf, Hazel Markus, Dale T. Miller, and Robert A. Scott. 1984. *Social stigma: The psychology of marked relationships.* New York: Freeman.

Jones, Elise F., Jacqueline Darroch Forrest, Noreen Goldman, Stanley K. Henshaw, Richard Lincoln, Jeannie I. Rosoff, Charles F. Westoff, and Deirdre Wulf. 1985. Teenage pregnancy in developed countries: Determinants and policy implications. *FPP* 17:53–62.

Jones, Jacqueline. 1985. *Labor of love, labor of sorrow: Black women, work and the family, from slavery to the present.* New York: Vintage.

Joyce, Gare. 2002. Britney's aura of innocence goes up in smoke: Photos catch singer smoking; claim to be a virgin "a joke," ex-boyfriend says. *Ottawa Citizen,* May 7.

Joyner, Kara, and Edward O. Laumann. 2001. Teenage sex and the sexual revolution. In *Sex, love, and health in America: Private choices and public policies,* edited by E. O. Laumann and R. T. Michael, 41–71. Chicago: University of Chicago Press.

Kakar, Sudhir. 1990. *Intimate relations: Exploring Indian sexuality.* Chicago: University of Chicago Press.

Kamen, Paula. 2000. *Her way: Young women remake the sexual revolution.* New York: Broadway Books.

Kaplan, David A., and Karen Springen. 1991. A battle over teaching sex ed. *Newsweek,* June 17.

Katz, Jonathan Ned. 1992. *Gay American history: Lesbians and gay men in the USA: A documentary history.* Rev. ed. New York: Meridian.

Keller, Wendy. 1999. *The cult of the born-again virgin: How single women can reclaim their sexual power.* Deerfield Beach, FL: Health Communications.

Kelly, Kathleen Coyne. 1999. Menaced masculinity and imperiled virginity in Malory's *Morte D'Arthur.* In *Menacing virgins: Representing virginity in the Middle Ages and Renaissance,* edited by K. C. Kelly and M. Leslie, 97–114. Newark, DE: University of Delaware Press.

———. 2000. *Performing virginity and testing chastity in the Middle Ages.* New York: Routledge.

Kelly, Kathleen Coyne, and Marina Leslie. 1999. Introduction: The epistemology of virginity. In *Menacing virgins: Representing virginity in the Middle Ages and Renaissance,* edited by K. C. Kelly and M. Leslie, 15–25. Newark, DE: University of Delaware Press.

KFF. 2000. *Sex education in America: A series of national surveys of students, parents, teachers, and principals.* Menlo Park, CA: KFF.

KFF. 2003. *National Survey of Adolescents and Young Adults: Sexual health knowledge, attitudes, and experiences.* Menlo Park, CA: KFF.

KFF. Entertainment Media Partnerships main page. Accessed September 1, 2004. http://www.kff.org/entpartnerships/index.cfm.

Kimmel, Michael. 1995. Misogynists, masculinist mentors, and male supporters. In *Women: A feminist perspective,* edited by J. Freeman, 561–572. Mountain View, CA: Mayfield.

Kinsey, Alfred C., Wardell B. Pomeroy, and Clyde E. Martin. 1948. *Sexual behavior in the human male.* Philadelphia: W. B. Saunders.

Kinsey, Alfred C., Wardell B. Pomeroy, Clyde E. Martin, and Paul Gebhard. 1953. *Sexual behavior in the human female.* Philadelphia: W. B. Saunders.

Kinsman, Sara B., Daniel Romer, Frank F. Furstenberg, Jr., and Donald F. Schwartz. 1998. Early sexual initiation: The role of peer norms. *Pediatrics* 102:1185–1193.

Kirby, Douglas. 1997. *No easy answers: Research findings on programs to reduce teen pregnancy.* Washington, DC: National Campaign to Prevent Teen Pregnancy.

———. 2001. *Emerging answers: Research findings on programs to reduce teen pregnancy.* Washington, DC: National Campaign to Prevent Teen Pregnancy.

———. 2002. *Do abstinence-only programs delay the initiation of sex among young people and reduce teen pregnancy?* Washington, DC: National Campaign to Prevent Teen Pregnancy.

Kitzinger, Celia, and Sue Wilkinson. 1994. Virgins and queers: Rehabilitating heterosexuality? *Gender and Society* 8:444–463.

Klassen, Albert D., Colin J. Williams, and Eugene E. Levitt. 1989. *Sex and morality in the U.S.,* edited by H. J. O'Gorman. Middletown, CT: Wesleyan University Press.

Knight, India. 2000. Virginity is pure mischief. *Sunday Times* (London), June 11.

Komter, Aafke. 1989. Hidden power in marriage. *Gender and Society* 3:187–216.

Ku, Leighton, Freya L. Sonenstein, Laura D. Lindberg, Carolyn H. Bradner, Scott Boggess, and Joseph H. Pleck. 1998. Understanding changes in sexual activity among young metropolitan men: 1979–1995. *FPP* 30:256–262.

Lakoff, George, and Mark Johnson. 1980. *Metaphors we live by.* Chicago: University of Chicago Press.

Landry, David J., Lisa Kaeser, and Cory L. Richards. 1999. Abstinence promotion and the provision of information about contraception in public school district sexuality education policies. *FPP* 31:280–286.

Laqueur, Thomas. 1990. *Making sex: Body and gender from the Greeks to Freud.* Cambridge, MA: Harvard University Press.

Larsen, Elizabeth. 1990. Censoring sex information: The story of *Sassy. Utne Reader,* July/August.

Laumann, Edward O., John H. Gagnon, Robert T. Michael, and Stuart Michaels. 1994. *The social organization of sexuality: Sexual practices in the United States.* Chicago: University of Chicago Press.

Lauritsen, Janet L. 1994. Explaining race and gender differences in adolescent sexual behavior. *Social Forces* 72:859–883.

Lee, Janet, and Jennifer Sasser-Coen. 1996. *Blood stories: Menarche and the politics of the female body in contemporary U.S. society.* New York: Routledge.

Lees, Sue. 1986. *Losing out: Sexuality and adolescent girls.* London: Hutchinson.

Leff, Leonard J., and Jerold L. Simmons. 1990. *The dame in the kimono: Holly-*

wood, censorship, and the Production Code from the 1920s to the 1960s. New York: Grove Weidenfeld.

Levine, Martin P. 1995. The life and death of gay clones. In *Men's lives,* edited by M. S. Kimmel and M. A. Messner, 55–67. Boston: Allyn and Bacon.

Levi-Strauss, Claude. 1969. *The elementary structures of kinship.* Boston: Beacon Press.

Lewis, Jon. 1992. *The road to romance and ruin: Teen films and youth culture.* New York: Routledge.

Lindisfarne, Nancy. 1994. Variant masculinities, variant virginities: Rethinking "honor and shame." In *Dislocating masculinity: Comparative ethnographies,* edited by A. Cornwall and N. Lindisfarne, 82–96. New York: Routledge.

Lindsey, Ben, and Wainwright Evans. 1925. *The revolt of modern youth.* Garden City, NY: Garden City Publishing.

Lingeman, Richard. 2000. Introduction to *Sister Carrie* by Theodore Dreiser. New York: Penguin Putnam.

Link, Bruce G., and Jo C. Phelan. 2001. Conceptualizing stigma. *Annual Review of Sociology* 27:363–385.

Lorber, Judith. 1993. Believing is seeing: Biology as ideology. *Gender and Society* 7:568–582.

Luker, Kristen. 1996. *Dubious conceptions: The politics of teenage pregnancy.* Cambridge, MA: Harvard University Press.

Lynd, Robert S., and Helen Merrell Lynd. 1929. *Middletown: A study in contemporary American culture.* New York: Harcourt, Brace and World.

MacClancy, Jeremy. 1996. Popularizing anthropology. In *Popularizing anthropology,* edited by J. MacClancy and C. McDonaugh, 1–57. London: Routledge.

Mace, David R. 1949. Is chastity outmoded? *Woman's Home Companion,* September.

MacKinnon, Catharine. 1989. Sexuality, pornography and method: Pleasure under patriarchy. *Ethics* 99:314–346.

Mahay, Jenna, Edward O. Laumann, and Stuart Michaels. 2001. Race, gender, and class in sexual scripts. In *Sex, love, and health in America: Private choices and public policies,* edited by E. O. Laumann and R. T. Michael, 197–238. Chicago: University of Chicago Press.

Malinowski, Bronislaw. 1929. *The sexual life of savages.* New York: H. Liveright.

Marks, Percy. 1924. *The plastic age.* New York: Century.

Martin, Karin A. 1998. Becoming a gendered body: Practices of preschools. *ASR* 63:494–511.

Mast, Coleen Kelly. 2001. *Sex respect: The option of true sexual freedom (student workbook).* Bradley, IL: Respect, Inc.

Maurstad, Tom. 1996. How NBC suddenly reset Susan. *Toronto Star,* September 27.

Mauss, Marcel. 1925. *The gift: Forms and functions of exchange in archaic societies.* Translated by I. Cunnison. Glencoe, IL: Free Press, 1954.

McCarthy, Tara. 1997. *Been there, haven't done that: A virgin's memoir.* New York: Warner.

McCaughey, Martha. 1997. *Real knockouts: The physical feminism of women's self defense.* New York: New York University Press.

McCaughey, William H. 1991. Brooke's example. *Los Angeles Times,* August 10.

McInerney, Maud Burnett. 1999. Rhetoric, power, and integrity in the passion of the virgin martyr. In *Menacing virgins: Representing virginity in the Middle Ages and Renaissance,* edited by K. C. Kelly and M. Leslie, 97–114. Newark, DE: University of Delaware Press.

Mead, Margaret. 1939. *From the South Seas: Studies of adolescence and sex in primitive societies.* New York: William Morrow.

Meier, Ann M. 2003. Adolescents' transition to first intercourse, religiosity, and attitudes about sex. *Social Forces* 81:1031–1053.

Mernissi, Fatima. 1991. *Women and Islam: An historical and theological enquiry.* Oxford: Basil Blackwell.

Meston, Cindy M., Paul D. Trapnell, and Boris B. Gorzalka. 1996. Ethnic and gender differences in sexuality: Variations in sexual behavior between Asian and non-Asian university students. *ASB* 25:33–72.

Methodius. 1958. *The symposium; a treatise on chastity.* Translated by H. Musurillo. Westminster, MD: Newman Press.

Mies, Maria. 1983. Towards a methodology for feminist research. In *Theories of women's studies,* edited by G. Bowles and R. D. Klein, 117–139. London: Routledge.

Miles, Matthew B., and A. Michael Huberman. 1994. *Qualitative data analysis.* 2nd ed. Thousand Oaks, CA: Sage.

Mills, C. Wright. 1959. *The sociological imagination.* New York: Oxford University Press.

Mitchell, William E. 1996. Communicating culture: Margaret Mead and the practice of popular anthropology. In *Popularizing anthropology,* edited by J. MacClancy and C. McDonaugh, 122–134. London: Routledge.

Modell, John. 1983. Dating becomes the way of American youth. In *Essays on the family and historical change,* edited by L. P. Moch and G. D. Stark, 91–126. College Station: Texas A & M University Press.

Modell, John, Frank F. Furstenberg, Jr., and Theodore Herschberg. 1976. Social change and transitions to adulthood in historical perspective. *Journal of Family History* 1:7–33.

Moffatt, Michael. 1987. *Coming of age in New Jersey.* New Brunswick, NJ: Rutgers University Press.

Moran, Jeffrey P. 2000. *Teaching sex: The shaping of adolescence in the twentieth century.* Cambridge, MA: Harvard University Press.

Mortimer, Jeylan T., and Reed W. Larson, eds. 2002. *The changing adolescent experience: Societal trends and the transition to adulthood.* Cambridge, UK: Cambridge University Press.

movies.com. Top 50 movies of 1999. Buena Vista Entertainment. Accessed September 21, 2004. http://movies.go.com/boxoffice/1999.html.

Mumford, Kevin J. 1993. "Lost manhood" found: Male sexual impotence and Victorian culture in the United States. In *American sexual politics,* edited by J. C. Fout and M. S. Tantillo, 75–99. Chicago: University of Chicago Press.

Muuss, Rolf E. 1970. Puberty rites in primitive and modern societies. *Adolescence* 5:109–128.

NARAL. 2001. *Who decides? A state-by-state review of abortion and reproductive rights.* Washington, DC: NARAL Pro-Choice America.

Nathanson, Constance A. 1991. *Dangerous passage: The social control of sexuality in women's adolescence.* Philadelphia: Temple University Press.

Nathanson, Constance A., and Robert Schoen. 1993. A bargaining theory of sexual behavior in women's adolescence. Paper presented at the General Conference of the International Union for the Scientific Study of Population, Montreal, Canada.

National Coalition Against Censorship. 2001. *Abstinence-only education: A joint statement.* http://www.ncac.org/issues/abonlypresskit.html#jointstmt.

Navarro, Mireya. 2004. Experts in sex field say conservatives interfere with health and research. *New York Times,* July 11.

Nemecek, Ottokar. 1958. *Virginity: Prenuptial rites and rituals.* New York: Philosophical Library.

Newcomb, Theodore. 1937. Recent changes in attitudes toward sex and marriage. *ASR* 2:659–667.

Newcomer, Susan F., and J. Richard Udry. 1985. Oral sex in an adolescent population. *ASB* 14:41–46.

New York Post. 1999. Still intact. August 1.

Office of National AIDS Policy. 2000. *Youth and HIV/AIDS 2000: A new American agenda.* Washington, DC: Government Printing Office.

Oldenburg, Ann. 2002. Britney Spears fears she's "not that innocent." *USA Today,* January 21.

Omolade, Barbara. 1983. Hearts of darkness. In *Powers of desire: The politics of sexuality,* edited by A. Snitow, C. Stansell, and S. Thompson, 350–367. New York: Monthly Review Press.

Ortner, Sherry B. 1976. The virgin and the state. *Michigan Discussions in Anthropology* 2:1–16.

Paradise, Jan E., Jennifer Cote, Sara Minsky, Ana Lourenco, and Jonathan Howland. 2001. Personal values and sexual decision-making among virginal and sexually experienced urban adolescent girls. *Journal of Adolescent Health* 28:404–409.

Parent, Anthony S., Jr., and Susan Brown Wallace. 1993. Childhood and sexual identity under slavery. In *American sexual politics*, edited by J. C. Fout and M. S. Tantillo, 19–57. Chicago: University of Chicago Press.

Parry, Jonathan. 1986. The gift, the Indian gift and the "Indian gift." *Man* 21:453–473.

Patton, Cindy. 1990. *Inventing AIDS.* New York: Routledge.

Payer, Pierre J. 1993. *The bridling of desire: Views of sex in the later Middle Ages.* Toronto: University of Toronto Press.

Peiss, Kathy. 1986. *Cheap amusements: Working women and leisure in turn-of-the-century New York.* Philadelphia: Temple University Press.

Penthouse Forum. 1985. De-virginized—both ways (Letter from Mr. J.N.). August.

Petersen, Larry R., and Gregory V. Donnenwerth. 1997. Secularization and the influence of religion on beliefs about premarital sex. *Social Forces* 75:1071–1088.

Phelan, Shane. 1989. *Identity politics: Lesbian feminism and the limits of community.* Philadelphia: Temple University Press.

Pittsburgh Post-Gazette. 2000. Britney's romance. July 12.

Pivar, David J. 2002. *Purity and hygiene: Women, prostitution, and the "American plan," 1900–1930.* Westport, CT: Greenwood Press.

Planned Parenthood Federation of America. 1999. *Equity in prescription insurance and contraceptive coverage.* http://www.plannedparenthood.org/rchoices/factsheet/viewer.asp.

Plummer, Kenneth. 1979. *Sexual stigma: An interactionist account.* Boston: Routledge and Kegan Paul.

Raffaelli, Marcela, and Lenna L. Ontai. 2001. "She's 16 years old and there's boys calling over to the house": An exploratory study of sexual socialization in Latino families. *Culture, Health and Sexuality* 3:295–310.

Raymond, Diane. 1994. Homophobia, identity, and the meanings of desire: Reflections on the cultural construction of gay and lesbian adolescent sexuality. In *Sexual cultures and the construction of adolescent identities*, edited by J. M. Irvine, 115–150. Philadelphia: Temple University Press.

Reinharz, Shulamit. 1983. Experiential analysis: A contribution to feminist research. In *Theories of women's studies*, edited by G. Bowles and R. D. Klein, 162–191. London: Routledge.

Reiss, Ira L. 1967. *The social context of premarital sexual permissiveness.* New York: Holt, Rinehart and Winston.

Reiter, Amy. 1999. Virginity: Going, going, gone! Love for sale on eBay? *Salon.* July 29. http://www.salon.com/people/col/reit/1999/07/29/ebay/.

Renfrew, Cliff. 2000. My wild nights of lust with bare Britney; First boyfriend of virgin pop queen tells how they fought desperate longing to go all the way. *The People,* June 11.

Respect, Inc. Our video series and workbook (online order form). Accessed August 12, 2004. http://www.sexrespect.com/videos.html.

Rexfelis. *Beverly Hills 90210* character frequently asked questions. Rex's *Beverly Hills 90210* obsessed fan sanctuary. Accessed July 16, 2001. http://members.aol.com/rexfelis/faq/faqchar.htm.

Rice, Tom W., and Diane L. Coates. 1995. Gender role attitudes in the southern United States. *Gender and Society* 9:744–756.

Rich, Adrienne. 1980. Compulsory heterosexuality and lesbian existence. In *Powers of desire: The politics of sexuality,* edited by A. Snitow, C. Stansell, and S. Thompson, 177–205. New York: Monthly Review Press.

Riessman, Catherine Kohler. 1993. *Narrative Analysis.* Newbury Park, CA: Sage.

Risman, Barbara, and Pepper Schwartz. 2002. After the sexual revolution: Gender politics in teen dating. *Contexts* 1 (1):16–24.

Roiphe, Katie. 1993. *The morning after: Sex, fear, and feminism on campus.* Boston: Little, Brown.

Roof, Wade C., and William McKinney. 1987. *American mainline religion: In changing shape and failure.* New Brunswick, NJ: Rutgers University Press.

Rosenberg, Charles E. 1973. Sexuality, class and role in 19th-century America. *American Quarterly* 25:131–153.

Rothman, Ellen K. 1984. *Hands and hearts: A history of courtship in America.* New York: Basic Books.

Rowson, Susanna Haswell. 1794. *Charlotte Temple.* Reprint, Oxford: Oxford University Press, 1986.

Rubin, Gayle. 1975. The traffic in women: Notes on the political economy of sex. In *Toward an anthropology of women,* edited by R. Reiter, 157–210. New York: Monthly Review Press.

———. 1984. Thinking sex: Notes for a radical theory of the politics of sexuality. In *Pleasure and danger: Exploring female sexuality,* edited by C. S. Vance, 267–319. Boston: Routledge.

Rubin, Lillian. 1976. *Worlds of pain: Life in a working-class family.* New York: Basic Books.

———. 1990. *Erotic wars: What happened to the sexual revolution?* New York: Farrar, Straus and Giroux.

Sanders, Stephanie, and June Machover Reinisch. 1999. Would you say you "had sex" if . . . ? *JAMA* 281:275–277.

Savin-Williams, Ritch C. 2003. Dating and romantic relationships among gay, lesbian, and bisexual youths. In *The gendered society reader,* edited by M. S. Kimmel and A. Aronson, 382–395. New York: Oxford University Press.

Schalet, Amy T. 1998. Raging hormones, regulated love: Adolescent sexuality and the constitution of the modern individual in the United States and the Netherlands. Paper presented at the annual meeting of the American Sociological Association, San Francisco.

Schecterman, Andrew L., and Roger L. Hutchinson. 1991. Causal attributions, self-monitoring, and gender differences among four virginity status groups. *Adolescence* 26:659–678.

Schlegel, Alice. 1991. Status, property, and the value on virginity. *American Ethnologist* 18:719–734.

———. 1995. The cultural management of adolescent sexuality. In *Sexual nature/sexual culture*, edited by P. R. Abramson and S. D. Pinkerton, 177–194. Chicago: University of Chicago Press.

Schmidt, Gunter, Dietrich Klusmann, Uta Zeitzschel, and Carmen Lange. 1994. Changes in adolescents' sexuality between 1970 and 1990 in West Germany. *ASB* 23:489–513.

Schwartz, Barry. 1967. The social psychology of the gift. *AJS* 73:1–11.

Seidman, Steven. 1991. *Romantic longings: Love in America, 1830–1980.* New York: Routledge.

———. 1992. *Embattled Eros: Sexual politics and ethics in contemporary America.* New York: Routledge.

———. 2002. *Beyond the closet: The transformation of gay and lesbian life.* New York: Routledge.

Shalit, Wendy. 1999. *A return to modesty: Discovering the lost virtue.* New York: Free Press.

Sheffield, Carole J. 1997. Sexual terrorism. In *Gender violence: Interdisciplinary perspectives,* edited by L. L. O'Toole and J. R. Schiffman, 110–127. New York: New York University Press.

Sherwin, Robert, and Sherry Corbett. 1985. Campus sexual norms and dating relationships: A trend analysis. *JSR* 21:258–274.

SIECUS. 1996. *Guidelines for comprehensive sexuality education: Kindergarten —12th grade.* 2nd ed. New York: SIECUS.

SIECUS Legislative Action Center. No new money for abstinence-only-until-marriage programs. Accessed October 10, 2004. http://www.nonewmoney.org/index.html.

Simon, Neil. 1986. *Biloxi blues.* New York: Random House.

Simson, Gary, and Erika Sussman. 2000. Keeping the sex in sex education: The first amendment's religion clauses and the sex education debate. *Southern California Review of Law and Women's Studies* 9:265–297.

Singh, Susheela, and Jacqueline E. Darroch. 1999. Trends in sexual activity among adolescent American women: 1982–1995. *FPP* 31:212–219.

———. 2000. Adolescent pregnancy and childbearing: Levels and trends in developed countries. *FPP* 32:14–23.

Sissa, Giulia. 1990. Maidenhood without maidenhead: The female body in ancient Greece. In *Before sexuality: The construction of erotic experience in the ancient Greek world,* edited by D. M. Halperin, J. J. Winkler, and F. I. Zeitlin, 339–364. Princeton, NJ: Princeton University Press.

Smith, Daniel Scott, and Michael S. Hindus. 1975. Premarital pregnancy in America 1640–1971: An overview and interpretation. *Journal of Interdisciplinary History* 5:537–570.

Smith, Tom W. 1994. Attitudes toward sexual permissiveness: Trends, correlates, and behavioral connections. In *Sexuality across the life course,* edited by A. S. Rossi, 63–97. Chicago: University of Chicago Press.

Smith-Rosenberg, Carroll. 1975. The female world of love and ritual. *Signs* 1:1–30.

Smoron, Paige. 1999. Bouncing, blushing Britney. *Chicago Sun-Times,* August 15.

Solin, Sabrina. 1996. *The* Seventeen *guide to sex and your body.* New York: Simon and Schuster.

Sonenstein, F. L., L. Ku, L. D. Lindberg, C. F. Turner, and J. H. Pleck. 1998. Changes in sexual behavior and condom use among teenaged males: 1988 to 1995. *American Journal of Public Health* 88:956–959.

Sontag, Susan. 1989. *AIDS and its metaphors.* New York: Farrar, Straus and Giroux.

South China Morning Post. 1995. Shields in virginity volte-face. April 9.

Sprecher, Susan, and Pamela C. Regan. 1996. College virgins: How men and women perceive their sexual status. *JSR* 33:3–15.

Sprecher, Susan, Anita Barbee, and Pepper Schwartz. 1995. "Was it good for you, too?": Gender differences in first sexual intercourse experiences. *JSR* 32:3–15.

Stacey, Judith. 1991. *Brave new families: Stories of domestic upheaval in late twentieth century America.* New York: Basic Books.

Staples, Robert. 1995. Stereotypes of black male sexuality: The facts behind the myths. In *Men's lives,* edited by M. S. Kimmel and M. A. Messner, 466–471. Boston: Allyn and Bacon.

Steele, Jeanne Rogge. 1999. Teenage sexuality and media practice: Factoring in the influences of family, friends, and school. *JSR* 36:331–341.

Stein, Arlene, and Ken Plummer. 1994. I can't even think straight: Queer theory and the missing sexual revolution in sociology. *Sociological Theory* 12:178–187.

Sterk-Elifson, Claire. 1994. Sexuality among African-American women. In *Sexuality across the life course,* edited by A. S. Rossi, 99–126. Chicago: University of Chicago Press.

Stern, Susannah. 2002. Sexual selves on the World Wide Web: Adolescent girls' home pages as sites for sexual self-expression. In *Sexual teens, sexual media*, edited by J. D. Brown, J. R. Steele, and K. Walsh-Childers, 265–285. Mahwah, NJ: Lawrence Erlbaum.

Strauss, Alix. 1991. *Britney Spears*. New York: St. Martin's.

Sutton, Michael J., Jane D. Brown, Karen M. Wilson, and Jonathan D. Klein. 2002. Shaking the tree of knowledge for forbidden fruit: Where adolescents learn about sexuality and contraception. In *Sexual teens, sexual media*, edited by J. D. Brown, J. R. Steele, and K. Walsh-Childers, 25–55. Mahwah, NJ: Lawrence Erlbaum.

Swidler, Ann. 1986. Culture in action: Symbols and strategies. *ASR* 51:273–286.

———. 2001. *Talk of love: How culture matters*. Chicago: University of Chicago Press.

Takagi, Dana. 1996. Maiden voyage: Excursion into sexuality and identity politics in Asian America. In *Queer theory/sociology*, edited by S. Seidman, 243–258. Cambridge, UK: Blackwell.

Tauber, Michelle, Todd Gold, and Dimitry Eliazs Leger. 2002. Britney's next act. *People*, September 2.

Teen-Aid. Accessed August 4, 2004. http://www.teen-aid.org/default.htm.

Thompson, Sharon. 1984. Search for tomorrow: On feminism and the reconstruction of teen romance. In *Pleasure and danger: Exploring female sexuality*, edited by C. S. Vance, 350–384. Boston: Routledge.

———. 1990. Putting a big thing into a little hole: Teenage girls' accounts of sexual initiation. *JSR* 27:341–361.

———. 1995. *Going all the way: Teenage girls' tales of sex, romance, and pregnancy*. New York: Hill and Wang.

Thornton, Arland, and Donald Camburn. 1989. Religious participation and adolescent sexual behavior and attitudes. *JMF* 51:641–653.

Tiefer, Leonore. 1995. *Sex is not a natural act and other essays*. Boulder, CO: Westview.

Time. 1973. The embarrassed virgins: Women and sexual pressures. July 9.

Tolman, Deborah L. 1994. Doing desire: Adolescent girls' struggles for/with sexuality. *Gender and Society* 8:324–342.

———. 1996. Adolescent girls' sexuality: Debunking the myth of the urban girl. In *Urban girls: Resisting stereotypes, creating identities*, edited by B. J. R. Leadbeater and N. Way, 255–271. New York: New York University Press.

Trowbridge, Lowell S. 1952. No "right age" for a girl to marry. *New York Times Magazine*, October 19.

Trudell, Bonnie, and Mariamne Whatley. 1991. Sex Respect: A problematic public school sexuality curriculum. *Journal of Sex Education and Therapy* 17:125–140.

True Love Waits. *Top 10 Risks of Having Sex before Marriage*. LifeWay Christian Resources. Accessed August 7, 2004. http://www.lifeway.com/tlw/tns_adv _top10.asp.

Turner, Victor. 1969. *The ritual process.* Ithaca, NY: Cornell University Press.

Union of Concerned Scientists. 2004. *Scientific integrity in policymaking: An investigation into the Bush administration's misuse of science.* http://www.ucsusa.org/global_environment/rsi/index.cfm.

Upchurch, Dawn M., Lene Levy-Storms, Clea A. Sucoff, and Carol S. Aneshensel. 1998. Gender and ethnic differences in the timing of first sexual intercourse. *FPP* 30:121–127.

U.S. Census Bureau. 2001. *Table MS-2. Estimated median age at first marriage, by sex: 1890 to the present.* http://www.census.gov/population/socdemo/hh-fam/tabMS-2.txt.

U.S. House of Representatives. 2004. *The content of federally funded abstinence-only education programs.* Report commissioned for Committee on Government Reform — Minority Staff, Special Investigations Division. http://www.waxman.house.gov/.

U.S. Surgeon General David Satcher. 2001. *The surgeon general's call to action to promote sexual health and responsible sexual behavior.* Rockville, MD: U.S. Department of Health and Human Services, Office of the Surgeon General.

Vance, Carole S. 1984. Pleasure and danger: Toward a politics of sexuality. In *Pleasure and danger: Exploring female sexuality,* edited by C. S. Vance, 1–27. Boston: Routledge.

van de Walle, Etienne, and Helmut V. Muhsam. 1995. Fatal secrets and the French fertility transition. *Population and Development Review* 21:261–279.

van Gennep, Arnold. 1908. *The rites of passage.* Reprint, Chicago: University of Chicago Press, 1960.

Vigarello, Georges. 2001. *A history of rape: Sexual violence in France from the 16th to the 20th century.* Cambridge, UK: Polity.

Walters, Suzanna Danuta. 2001. *All the rage: The story of gay visibility in America.* Chicago: University of Chicago Press.

Weber, Max. 1946. The social psychology of world religions. In *From Max Weber: Essays in sociology,* edited by H. H. Gerth and C. W. Mills, 267–301. New York: Oxford University Press.

Weeks, Jeffrey. 1985. *Sexuality and its discontents.* London: Routledge.

Weinberg, Martin S., and Colin J. Williams. 1980. Sexual embourgeoisment? Social class and sexual activity: 1938–1970. *ASR* 45:33–48.

Weis, David L. 1985. The experience of pain during women's first sexual intercourse: Cultural mythology about female sexual initiation. *ASB* 14:421–438.

Welter, Barbara. 1983. The cult of true womanhood: 1820–1860. In *The American family in socio-historical perspective,* edited by M. Gordon, 372–392. New York: St. Martin's.

West, Candace, and Don H. Zimmerman. 1987. Doing gender. *Gender and Society* 1:125–151.

Westoff, Charles F. 1988. Unintended pregnancy in America and abroad. *FPP* 20:254–261.

White, Kevin. 1993. *The first sexual revolution: The emergence of male heterosexuality in modern America.* New York: New York University Press.

White, Renee T. 1999. *Putting risk in perspective: Black teenage lives in the era of AIDS.* Lanham, MD: Rowman and Littlefield.

Widmer, Eric, Judith Treas, and Robert Newcomb. 1998. Attitudes toward nonmarital sex in 24 countries. *JSR* 34:349–358.

Wight, Daniel. 1994. Boys' thoughts and talk about sex in a working-class locality of Glasgow. *Sociological Review* 42:703–738.

Wight, Daniel, Marion Henderson, Gillian Raab, Charles Abraham, Katie Buston, Sue Scott, and Graham Hart. 2000. Extent of regretted sexual intercourse among young teenagers in Scotland: A cross-sectional survey. *British Medical Journal* 320:1243–1244.

Willis, Ellen. 1992. *No more nice girls: Countercultural essays.* Hanover, CT: Wesleyan University Press.

Wilson, Pamela M. 1986. Black culture and sexuality. *Journal of Social Work and Human Sexuality* 4:29–46.

Wolf, Naomi. 1997. *Promiscuities: The secret struggle for womanhood.* New York: Fawcett Columbine.

Woodberry, Robert D., and Christian S. Smith. 1998. Fundamentalism et al.: Conservative Protestants in America. *Annual Review of Sociology* 22:25–56.

World Health Organization. 2000. *Effectiveness of male latex condoms in protecting against pregnancy and sexually transmitted infections.* Fact sheet 243. http://www.who.int/mediacentre/factsheets/fs243/en/.

———. 2002. *Definition of sexual health.* WHO International Technical Consultation on Sexual Health. http://www.who.int/reproductive-health/gender/sexual_health.html.

Wray, Jennifer, and Jeanne R. Steele. 2002. Girls in print: Figuring out what it means to be a girl. In *Sexual Teens, Sexual media,* edited by J. D. Brown, J. R. Steele, and K. Walsh-Childers, 191–208. Mahwah, NJ: Lawrence Erlbaum.

Wyatt, Gail Elizabeth. 1997. *Stolen women: Reclaiming our sexuality, taking back our lives.* New York: Wiley.

Wylie, Margie. 1999. Ad offers virginity to highest bidder on eBay auction site; company pulls offer, insists it was a hoax. *Times-Picayune,* August 19.

Zabin, Laurie S., Marilyn B. Hirsch, Edward A. Smith, and Janet B. Hardy. 1984. Adolescent sexual attitudes and behavior: Are they consistent? *FPP* 16:181–185.

Zerubavel, Eviatar. 1996. Lumping and splitting: Notes on social classification. *Sociological Forum* 11:421–433.

Index

Abortion, 191

Abstinence: among nonvirgins, 87, 94; as birth control, 42, 197–198; as gift from God, 222n. 15; and masculinity, 24, 29; rarity of life-long, 145; religious vs. secular, 186–187, 197–198. *See also* Chastity; Premarital virginity

Abstinence-focused sex education: challenges to, 201–202; effective-ness, 180, 198–200; expansion, 42, 54–55, 74, 178–179, 199–200; federal definition, 180–181; gender/sexual identity in, 180–181, 201; gift metaphor in, 70, 195, 198; medical inaccu-racies, 199–201, 249–50n. 7; sci-entific evaluations, 191, 199–200; secular vs. religious, 181–182, 197–198, 250n. 22. *See also* Sex education

Abusive relationships, 86–87, 195–196

Acquaintances, virginity loss with, 105–106, 133

Act-of-worship metaphor, 182–190; conservative Christian support, 189; distinguished from gift metaphor, 182–183, 189, 251n. 29; effects evaluated, 197; male ad-herents, 251n. 29

Adolescence, as distinct life stage, 33

Adolescent Family Life Act (AFLA), 3, 42, 180

Adulthood: postponement of, 33, 38–39, 203; virginity loss as transi-tion to, 14, 111, 136, 143, 145–146, 175–176, 203–204

Advice literature, 5, 32, 38, 49, 141, 182, 228n. 101. *See also* Mass media

Advocates for Youth, 192

Affection: as precondition for sex, 39–40, 185; for virginity loss part-ner, 78, 163. *See also* Emotional intimacy; Love

African Americans: approaches to vir-ginity/sexuality, 21, 33–34, 39–40; gender differences, 98–99, 109–111; religious beliefs, 240n. 77, 245n. 50; sexual conservatism of middle-class, 25–26, 33; sexual-ity under slavery, 25–26, 243n. 29; stereotypes, 21, 23, 25, 100, 130, 152, 245n. 50. *See also* Race/eth-nicity

Age: and concealing virginity, 121; ideal for virginity loss, 244n. 43; and imperative to lose virginity, 71, 111–112, 117, 125–126, 132, 205; mitigating stigma, 106, 114, 127; at virginity loss, 4, 43, 51, 58, 113. *See also* Timing

Age of consent, 28

Sympathy, for stigmatized, 124, 127, 244n. 42

Take Back the Night marches, 52–53
Teachers, and sex education, 179–180
Technical virginity: among conservative Christians, 154; critiqued, 49, 229n. 128; delineated, 113; and oral sex, 41; origins of term, 34; secondary, 96; among participants, 49, 77, 92. *See also* Petting; Sexual activity
Teen-Aid (curriculum), 191
Telephones, and dating, 33
Thompson, Sharon, 79, 93
Timberlake, Justin, 58–59
Timing, of virginity loss, 51, 112–113, 118, 125–126, 129. *See also* Age; College
Tolman, Deborah, 100
Transformation: at virginity loss, 87, 136, 145–146, 163–164. *See* Rite of passage
True Love Waits (TLW), 182
Trust: of partner, 78, 110, 163; in interviews, 211
Truthfulness. *See* Honesty
Turner, Victor, 143, 170
Turning points: other than virginity loss, 68, 123, 135–136, 160, 164, 170, 186; virginity loss as, 184–185, 206

Union of Concerned Scientists, 199
Uniqueness, of virginity, 71, 95
United States, compared with Europe, 191–192, 198, 200
Urbanization, 26–27, 29, 33

Vaginal sex: and definitions of virginity loss, 44–45, 68, 83, 162; moral privileging of, 233n. 4; pleasure/discomfort, 149
Van Buren, Abigail, 41

van Gennep, Arnold, 151, 245n. 1, 245n. 2
Vance, Carole, 42
Victorian sexual culture, 23–26, 30, 54
Virginity: as challenge, 133; as choice, 207; detection of, 102, 222–223n. 16, 241n. 9; idealized, 19–21, 32; irrelevant to gays/lesbians, 45–46, 204, 220n. 36; as part of self, 49, 61–63, 69, 81, 86–87; rarity presumed, 75; signs of, 2, 38, 96, 102, 153; as social category/cultural phenomenon, 5, 217–218n. 11, 254n. 26; linked with homosexuality, 108; supernatural powers, 18; transgressive potential, 233n. 5. *See also* Premarital virginity
Virginity loss: ages at, 4, 43, 51, 58, 113, 191, 238n. 47; coming out, links with, 160, 164, 248n. 29; compared to other transitions, 39, 143, 167; and construction of gender identity, 99–100, 130, 138–139, 144, 176, 246n. 5; and construction of sexual identity, 117, 138–139, 152, 155–156, 159, 164, 176; and construction of social identities, 203, 205; defined, 4, 6, 10, 18–20, 44–56, 68, 83, 89, 101, 136, 138, 157, 162, 207; as end in itself, 105; equated with vaginal sex, 44–45, 68, 83, 162, 217n. 9; etymology, 18–19; expectations about sex altered by, 186; marriage, links with, 80, 118, 141; significance attributed to, 6, 14, 16, 39, 73, 88–90, 128, 131, 136, 161–162, 165–166, 195–196, 202–204; term critiqued, 217–218n. 11; as transition to adulthood, 14, 111, 136, 143, 145–146, 175–176, 203–204; as turning point, 184–185, 206. *See also* Definitions of virginity loss

About the Author

Laura M. Carpenter is Assistant Professor of Sociology at Vanderbilt University, where she conducts research and teaches courses on gender, sexuality, and health over the life course. She received her Ph.D. in sociology from the University of Pennsylvania and held postdoctoral fellowships from the Social Science Research Council—Sexuality Research Fellowship Program and National Institute of Aging at the Johns Hopkins University Bloomberg School of Public Health.